YALE UNIVERSITY PUBLICATIONS
IN ANTHROPOLOGY
NUMBER 51

THE KASKA INDIANS:
AN ETHNOGRAPHIC RECONSTRUCTION

JOHN J. HONIGMANN

NEW HAVEN

PUBLISHED FOR THE

DEPARTMENT OF ANTHROPOLOGY, YALE UNIVERSITY

BY THE

YALE UNIVERSITY PRESS

London: Geoffrey Cumberlege, Oxford University Press

1954

IRVING ROUSE
Editor

PRINTED IN THE UNITED STATES OF AMERICA

ACKNOWLEDGMENT

THE PUBLICATION OF THIS PAPER HAS BEEN MADE POSSIBLE THROUGH THE GENEROUS AID OF THE WENNER-GREN FOUNDATION FOR ANTHROPOLOGICAL RESEARCH, INC.

PREFACE

MY first direct contact with Athapaskan Indians came in the summer of 1943 with the Slave Indians at Fort Nelson, B. C.[1] The original and unattained objective of that field trip had been the Kaska Indians, whom I then believed to be trading into a post located at the confluence of McDame Creek and Dease River, British Columbia, some 300 miles northwest of Fort Nelson. In June 1944 I succeeded in winning another opportunity to work with the Northern Athapaskans, again setting out for McDame Creek and the Kaska Indians. In Edmonton, district officials of the Hudson's Bay Company informed me that not many Indians were left at McDame Creek. Following the coming of the Alaska Highway, they explained, the McDame trade had been deflected to Lower Post, where the Dease and Liard rivers meet. Here the Dease River Kaska now came to spend the summer with other Kaska Indians who lived on the northern drainage of the Liard. The advice proved encouraging, since it meant that an 80-mile boat trip from Lower Post to McDame Creek could be avoided.

Contrary to the previous year, in 1944 I went North accompanied by my wife and two children: David, age three, and Karen, eight months. On June 15 we started from Dawson Creek, the end of rail, comfortably seated in a very up-to-date Greyhound Bus. The Northwest Division of the United States Army provided this facility for "essential" transportation over the Alaskan Highway. Many changes from the previous summer could be noted during the first lap of the journey. Not only had the Highway been vastly improved, but many of the army and construction camps were closed and some had already been demolished. The "town" of Mile Eight, eight miles above the spur road that leads eastward to Fort Nelson airport, now revealed only a few structures. (When we returned in September the locale appeared to be even more abandoned.) Twenty-three hours sufficed to cover the 620 miles to Lower Post. Early on a glorious summer morning the huge vehicle turned off the Highway and wheeled onto the dirt track leading to the front of the settlement, which then faced the sparkling Liard River.[2]

We spent 13 happy weeks in Lower Post, coming to know a few Kaska Indians so well that we were able to return in 1945 confident of being able to live with them in their winter settlements.[3]

The intention behind my initial visit to the Kaska in 1944 was to acquire gradually an intimate knowledge of their contemporary culture and personality by approaching them with questions about their aboriginal way of life. These data about pre-contact times form the subject matter of the present monograph. In the following year five additional months residence with the people, including part of a winter, helped elucidate many more aboriginal problems. On that field trip, however, contemporary Kaska life constituted the focus of study. The latter material has already been published in *Kaska*

[1] Honigmann, *Ethnography and Acculturation of the Fort Nelson Slave* (1946).

[2] Recently published material suggests that the town has turned its face toward the Highway, a process which commenced in 1944 when a new Hudson's Bay Company store opened on the Highway and the old store, facing the river, was abandoned. Cf. Harrington, *Alaska Highway* (1951).

[3] Honigmann, *Culture and Ethos of Kaska Society* (1949), 3–4.

Culture and Ethos (1949). In 1948, while spending a relatively lonely winter with the Cree Indians of Attawapiskat, Ontario, I managed to salvage sufficient time to write up the first draft of the present manuscript from field notes which I had designedly taken North the previous summer. The following pages are published substantially as they came from the typewriter in 1951.

Conditions for work among the Kaska Indians remained almost unbelievably excellent when compared with the problems which anthropologists have encountered in Northern Apathaskan field work. Relatively little of the reticence, diffidence, and disinterest, that made previous work with the Fort Nelson Slave so difficult, manifested themselves at Lower Post. Willing male informants were easy to secure. However, in recent years I have become very conscious of the sampling deficiencies inherent in the traditional method of ethnography. This method has led to disproportionate amount of information being secured from informants belonging to the upper Liard River region. That group provided the most cooperative informants as well as those possessing considerable facility in English. In 1945 I spent part of the winter with these same willing upper Liard River folk.

For their generous hospitality, gratitude goes to Mr. and Mrs. J. Stewart, of the Hudson's Bay Company. At their door early that June morning appeared my family inquiring about a place in which to get breakfast. We were not turned away. I recall, too, the friendliness of Mr. and Mrs. Rupert Brooks, the always ready helpfulness of Mr. Clarence Millspaugh, and the open heartedness of Mr. Hans Anderson, one of the most unforgettable characters whom I have met in the North. Transportation was arranged through the cooperation of Major F. C. Barger, Lieutenants C. E. Barger and E. Waters, and Sergeant V. Kelly, all of the United States Army. Major D. M. MacKay, then Indian Commissioner for British Columbia, facilitated certain aspects of field work and his office supplied useful census data. My intellectual debt to Professor Cornelius Osgood is a pervasive one. To him I owe my original orientation to the peoples and cultures of northern North America. My sincere thanks for financial assistance to do field work go to the Department of Anthropology, Yale University, the Yale Peabody Museum, and to Mr. and Mrs. William A. Castleton. Professor Lucy Chamberlain, Chairman of the Department of Sociology-Anthropology, Washington Square College, New York University, helped me arrange a teaching schedule that left a maximum time for writing. For assistance in completing final typing of parts of the manuscript I acknowledge the help received from the Institute for Research in Social Science of the University of North Carolina.

Chapel Hill, 1954.   JOHN J. HONIGMANN

CONTENTS

7

TEXT FIGURES

PHONETIC KEY

VOWELS:

i as in English eat.
e as in English mate.
a as in German Mann.
u as in English soon.
ü as in German Küche.
ɔ as in English law.
Duplication indicates lengthening of the vowel.
( ) indicates subject to elision.

SEMIVOWELS:

j high front unrounded semivowel.
w high back rounded semivowel.

CONSONANTS:

θ voiceless coronal spirant, as in English thick.
ł voiceless lateral spirant.
x voiceless dorsal spirant.
γ voiced dorsal spirant.
c voiceless frontal spirant, as in English ship.
ʔ glottal stop.
Other consonants as in English.

˛ indicates nasalization.
ʹ accent (usually omitted).

Transcriptions are not phonemic and no doubt reflect a relatively poor ear for phonetic values.

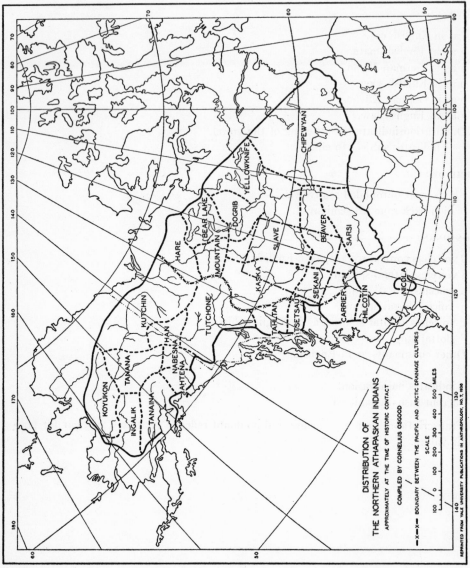

DISTRIBUTION OF
THE NORTHERN ATHAPASKAN INDIANS

APPROXIMATELY AT THE TIME OF HISTORIC CONTACT

COMPILED BY CORNELIUS OSGOOD

━ ✕ ━ ✕ ━ BOUNDARY BETWEEN THE PACIFIC AND ARCTIC DRAINAGE CULTURES

SCALE

100   0   100   200   300   400   500   MILES

REPRINTED FROM YALE UNIVERSITY PUBLICATIONS IN ANTHROPOLOGY, NO.7, 1936

Fig. 1. Distribution of the Northern Athapaskan Indians (after Osgood).

INTRODUCTION

THE present monograph is intended primarily to describe the aboriginal and time-of-contact lifeways of the Kaska Indians of northern British Columbia and southern Yukon Territory, Canada (Fig. 1). The writer's principal object has been to add to present knowledge concerning the Northern Athapaskan Indians. As far as the organization of the material is concerned, the cultural data follow this introduction, which includes, in addition to these preliminary remarks, a description of the environment (based mainly on contemporary observation), tribal distribution and nomenclature, population data, a sketch of psychological types, and an index of principal informants.[1] The description of aboriginal Kaska culture is divided into five main sections covering, respectively, data pertaining to the food quest, camp life and some associated activities, social organization, ideological system, and the life cycle. These main divisions are in turn further broken down. For many of the dress patterns, implements, and behaviors, alternatives are indicated. It must be kept in mind that evidence does not warrant the assumption that all such alternatives existed simultaneously.

Information has been obtained primarily from the Upper Liard and Dease River Kaska (Fig. 2). When available, data from other Kaska groups follow these two in the following order: Tselona, Espatotena, and Frances Lake Kaska. References to adjacent tribes, like the Tahltan, Pelly River people, Bear Lake Sekani, and Tlingit will be found in footnotes.

ENVIRONMENT

To the person who has not been raised to love the prairie the Cassiar, as the northwestern area of British Columbia and southern Yukon Territory is often called,[2] must appeal as a colorful and exciting region. Lying between the Rocky Mountains on the east and the Coast Range to the west the country is bounded north and south by water sheds of considerable height. Geologically the Cassiar may be considered as a portion of the Yukon Plateau.[3] Between the eastern and western ranges the land is rolling and crossed from northwest to southeast by the Cassiar Mountains, which extend from Teslin Lake to the headwaters of the Finlay River (Fig. 2). Below McDame Creek, 80 miles south of Lower Post, the Dease River cuts a gorge through the Cassiar Mountains

---

[1] The history of the Cassiar and its people will not be presented in this monograph, since it has already been written in some detail. See Honigmann, *Culture and Ethos of Kaska Society* (1949), 38–50; Scidmore, *Stikine River in 1898* (1899).

[2] For an impressionistic picture of the area see Turton, *Cassiar* (1934). The term Yukon is apparently derived from the Athapaskan word for Northern Lights, yokąąn. (Cf. Osgood, *Ingalik Material Culture* [1940], 459.) Le Jeune, however, derives the territory's name from a supposed "Yuki" (Wicked Ones) Indian tribe. Le Jeune, *Dictionnaire Générale du Canada* (1931), II, 826.

[3] Lees, *Geology of Teslin-Quiet Lake Area, Yukon* (1936), 5. See also Hanson and McNaughton, *Eagle-McDame Area, Cassiar District, British Columbia* (1936), 2–3; Kerr, *Dease Lake Area, Cassiar District, B. C.* (1926). For maps the reader is referred to Honigmann, *Culture and Ethos of Kaska Society* (1949), 32, 34.

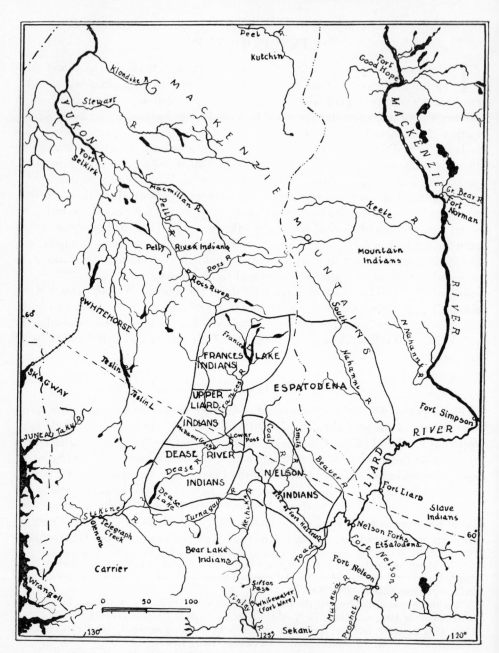

FIG. 2. Map of the Cassiar and Its People.

at Pine Rapids. Above McDame the river passes west of the Horseranch Mountains, a spur of the Cassiar Range. The more rugged features of the district are somewhat softened at the confluence of the Dease and Liard rivers, the site of Lower Post. It is this region, actually extending westward from Smith River to Watson Lake, which Williams has described as "a rolling plateau deeply covered with sand and gravel, and varied by low rounded hills and deep, well forested stream valleys."[4] Bisecting the Cassiar from north to south is the so-called Rocky Mountain Trench, one of the proposed routes for the Alaska Highway that has also been surveyed from Prince George to Watson Lake for a railroad. The survey line can still be followed and crosses the Alaska Highway a few hundred feet east of Lower Post.[5]

The Cassiar is drained by several large rivers including, from west to east, the Frances, Dease, Hyland, Kechika (Muddy), Coal, Rock, and Smith. The lower reaches of the Kechika or Muddy River are sometimes referred to as the Turnagain or Black River. All of these run into the easterly flowing Liard, which in turn enters the Mackenzie at Fort Simpson, Northwest Territories, whose waters finally reach the Arctic Ocean. In spring and early summer the streams are swift and deep. Toward autumn the water level recedes considerably but the numerous rapids always render river navigation difficult and sometimes hazardous. "Rising in the elevated country west of the Rocky Mountains, the Liard falls rapidly toward the east, the difference in elevation between the mouth of the Dease and the Mackenzie amounting to nearly 1,650 feet, and is characterized nearly everywhere by impetuous currents, by dangerous rapids and narrow whirlpool cañons."[6] About 50 miles below Lower Post is Hell's Gate, the most famous of the Liard's rapids. Here the river cuts its torturous route through the barrier of the Rockies. The spring break-up of the frozen Liard is reported to be particularly spectacular in this canyon where huge slabs of ice pile up with pressure increasing behind them until, with a terrific roar that can be heard for miles, the mass gives way and charges through the narrow, cavelike opening. The difficulties associated with water transportation up the Liard from Fort Simpson were largely responsible for the abandonment, in 1865, of Fort Halkett, the Hudson's Bay Company post at the confluence of the Liard and Smith rivers (Fig. 2). Since that date the principal means of access to the Cassiar has been from the south, travelers, among whom gold seekers occupied a prominent place, journeying up the Stikine River from Wrangell, Alaska, to Telegraph Creek, B. C. From here they crossed the height of land to reach the foot of Dease Lake, 200 miles south of Lower Post. By 1946 this route was rapidly falling into abeyance as the Alaska Highway provided a new and modern means of access.

The climate of the intermontane Cassiar is seasonally variable. In summer, as elsewhere in the northern forest, the days are hot and temperatures reach 90 degrees in the

---

[4] Williams, *Geological Reconnaissance along the Alaska Highway from Fort Nelson, British Columbia, to Watson Lake, Yukon* (1944), 2. See also McConnell, *Report on an Exploration in the Yukon and Mackenzie Basins* (1890), 80.

[5] In 1950 the New York newspapers reported fresh talk of a proposed railroad to extend from Prince George to Fairbanks, Alaska, passing through Lower Post.

[6] McConnell, *Report on an Exploration in the Yukon and Mackenzie Basins* (1890), 34D.

sun. With the onset of evening the heat declines so that the nights are cool. Frosts begin in August. In winter periods of extreme cold occur but the season is relatively windless, a condition that helps to make the low temperatures bearable. In 1943–44 and again in January, 1947, the mercury is said to have approached 70 degrees below zero Fahrenheit. The winter of 1944–45 was described as relatively mild, the coldest day being about 55 degrees below zero.[7] The winter climate is greatly influenced by the Polar Continental air masses of the interior. When these cross the eastern mountains they bring the particular quality of cold which Indians describe as coming from the east or northeast. Snowfall is apt to be heavy, beginning in late September and remaining in the mountains until late June.

Like other parts of the North American taiga, the Cassiar remains well stocked with game and fur bearers. The coniferous forest of spruce and jackpine, interspersed with dense clumps of willow, quaking aspen,[8] birch, and cottonwood (*liard*), proves hospitable to the fox, ground hog, gopher (marmot), lynx, mink, marten, otter, weasel, porcupine, muskrat, rabbit, red squirrel, wolf, coyote, mouse, and beaver. Amid the spruces the ground is covered with a luxuriant blanket of sphagnum moss attractive to caribou. Snakes are apparently absent, though not unfamiliar to the Indians. Patches of raspberry, saskatoon, strawberry, cranberries (low and high bush), and soap berry are inviting to grizzly, brown, and black bears. Jenness reports native traditions of buffalo having been plentiful in the Kaska country during the precontact period.[9] Is he perhaps influenced by Indian tales of people running across huge "elephant" bones and teeth, probably belonging to some prehistoric species of dinosaur?[10] The available evidence indicates the range of wood buffalo to have been restricted to the east of the Fort Nelson River.[11] Various authors as well as local Indians agree that at some time in the past moose were lacking in the country. According to Pike, "twenty-five years ago there were few moose along the Liard, and the animal was unknown to the Indians hunting to the westward of Dease Lake. Then there began to be frequent rumours of a big track seen in the snow, and momentary glimpses of a beast whose size varied according to the fancy of the startled hunter. Then a young brave stood face to face with a moose and slew it; and the Cascas discovered that a new animal . . . had invaded their country."[12] George Adsit, a now deceased, long-term resident of the Cassiar, told the writer

[7] Personal communication. According to Pike, "the winters in the Cassiar are mild in comparison to the climate in the same latitude to the eastward of the Rockies, the warm Chinook winds from the Pacific penetrate the coast ranges, modifying the intensity of the cold to such an extent that there is usually a thaw with rainfall during some part of the winter." (Pike, *Through the Subarctic Forest* [1896], 99–100.) According to information personally received from George Adsit, long-term Cassiar resident, the Chinook does not blow until April and therefore has no effect on winter temperatures.

[8] This species of tree is especially found as a second growth in burned areas, where the rose bay or fireweed also flourishes. For an interesting account of the latter plant, lately returned to London, England, after 300 years, see Vadeboncoeur, *Flower of the Blitz* (1946).

[9] Jenness, *Indians of Canada* (1932), 397.

[10] Sternberg, *Canadian Dinosaurs* (1945).

[11] Allen, *American Bisons* (1876).

[12] Pike, *Through the Subarctic Forest* (1896), 89. Williams also reports the former absence of moose in the Cassiar in his *Game Trails in British Columbia* (1925), 256.

that the Kaska Indians had known moose "a long, long time ago." Subsequently the animal disappeared and when it returned the people had lost the art of hunting the animal. Informants spoke of aboriginal techniques for hunting moose, indicating that the animal entered the region prior to the beginning of acculturation. Linguistically it is interesting to compare the Kaska word for moose, gatɔ or ketɔ, with the terms kǫlǫn and ulǫn used by the Fort Nelson Slave. Elk and deer were more certainly originally absent in the Cassiar and have only recently begun to appear west of the Rockies. Thus a deer was killed about seven miles southeast of the confluence of the Liard and Frances rivers about 1928. In the summer of 1944 Indians expressed great interest in what were presumed to be deer tracks encountered in the soft shoulders of the Alaska Highway near Lower Post. Similar tracks appeared along the Liard near the confluence of the Frances River. Perhaps the highway has been responsible for the animal's intensified westerly migration. According to Williams, "the most northerly herd of wapiti (elk) is resident in the vicinity of Tuchodi Lake," the source of the Smith River.[13] Weasel and skunk are also reported to be recent arrivals in the district. Wild fowl include grouse, spruce (fool) hens, ptarmigan, owl, eagle, crow, swan, loon, and a relatively small number of geese and duck. In summer Lower Post harbors a small colony of swallows but they originally came from England. Rivers and lakes contain grayling sucker, trout, whitefish, loche (ling), and pike. Watson Lake, 23 miles northwest of Lower Post, once provided an important source of whitefish for the Indians.[14] Salmon are known to run in the Stikine, Pelly, and Ross rivers but are absent from the region of which we speak.

A geographically interesting feature of the region is the hot springs that erupt about 100 miles east of Lower Post. These warm, sulphurous waters have long excited interest in the Cassiar, giving rise to stories of hidden and mysterious "tropical valleys."[15] The writer visited one of these springs located about a mile west of the bridge where the Alaska Highway makes its easternmost crossing of the Liard. The vegetation is indeed more luxuriant near the pool of warm water and photographs prove that the springs resist freezing in winter. The area of such exuberant growth, however, is extremely circumscribed.[16]

KASKA TRIBES AND THEIR NEIGHBORS

Sometime within the past 20,000 years man probably first set foot in the Cassiar. The immediate point from which those early settlers had migrated presumably lay somewhere to the northwest. At a somewhat greater distance in time and space the forefathers

[13] Williams, *Geological Reconnaissance along the Alaska Highway from Fort Nelson, British Columbia, to Watson Lake, Yukon* (1944), 3.

[14] Named after a Yorkshireman who settled there and married an Indian woman. Watson is dead but in 1945 Mrs. Watson continued to live near the airdrome at the Lake with her daughters, a son-in-law (a Beaver Indian *métis*), and two grandchildren.

[15] Johnston, *Gold Placers of Dease Lake Area, Cassiar District, B. C.* (1926), 38A; Godsell, *Romance of the Alaska Highway* (1944), 86–92.

[16] See also Williams, *Geological Reconnaissance along the Alaska Highway from Fort Nelson, British Columbia, to Watson Lake, Yukon* (1944), 31.

of the people called Kaska must have crossed Bering Strait enroute from Asia. Leech-man, who assumes migration movements toward the headwaters of the Yukon and thence along the Pelly, Liard, and Frances rivers, discovered along the Whitehorse and Snag sections of the Alaska Highway "chipped points, scrapers, large blades, a few other implements and large numbers of chips and flakes. The material employed was for the most part a fine-grained grey chert with a fairly well-marked conchoidal frac-ture; a certain amount of jasper and obsidian was also used."[17] Such may perhaps have been the primary tools of the early intermontane people, Whitehorse being only 300 miles northwest of Lower Post. Further south along the Highway Frederick Johnson discovered other cultural remains whose age he estimates to be about 7,000–9,000 years.[18] At least it is certain that the remote ancestors of the Kaska lived by food gather-ing and possessed the general pattern of social organization associated with such a tech-nological base.

Between the time of the earliest arrival of the human stock and the day when the white man began to bring goods to trade for the Indians' furs there were undoubtedly many shifts in the Cassiar population. Evidence exists today that migration brought people from the Fort Nelson River valley into Kaska territory. Once the trader arrived, more extensive shifts of people took place, the movement now being inspired by the desire for favorable fur prices and the trader's goods. Between 1890 and 1900 the peak of such mobility appears to have been reached and it thoroughly scrambled the Cassiar population.

At the time when the more easterly Cassiar people first contacted the white man in the Mackenzie basin the group collectively and gratuitously referred to as Kaska (synonymy: Casca) was divided into a number of macrocosmic groups or tribes. These units have been variously named, the confusion being due to the fact that the groups were loosely organized and failed to adopt fixed tribal designations of their own. The nomenclature to be given here reflects ideas in the minds of Indian informants concern-ing more or less delimited human aggregates. It is not likely that if different informants had been consulted the same designations would have been obtained. As a matter of fact the same informants might have altered their classifications from time to time. Before presenting this scheme, it is proposed to examine earlier writers' subdivisions of the Cassiar people.

According to Dawson the Kaska, bounded on the west by the Tahltan, hunted in the country drained by the Dease River "but north of the sources of streams reaching the Dease, they wander seldom" except as far "as Frances Lake."[19] East of the Dease they occupied the drainage of the Turnagain (Black) River "but not to the headwater of that stream, as the country there is claimed by the Al-ta'-tin ('Sicconie') of Bear Lake re-gion. . . ." They also exploited the country northeast as far as Fort Halkett, where

---

[17] Leechman, *Prehistoric Migration Routes through the Yukon* (1946), 387–388.

[18] Johnson, *Archaeological Survey along the Alaska Highway* (1946). He discovered no sites between Teslin village and Muncho Lake. The latter place is already outside of the Cassiar proper.

[19] Dawson, *Report of an Exploration in the Yukon District, N. W. T., and Adjacent Northern Portion of British Columbia, 1887* (1887–88), 200.

Smith River joins the Liard, and north to the head of the Smith. In this general area
Dawson distinguishes two groups, the Sa-ze-oo-ti-na and Ti-tsho-ti-na. The first of
these he localizes in the "corner" of the Liard and Dease rivers and in the basin of the
Turnagain as far south as the country of the Bear Lake Sekani. The Ti-tsho-ti-na, Dawson says, occupied the area east of the Sa-ze-oo-ti-na. This latter name designated their
easterly neighbors (i.e., the Indians dwelling along the Liard below Fort Halkett),
A-tsho-to-ti-na.[20]

A few comments are in order. Dawson seems to have erred if he intended to show per-
sistent penetration by the Dease River Kaska (Sa-ze-oo-ti-na) of Frances Lake country.
His designation, Sa-ze-oo-ti-na, confuses the Dease River and Bear Lake Indians and
probably relates to the fact that some of the latter were encountered near the juncture
of the Liard and Dease. It is not clear to what group the name Ti-tsho-ti-na (Big Water
People) refers unless it is a synonym for the tribe that we will later call Tselona.

Hodge in the *Handbook of American Indians* subdivides the Kaska into the Tishotina
and Etagottine, both occupying the Liard and Dease River basins. To the east of these
are placed the Esbataottine, extending from the Liard south to the Peace. North of the
latter is found an extension of the Etagottine. Between the Dease and Turnagain rivers
(a position that seems already to have been assigned to the Esbataottine) are placed the
Sazentina and around Fort Halkett the Ettcaottine. To the north and west of the Kaska,
Hodge introduces the Abbatottine, living in the Pelly, MacMillan, and Stewart river
valleys.[21]

Teit, in his discussion of Kaska subdivisions, appears correct on linguistic grounds in
objecting that the *Handbook's* Abbatottine and Esbataottine are probably identical.[22]
He discards the general term "Kaska" in favor of the highly equivocal word "Nahani,"
a term that will be discussed presently. He includes as Kaska, or Nahani, not only the
Tahltan but also the Sezotena of the Muddy (Kechika), Dease, and McDame rivers as
well as the Tittcotena, Na·ani, eiyo·na, Little Salmon Indians, Espätoten, and Tsetsexo-
tena. The Titcotena he locates on the Upper Liard and along the Highland River. To
the Na·ani is allocated the upper Pelly basin and they are said to have spoken a dialect
akin to Titcotena. The eiyo·na Teit identifies with the MacMillan and Stewart rivers,
north of the Pelly. On Little Salmon River, in Yukon Territory, he locates the Little
Salmon Indians. East of the Titcotena and along the North and South Nahani rivers,

[20] Probably a cognate of Etca? otena. See below, p. 23.

[21] Hodge, *Handbook of American Indians* (1907–10), I, 661.

[22] Teit, *Unpub. manuscript* (1915?). Petitot corrected Franklin's designation of Am baw law hoot-
dennèh, saying that these were the Sheep Indians or Es pa-tρa ottinè, "People among the Antelopes."
(Petitot, *Autour du grand lac des Esclaves* [1891], 96.) Considerable discussion has been spent in ascertaining whether the radical (e)spa- is to be translated "sheep" or "goat." (Cf. Osgood *Distribution of the
Northern Athapaskan Indians* [1936], 13; Honigmann, *Ethnography and Acculturation of the Fort Nelson
Slave* [1946], 24.) Translation of the word as "goat" by several Kaska informants leads to the usage
adopted in this monograph. According to Morice, "deceived by appearances, modern Carriers have
denominated goat what is really a sheep and sheep what should be called goat." He gives tepê as the
Carrier term for "goat" and espai as their word for "sheep." (Morice, *Carrier Language* [1932], I, 34.)
See footnote 27.

between the Liard and Mackenzie, dwelt the Espätoten or histoten. Finally, the Tset-sexotena exploited the region north of the Espätoten.

By way of comment, it is obvious that Teit means to group the Bear Lake Sekani with the Kaska or Nahani. He maintains that the former speak a dialect "exactly the same as the Upper Liard and Hyland Indians," a dubious assertion judging from contemporary evidence. Working with the word Nahani Teit got exactly the results that one could now predict would be secured by presenting this term to a number of informants from different parts of the country. The term denotes little known and potentially hostile strangers. It is certainly a cognate of Na·ani, a group which is included in the larger class.

Allard gives the Kaska a territory which in about 1925 extended from Dease Lake "down the Dease to about twenty miles west of the Upper Liard Rivers."[23] Southeast of Dease Lake and Dease River he would extend the Kaska to longitude 126°, or just west of Muncho Lake and considerably east of the Kechika River. South he continues them to the fifty-eighth parallel, that is almost to the headwaters of the Stikine and to Sifton Pass. Northwest they are said to range along the Liard to the height of land but not beyond the Yukon border. The divide, however, which is where the Liard River rises, is clearly north of the British Columbia-Yukon border.

On the basis of available evidence Jenness in 1932 divided the Kaska (whom he extends from McDame Creek eastward to the Beaver River, a little west of Fort Liard) into two groups, the Tsezotena or "Mountain People on the east" and the Titshotina, "Big Water People on the west."[24] The boundary between the Mountain and Big Water peoples is put at the junction of the Kechika and "Dease rivers." This latter statement certainly reflects an oversight since the Kechika flows northwest from Sifton Pass to join the Liard and not the Dease. The confluence of the Kechika and Liard occurs about 70 miles below Lower Post. Jenness probably meant the Liard River. East and northeast of the Mountain people, on the Beaver and South Nahanni rivers, Jenness places the Esbaottine. We would argue that a distinction of the groups on either side of the Kechika River appears valid, regardless of how those groups may be designated. Jenness did not know that the westerly Indians by no means regard themselves as a single, homogeneous unit, the Upper Liard people, for example, distinguishing themselves from the Dease River dwellers. Still further north lie the also distinct Frances Lake Indians.

Osgood extends the classification by Jenness to include as Kaska the Tsezotena Titshotina, and Esbaottine, as well as "the little known people of the Upper Liard River drainage who have frequently been called Nahani."[25] We would add the Frances Lake people, especially if similarity of dialect be regarded as an important criterion of classification.

On the basis of long-standing relations, intermarriage, mutual intelligibility, and absence of serious geographical barriers it appears reasonable to group the people living around Frances Lake, the Upper Liard, Dease, and Middle Liard rivers in a single

[23] Allard, *Notes on the Kaska and Upper Liard Indians* (1928), 24.
[24] Jenness, *Indians of Canada* (1932), 396.
[25] Osgood, *Distribution of the Northern Athapaskan Indians* (1936), 13.

category. Since the name "Kaska" has already been applied to the Indians of this area we will continue to follow this nomenclature for the several tribes who aboriginally inhabited the region delimited above. Constituting the Kaska community or nation were five macrocosmic bands or tribes here designated Natitu?agotena, Kistagotena, Tselona, (E)spatotena, and Tutcogotena. Each of these will now be identified more closely.

1. The Natitu?a'gotena, "Dwellers at a High Sharp Mountain Where a Little River Starts" (synonymy: Upper Liard Kaska) are the Indians who occupied the area close to the source of the Liard River as well as the banks of that stream extending southeast to the canyon located where today the border of Yukon Territory crosses the Liard. This canyon is about eight miles above Lower Post. Some of the Upper Liard people spent every winter at Watson Lake and in season others visited the Pelly River to fish for salmon.

2. South and southeast of the Natitu?agotena were the Ki'stagotena, "Mountain Dwellers" (synonymy: Dease River Kaska), who might also be referred to as the Kaska proper because it is this group to whom the name originally applied. The designation Mountain Dwellers becomes somewhat gratuitous when applied to a single group, since in the fall most of the Cassiar Indians hunted on the mountain slopes. The people living along McDame Creek above its junction with Dease River were also known as Onzana. The total range of the Kistagotena included the valleys of the Dease south from the Liard to the head of Dease Lake, where a divide separated them from the Tahltan. Eastward they extended about halfway to Sifton Pass, where the Kechika River is formed. West the Dease River Kaska ranged as far as the Cordillera.

3. The Tse'lona (synonymy: Nelson Indians), a word variously translated as "Mountain Top," "End Point," or "Point at Which is Located the End of the World," are apparently Jenness' and Osgood's Tzezotena. They occupied the area east of the Kistagotena and along the Kechika River. The establishment of Fort Nelson after 1800 attracted these people beyond the borders of the Cassiar to trade at that post on the other side of the Rocky Mountains. Among the Sekani and Slave Indians who frequented the Nelson River Valley the Tselona became known as Grand Lakers and came much to be feared for sorcery.[26] Today in Lower Post at least some Indians from the middle Liard are called Nelson Indians. Morice identified the "Tse-loh-me" with the Etchere-ottine or Brushwood People and estimated their population at 350. He located them on the Liard, immediately east of the Rocky Mountains.[27] We would be less inclined to overlook distinctions between the people of the middle Liard (Tselona) and the Etca?otena of Fort Nelson. Contemporary members of the former group complained of being unable to understand the speech of the Fort Nelson Slave. Historically, after the European traders crossed the Rocky Mountains, the Tselona traded at Chee House, which was built about 1880 at the mouth of the Kechika. This post was later shifted inland. Today

[26] Honigmann, *Witch-Fear in Post-Contact Kaska Society* (1947), 223.

[27] Morice, *Great Déné Race* (1906–10), 270–271, 507. The dictionaries of the Oblate Fathers, which the author consulted at Fort Nelson, define the Slave word sayonne as "male mountain sheep." If sayonne and tselona are cognates we conclude that there could have been both Sheep People and Goat People in the eastern Kaska area or that the same group was designated in two ways.

the people visit Forts Ware and Grahame as well as Lower Post. In some census reports: the Tselona are listed as "Fort Grahame Nomads."

4. North and northeast of the Tselona were the (E)spa'totena, "Dwellers among the Wild Goats," or "Goat Indians," also referred to as Gata'otena, "People who Hunt Rabbits" (synonymy: Abbatotine, Esbataottine, Ambawlawhoot dennèh, Espätoten, Histotina). These people inhabited the area north of the Liard, including the drainages of the Beaver, South Nahanni, and perhaps Upper Nahanni rivers. With contact some came to trade at Fort Halkett and Lower Post while others congregated at Fort Liard. At the latter place Bishop Grouard designated them People of the Mountains and Bad People. Future research may indicate more clearly where the eastern boundary of the Espatotena is to be drawn in order to separate them from the Mountain Indians. One informant (O) denied that, on the basis of dialect similarity, the Espatotena could be related to their western neighbors. Claiming to have spent a year with this group, he illustrated some differences between the Natitu?agotena and Espatotena dialects. Thus his word for meat, etsun, was said to be rendered a?apa by the latter, a reference probably to goat; moose, gatɔ, becomes gulon (as in Fort Nelson); caribou, gutzi, becomes matsi, and sheep, depe, becomes duga.

5. By Tu'tcogotena, "Big Water Dwellers" (synonymy: Frances Lake Kaska; Titshotina; Titcotena; Tzazi?a?otena, "Flint Mountain Dwellers," and Tutcomenagotena, "Big Water Lake Dwellers") is indicated the Indians who formerly and at the present time occupy the area around Frances Lake and upper Frances River. Sometimes these people ranged east and south to the headwaters of the Hyland and Smith rivers. Like the word Kistagotena the designation Big Water People is not descriptively exclusive since the Finlay, Liard, and Dease rivers have all at various times been called "Big Water" by Indians.[28] Hence the people inhabiting the shores of these streams may logically be referred to as Big Water Dwellers. In 1926 a police patrol to Frances Lake reported that "the country between the canyons on the Frances River is a natural game preserve. The Frances Lake Indians do not hunt south and the Liard Indians do not go further north than the first canyon. The country between is therefore untouched."[29] This statement may be taken as evidence of a distinction between the Upper Liard and Frances Lake Indians. The designation for the people, Flint Mountain Dwellers, was suggested by an informant familiar with the habit of the Indians to hunt in the vicinity of a certain source of flint. Two informants said that the Frances Lake people could also be called Terahan, a term otherwise used for the Pelly River people.

These then constitute the groups whom it is proposed to include in the Kaska nation. The meaning of the term Kaska is itself difficult to elucidate. According to George Adsit, a white man with a fair knowledge of the Athapaskan language, the word means "old moccasins" and was originally bestowed on the Dease River Indians as a term of opprobrium by their Tahltan neighbors. According to a Tahltan informant from Telegraph Creek, the Tahltan refer to the Kaska as Kɔswa, a word whose meaning was inexplicable to him. A Kaska Indian (WT) said that the people referred to themselves as

---

[28] Morice, *Fur Trader in Anthropology* (1928), 63.
[29] Canada, *Report of the Royal Canadian Mounted Police* (1926), 83.

kaca, a word that he could not define. No informant pointed out that the term could be related to the local word for boot, keske. Morice opines that "Kaska is the name of no tribe or sub-tribe, but McDane [sic!] Creek is called by the name Na·ane KasHa—the H representing a peculiar gutteral-sibilant aspiration—and this is the real word which corrupted into Cassiar by the whites, has, since a score of years or more, served to designate the whole mining region."[30] Although it is difficult to be definite concerning the associations of the term Kaska, enough data are at hand to criticize with some finality the use of the term Nahani for any group of Indians. Various widely scattered people have at various times been called by this appellation. Thus the present writer heard in the field that long ago the Nahani Indians hunted in the area between McDame Creek Post and Kechika River. These people were said to have been giants who died out because of incestuous practices, sons even copulating with mothers and fathers with daughters (WT).[31] Another informant identified the Nahani with the Pelly River people, while another man applied the word to the Tahltan. Writing early in the nineteenth century Keith describes the country around Fort Liard as having been abandoned by the "Na ha né tribe" under pressure from a new population.[32] The reports of the Department of Indian Affairs frequently contain references to "nomadic" Nahani Indians said to reside in the corner made by the Fort Nelson and Liard rivers. In 1915 a report stated that these people "are gradually merging into surrounding bands in the north and that in a few years they will have entirely lost their identity and standing as a band."[33] In 1943, in Fort Nelson, the writer was assured by the game warden of northern British Columbia that Nahani was another name for certain Kaska Indians inhabiting the area around Nelson Forks and west of Fort Nelson. From all this the conclusion follows that numerous Athapaskan groups themselves designated as Nahani (na- indicates "enemy" or "hostile"[34]) other remote and distrusted Indian bands with whom they lacked frequent relations. European and Canadian writers have tried to apply the term to specific population units.

Surrounding the Kaska Indians were a number of other Athapaskan speaking groups. In clockwise order, immediately to the southwest and west were the Tahltan Indians (synonymy: Tatcotena, Tutcotena). Various equivalents were received for this group, including People who Fish Salmon in the River and People who Stay in a Low Place. Beal Carlick, a Tahltan informant, derived the name from the village of Tahltan, located at the juncture of the Tahltan and Stikine rivers. The village itself received its appellation from a woman who descended the Tahltan River and at its mouth met a man who had originally come from the south. This man heard a voice calling from the opposite bank of the Stikine and so discovered the woman. They exchanged names. He asked her if she belonged to the Crow or Wolf moiety and she replied that she was Crow. The man

---

[30] Morice, *Nah·ane and their Language* (1900–03), 519.

[31] The Dease River was once called the "Nahany." See Parnell, *Campbell of the Yukon* (1942), 5.

[32] Keith, *Letters to Mr. Roderic McKenzie* (1890), 66–68. See also Hodge, *Handbook of American Indians* (1912), II, 11.

[33] Canada, *Annual Reports of the Department of Indian Affairs* (1915), 103.

[34] Hoijer, *Linguistic History* (1946), 225. See below, p. 92, 97.

was Wolf. Her name was Tahltanma, a word whose meaning the informant did not know. The Tahltan tribe (or macrocosmic group) in closest proximity to the Kaska was the Nalotena, "People who Live in a Country Where There is Not Much Snow" or North People. These people ranged from about 40 miles north of the present site of Telegraph Creek on the Cheseli River to as far as Teslin Lake.[35] To the west the Nalotena met the Tlingit. The latter Indians sometimes brought trade goods up the Cheseli River to the Tahltan fishing village of Naliin, at the confluence of the Naliin ("Waterfall") and Cheseli rivers. Near Naliin was the Tahltan village of Tselɔ in a canyon that the Indians bridged. Other villages were located at hunting and fishing sites on salmon streams and fish lakes like Tstałue, "Flat Rock Fish Lake." In the spring the people fished for rainbow trout in that lake. Another village, Tediititc, "Hand in the Water All the Time for Fish," lay inland from Naliin and was frequented by Indians fishing for grayling with a hand net.

North of the Tahltan and northwest of the Upper Liard Indians dwelt the Taku people, grouped around Teslin Lake and River and occupying the drainage of Nisutlin River. Kaska informants identified the Taku as Tlingit (a feature also noted by Teit[36]), indicating perhaps a displacement of the original Taku population by Tlingit immigrants. The people of the Teslin area were also known as Totena. Taku people used to meet the Kaska at a Groundhog Lake near the headwaters of the Rancheria River. Here the Kaska went in autumn to hunt groundhog. Most of the Kaska also knew of the existence of "Salt Water Indians" situated west of the Taku. In recent years visitors from the Cassiar have met Tlingit Indians at Wrangell in Alaska. According to Parnell, a party of Tlingit under a female chieftainess visited Dease Lake Hudson's Bay Post in the winter of 1938–39.[37]

North of the Kaska were the inhabitants of the Ross and Pelly River basins, the Akidixtinitu?agotena, "Dwellers Where Two Rivers Join at Right Angles," also called Terahan(i), "Over the Ridge People." The Upper Liard and Frances Lake people occasionally sought salmon at Pelly Banks and there encountered Pelly Indians. The latter also traveled south to what is now called Albert or Cormier Creek, near Watson Lake. They made this journey in order to contact the Tahltan traders who after 1700 became middlemen carrying European trade goods inland from the Tlingit. The Frances Lake Kaska easily understand the dialect of the Pelly River Indians. According to an Upper Liard informant (O) the dialect of the Frances Lake people is closer to that of the Pelly people than it is to the Liard River dwellers.[38] According to Jenness, citing a

[35] Barbeau has the Tahltan coming to trade at Frances Lake about 1849. This was possible, but his work is completely fictional, and better source material is needed before such a range for the Tahltan becomes accepted even for post-contact times. (Barbeau, *Mountain Cloud* [1944].) One informant (RJ) claimed the Tahltan went to within 20 miles of the confluence of the Frances and Liard rivers.

[36] Teit, *Unpublished manuscript* (1915?).

[37] Parnell, *Campbell of the Yukon* (1942), 6.

[38] Sheldon saw the Pelly people "closely allied to that branch of the Nahanni group designated as Kaska." Perhaps such similarity is late and related to Kaska emigrants in the Pelly basin. Sheldon, *Wilderness of the Upper Yukon* (1919), 190.

manuscript of Poole Field, a band of Mackenzie Indians wiped out the original Pelly and Ross River populations about 1886. One or two survivors found refuge with the Frances Lake people, some of whom extended themselves northward. Their descendants are today in possession of the Pelly drainage basin. Teslin Lake Indians (Taku?) also moved in to the country vacated by the autochthonous Pelly population.[39] In the field the present writer heard that the establishment of a trading post at Ross River in about 1898 caused some Indians to leave off trading at Lower Post and to take up trapping around Frances Lake. They went to trade at Ross River post where prices were lower. The movement north included Indians like Old Ceasar and coincided with the Yukon gold rush, when a horse trail was cut from Lower Post across the divide separating Frances Lake from Pelly River.

To the northeast the Frances Lake Kaska bordered on the territory of the Mackenzie River People, the Klukotena. To the east and southeast the Espatotena adjoined the Beaver Indians, Tsapagotena, of the lower Liard, and the Fort Nelson Slave, Etca?otena (synonymy: Atcotena "People Who Hunt in a Brushy Place," and Gutzitotena, "People Who Work all the Time.") The Atcotena obviously correspond to Petitot's Étca-ottinè, "gens a l'abri."[40] On the south the Kaska contacted that branch of the Sekani known as the Bear Lake Indians. In recent years this tribe has penetrated far down the Kechika River, almost to the Liard, and came to trade at McDame Creek as well as at Fort Ware.[41] Considerable intermarriage has occurred between the Kaska and Bear Lake people. In Kaska their name is rendered Sastotena (synonymy: Sateune; Tsekona, "Mountain People"; Satełune; Sazeootina; Sazentina; and Sezotena). The frequency of intermarriage and the penetration of the Liard country by the Bear Lake are probably jointly responsible for the frequency with which these people have been included in the Kaska nation. Moderately strong differences in dialect[42] plus the fact that Jenness has already grouped them with the Sekani[43] recommend their exclusion from the Kaska category. The Bear Lakers' movement down the Kechika probably followed the closing of their trading post, Fort Connell, on Bear Lake at the head of the Skeena River, in 1890.

Apart from these Athapaskan speaking neighbors the Kaska aboriginally also knew the troublesome Cree Indians, teciina, "They Hide Themselves."

POPULATION

Few helpful data are available with which to estimate the aboriginal population of the Kaska tribes. Kroeber, following Mooney, gives a population of 500. Since he allots a somewhat smaller area to the nation than we do his density figure of 1.00 per hundred

[39] Jenness, *Indians of Canada* (1932), 396.

[40] Honigmann, *Ethnography and Acculturation of the Fort Nelson Slave* (1946), 24–25; cf. Petitot, *Autour du grand lac des Esclaves* (1891), 363; also pp. 344–358.

[41] See Hunter, *Frances Lake, Yukon* (1924), 98; Stanwell-Fletcher, *Naturalists in the Wilds of British Columbia* (1940).

[42] See below p. 80. A Frances Lake youth said he could understand hardly a word of Bear Lake.

[43] Jenness, *Sekani Indians of British Columbia* (1937), 9–10.

square kilometers probably needs reduction if it is to conform to the Cassiar as we have defined it.[44] Available information concerning population movements in the early contact period has been presented in another monograph and need not be repeated here.[45]

PSYCHOLOGICAL TYPES

It is manifestly impossible to utilize direct observation as a method for learning the personal characteristics of the aboriginal Kaska Indians. Such a picture, it cannot be denied, would give depth to the cultural reconstruction that we intend to present. One means of gauging the personality of a past people is to rely on the impressions of early travelers. Such visitors may not have had contact with the Kaska but with their neighbors and so it must be assumed that relatively common behavior patterns obtained throughout a relatively large culture area. Personal observations by the writer and recent psychological studies by Hallowell, Caudill, Barnouw, and others suggest that the facts support an assumption of behavioral homogeneity in the northern forest, although differences can certainly be discovered even between adjacent tribes or nations. Richardson has given a very full and intimate impression of the Dogrib. He says:[46]

Few traces of the stoicism popularly attributed to the red races exist among the Dog-ribs: they shrink from pain, show little daring, express their fears without disguise on all occasions, imaginary or real, shed tears readily, and live in constant dread of enemies, bodied and disembodied. Yet all, young and old, enjoy a joke heartily. They are not a morose people but, on the contrary, when young and in a situation of security, they are remarkably lively and cheerful. The infirmities of age, which press heavily on the savage, render them querulous.

According to Dawson, "the Kaska have the reputation of being a very timid people and they are rather undersized and have a poor physique. They are lazy and untrustworthy."[47]

Another means of securing personality data suggested itself in the course of field work. What could a sophisticated informant say about aboriginal character types? Asked to describe some "old fashioned" individuals an Upper Liard informant provided the following patterns:

"Quiet man" (maza?unt?etena). Such a person spoke infrequently and briefly. However excessive taciturnity disturbed other people. A man who didn't speak for two or three days was suspected of holding murderous intentions toward somebody.

"Highest man talking" (maza?anu?utiihiitena). This refers to a man capable of many tasks and confident enough in his ability to see that other people became aware of his capacities.

"He knows everything man" (enatayatiihiitena). Very few people in the aboriginal community measured up to this type, a man skillful in providing all the implements and apparatus needed for making a living and doing all of the required tasks with consummate skill.

[44] Kroeber, Cultural and Natural Areas of Native North America (1939), 141.
[45] Honigmann, Culture and Ethos of Kaska Society (1949), 37.
[46] Richardson, Arctic Searching Expedition (1852), 250.
[47] Dawson, Report of an Exploration in the Yukon District, N.W.T. (1887–88), 200.

"*Nice fellow to anybody* [*i.e., everybody*]" (tenametii?a?etiia). This person was suffused with warmth toward all his neighbors. He was universally liked. "People in the old days used to think about each other rather than talk to each other."

"*Tell them about anything man*" (?utetciitena). A talkative person or gossip is indicated.

"*Crazy man*" (tena?atutatii). Such an individual played many jokes on his neighbors and teased other people. "He told young girls he's going to marry them." Few people belonged in this category and rarely did old people demonstrate such behavior. Our chief informant, Old Man, tended to manifest this kind of humor.

"*Mind about woman*" (e?uteniitciitsuna). Refers to a man so preoccupied with the thought of women and sex that he could not apply himself to hunting and other work. In other words we have here the rake.

"*He gets around all right this little man*" (tatzile eɣtintena su?ate). A fellow who just got by in the course of making his living.

"*Poor man*" (etuyatiieɣitiniitena). People were kind to an unfortunate person of this type. If, after a suitable period of aid, he failed to make his own living their assistance might be discontinued. In return for receiving aid a person should help his benefactor, for example by visiting deadfalls. We have here the germ of specialization and the kind of relationship found in the Plains where poor men served rich patrons.

"*Lazy man*" (katsatsetena). He lacked both knowledge and skill and wasted much potentially productive time.

"*Lazy man starving*" (tenakatsatsetena seklii). "You helped him, gave him nets, and what he needed. Pretty soon his wife came back and said that they're starving."

"*Full of prunes man*" (?utsiiɣiitena). A person who boasted but without telling the truth. People disliked a liar and tended to ignore the windbag to whom this designation refers.

INFORMANTS

The informants to be identified did not themselves experience directly all of the aboriginal lifeways which they recounted. In some cases, of course, aboriginal patterns have survived to contemporary or near contemporary times. Of these the informants enjoyed first hand knowledge. Other data, however, were verbally transmitted to living persons by parents and grandparents. Where such information is involved time has often fogged memories and distorted facts. If any value is seen in ethnographic reconstruction, such facts nevertheless must be accepted with a measure of caution and preserved. No great gift of prophecy is required to point out that the pace of culture change in the North is bringing about a rapid displacement of aboriginal tradition so that in the near future generations will grow up without understanding the culture of their forefathers.

Because a number of the informants employed to complete this reconstruction also served as subjects of a somewhat intimate, psychologically oriented, contemporary community study[48] the actual identity of these field assistants must be concealed. The

---

[48] Honigmann, *Culture and Ethos of Kaska Society* (1949).

following names are keyed by initials. Wherever it seems pertinent in the course of this monograph, the source of information is designated by the initials of the informant.

Jack Abou (A) is the true name of an early middle aged man who, like so many Indians, has for several years been troubled with failing eyesight. Doctors could do little for him beyond recommending spectacles. His great wish was to earn enough money by trapping to be able to visit an optician at Whitehorse. Jack's father was a Tselona. His mother, probably a Sekani, came from McLeod Lake. He served briefly to provide information about the Tselona tribe. The fact that he had to travel far to reach his trap line and therefore quit Lower Post early in the fall limited his usefulness.

Old Man (O) proved to be our most valuable informant. A genial, highly cooperative, 50-year old Upper Liard Indian, his paternal grandparents were Tlingit and his maternal grandfather an Upper Liard Indian. His father was born at Ross River and after his marriage moved to the country of the Upper Liard. Old Man possessed a high intelligence. His long association with white men had further given him a fair knowledge of English and a relatively objective perspective on Indian life. He was completely trustworthy, although there remains the danger that some of the patterns he reported (for example warfare) pertain more closely to the Teslin Lake and upper Taku River people than to the Upper Liard dwellers and may even represent traditions heard from his Tlingit grandfather.

River Joe (RJ) served as another reporter of aboriginal Upper Liard River life. Pretentious and not overly bright, he was not one of our most valuable assistants. He stems from Taku (possibly Chilkat) parentage.

Skipper (S), a man of about 60, constituted one of the main sources of information concerning the Dease River people. Generally he was a taciturn person, a quality that made him difficult to work with. At one time he had been suspected of killing a white man and stealing the latter's fur. Investigation, however, had failed to prove his guilt. It is not likely that Skipper deliberately lied during his relationship with the anthropologist but for some reason he showed a propensity to assent readily when various possible traits were brought to his attention with the query whether he had heard of them in the Dease River valley. Dubious cases were rechecked whenever possible.

Willy Tsiga (WT), the true name of a 45-year old man, served as a second informant for the Dease River basin. His father was a Tlingit Indian. Serving as an informant manifestly augmented his pride. In effort he made up what he may have lacked in the way of developed intellectual ability.

Xavier (X) volunteered briefly to contribute data for the Upper Liard area. About 70 years old, he migrated west from Fort Simpson at a very early age and later married an Upper Liard woman. His parents were perhaps Espatotena. Of all informants he seemed to retain the greatest emotional involvement with aboriginal supernaturalism. His conversation was most rewarding when informal.

MAKING A LIVING

TECHNOLOGY

UPPER LIARD KASKA. The basic techniques through which the aboriginal peoples of the upper Liard converted stone, skins, and other materials into tools, clothing, and similar useful products were as uncomplex as the group's social organization. The basic tools came from pecked and polished, close-grained stone or flaked, siliceous rock. Lithic implements included axes, knives, scrapers, and crude pestles. The last need little further description than to say that they consisted of naturally smooth stones employed for pounding meat or cracking bones to expose the much relished marrow. The degree of refinement that these pounders originally lacked was soon acquired through repeated usage. While simple adzes of unhafted caribou could be recalled clearly by informants, memories remained much less reliable concerning the process by which the stone ax came into being. According to one man a "smooth" rock was thrown against another stone causing the former to fracture. Pecking then produced a cutting edge on one of the fractured edges. Finally the head, probably after polishing, was hafted in a birch handle and securely lashed in place. The efficiency of such an ax remained so limited that horn adzes were regarded as eminently more satisfactory for cutting down growing timber. A careful man took good care of his ax, probably because of the time and energy required to work not only the stone but also the hard birch wood. Knives varied in size depending upon their intended use, the smaller blades serving for woodworking and the larger for skinning and butchering. The handling of stone in the process of blade making could not be recalled. Our principal informant (O) spoke of the stone being fractured between two flint wedges and claimed that men wore double gloves in this task. Blades were usually hafted in handles of goat's horn. In use a woodworker drew his knife toward the body. The existence of a beaver tooth drawknife such as Osgood describes could not be certified.[1] For women to use in skin processing men made a variety of scrapers. One of these instruments, used to soften a hide after the hair had been removed, consisted of a thin chipped stone mounted in a wooden handle from one to three feet in length. No semilunar knife could be recalled.

Clay found little employment in technology except for preparing fireplaces on rafts. The most dependable informant (O) knew nothing about solid clay vessels but his contemporary (X) had heard of clay-lined spruce-bark containers for boiling meat.

Bone possessed utilitarian value and provided knives, scrapers, awls, needles, and arrow points. Eating knives resulted from cutting with a flint knife a piece of softened bone taken from the lower joint of an ungulate and then hafting the blade in a handle of goat's horn. Fleshers used in cleaning hides were obtained by cracking the shaft of a caribou leg bone and sharpening the transverse fractured surface until it formed a smoothly tapering edge. Awls for sewing and bark basketry consisted of sharpened

---

[1] Osgood, *Ingalik Material Culture* (1940), 87. A beaver-tooth knife for woodworking is found among the Tsimshian and Tlingit. Drucker, *Culture Element Distributions: XXVI, Northwest Coast* (1950), 183.

bone splinters. Needles with eyes appear to have been manufactured prior to contact, their use being aided by a "thimble" consisting of a flat piece of bone held in the palm. The bone arrow points will be described in connection with weapons.

As already indicated, horn from mountain sheep, goats, and caribou found a place in the technology. To prepare spoons and blades from goat or sheep horn the material was boiled until soft, split with a stone ax, and then shaped with a stone knife. Without previous boiling, caribou horn could be sharpened (by grinding ?) to provide an adze or scraper with an edge sharp enough to cut through the hairs on a caribou hide. The sharp point of a caribou horn made a useful tool for drilling through wood. Another drill consisted of a beaver tooth mounted in a wooden handle.

Although objects of wood and bark played important roles in daily living, woodworking remained a relatively undeveloped industry carried out with simple apparatus. Spruce appears to have been the most frequently used wood. The available cutting tools made it relatively impossible to cut down any tree larger than a sapling so that older trees had to be weakened by firing the base. Then came the problem of cutting the trunk into planks of desired length and thickness. A felled tree was split with a birchwood wedge driven with a maul made by hafting a heavy stone in a wooden handle.[2] In the course of using a maul of this type a man sometimes chanted "gu guk, gu guk," the charm urging the lashing around the head of the maul to remain strong and not to loosen. Fabrication of the resultant planks into snowshoes, snow shovels, handles, and other objects demanded use of the cutting tools previously described. Spruce bark provided a variety of objects ranging from canoes to drinking and storage vessels. Large pieces of bark were often peeled by a skilled man who, after selecting a suitable tree, climbed into it on a ladder consisting of a spruce sapling leaned into the branches. After clearing the trunk of branches he cut a girth around the tree with a caribou-horn adze. He then split the bark lengthwise for about four feet and peeled it free from the trunk with a wooden barking tool fitted with a crook. This implement partly encircled the tree, under the bark. The loosened rind was tied in place around the trunk with babiche line while the worker lengthened the split downward by cutting. This continued until the bottom of the tree was reached. Here another girth was cut and from the ground several men now pulled the strip fanwise from the tree. The lashing at the top of the piece had been left loose enough to permit the large sheet to gradually slip down as the men drew the lower edges free. White birch bark, scarce along the upper Liard River, found little place in technology.

From the pelts of slain animals the people secured garments, sleeping robes, and storage bags. First, however, the skins had to undergo processing to render them fit for these purposes. Fur covered pelts required thorough fleshing after which they were dried and perhaps stretched. Beaver skins were dried and stretched on oval frames of willow very similar to the type still in use. People stretched lynx, fox, muskrat, and similar pelts, peeled whole from the animal's body, over form boards that slipped into the skins. Rabbit skin, intended for cutting up into plaiting line, could be best dried

[2] Hafted stone sledge hammers as well as plain wooden mauls are specified to have been made by the Tlingit. Drucker, *Culture Element Distributions: XXVI, Northwest Coast* (1950), 183.

in cold weather. The tanning of caribou, goat, and moose hide involved a relatively more complex process to which women devoted considerable time.[3] First the skin needed to be scraped clean of flesh and fat with the aid of a bone fleshing tool. Next greater muscular effort had to be applied in wielding the horn scraper with which to free the hide of hair. The woman then rubbed a mixture of brain and water into the skin and left it to soften.[4] Afterwards the hide must be washed and then twisted or wrung out to remove the excess moisture, dried in the sun, and stretched. Thereupon came the labor of softening, accomplished by scraping the spanned white hide with a long handled stone scraper. A second or third brain soaking and scraping followed. Now the skin could be sewn into a tube loosely closed at the end from which it was suspended for an hour or so over a smudge fire kindled with rotten spruce wood. When the inside had been thoroughly smoked the surfaces were reversed and smoking continued for about another hour. The result appeared in a golden yellow skin which the worker suspended in the sun to dry and then fabricated into containers and tailored clothing. The dried whole skin of a large fish (probably loche) provided material for a bag widely used to store sewing materials.

Line ranked as an indispensable requirement in aboriginal times. Material used in line making included sinew, caribou hide taken at various stages of the tanning process, spruce root, whole willow, willow bark, willow root, and grass. Fish skin, willow bast, and spruce wood do not appear to have provided material for cordage. Sinew line originated along the backbone of a caribou or, in emergencies, from the tendons of mountain sheep and goats. A woman scraped the sinews clean of flesh with a knife and hung them overnight to dry. On the following day she flexed and loosened a bunch by grasping the upper and lower ends with the hands and rotating the mass in opposite directions. The process separated the individual strands which could then be stored until needed. Before being used the sinew was moistened by drawing individual strands through the mouth thus rendering them soft and pliable. From caribou hide came rawhide, babiche, and smoked (or tanned) skin line. Rawhide designates a skin from which the hair and flesh have been removed but which has not been treated with the brain mixture. Such skin provided a strong cordage difficult to untie once it had dried and hardened. Ordinary babiche (semi-tanned skin) line generally came from the skin of a bull caribou. Bear skin provided the strongest variety of this type of line while mountain sheep skin yielded a particularly fine babiche highly desirable for filling the front and rear panels of snowshoes. More often "fine" babiche came from the hide of a cow caribou. Hide to be used in the manufacture of semi-tanned skin cordage had been fleshed, cleaned of hair, and softened. It might be dyed in moose blood if the maker fancied the deep rusty color. Newly cut babiche was stretched between two trees and left to dry for 24 hours

[3] For fairly detailed descriptions of skin working observed in contemporary Kaska setting see Honigmann, *Culture and Ethos of Kaska Society* (1949), 59, 76–79. Skin working among other Northern Athapaskans is illustrated in Leechman, *Caribou for Chipewyans* (1948), and the same writer's *Pointed Skins* (1948).

[4] The Tlingit (including the Chilkat) used brains as a tanning mixture, while southerly tribes on the coast tended more to use salmon roe and oil. Drucker, *Culture Element Distributions: XXVI, Northwest Coast* (1950), 196.

in warm weather but for a week during winter. Summer babiche broke easily in comparison to the winter variety. Cold weather drying also rendered the line softer and more flexible. Stretching frames for drying babiche were not generally used, although for hasty drying such line might be wrapped around a snowshoe. From fully tanned and smoked hide came smoked-skin line, of whose manufacture little need be said. Men collected the roots for spruce-root cordage but all subsequent stages of manufacture were carried out by women who scraped the roots with a stone knife and then boiled them for about half an hour. The worker then split each root, smaller ones being split only once but very thick roots four times. Occasionally spruce roots were braided. This line kept best when loosely hung up and tended to spoil if wound tightly. When spruce roots became hard and dry, they could be softened with grease but urine was never used for this purpose. Whole willow line, made in emergencies to pack meat, consisted of a long willow branch softened by heating over fire and then twisted until the fibers had been well broken. Willow bark line found a host of uses and yielded material for fish nets. Willow roots, collected by men, were softened through an hour's boiling, split, and then used for cordage. To manufacture grass line women gathered the high sedge growing along lake shores. Bundled into sheaves for transportation back to camp, the material had to be fabricated quickly before it dried. Twisting converted the grass into line that remained useful for only a short period of time. When confronted with the information that the Tahltan had woven goat's wool into blankets our informant (O) opined that the Kaska must have done the same thing.[5] Among the knots commonly applied to the foregoing types of cordage are the running noose, bowline, and overhand. Two ends of babiche were spliced by means of a sheet bend.

Dease River Kaska. Stone tools constituted the basic equipment in the Dease River area. A flintlike stone as well as obsidian provided materials for blades which were then hafted in handles of horn or spruce and birch wood. Sinew or babiche line secured the hafting. To protect blades men or women manufactured scabbards from smoked caribou hide. The container attached under the outer belt of a person's garments. Although a woman had her own knife its form did not differ from the man's and the objects were designated by a common term. Before beginning to chip stone a man might swing a bullroarer while repeating the song, "tłunatis, tłunatis." The charm caused his magical power to aid him in the work.

Concerning work in clay, we found it impossible to check the testimony of one informant (S) that vessels used to be shaped from this substance and hardened by firing.

The caribou or goat's horn adze served as a basic tool for woodworking and stone axes were denied. Men split logs with wooden wedges and used spruce barking tools to assist them in peeling spruce bark.

Bone constituted an important material for knife blades, the material being "scraped" to an edge and hafted in a horn or wooden handle. Women used skin fleshers derived from the leg bone of the caribou as well as obsidian scrapers for removing the hair of a hide. Sewing needles of fish bone are said to have been of recent introduction, supplanting bone awls. Unprocessed moose horn provided an ice chisel as well as material for

---

[5] Teit, *On Tahltan (Athabaskan) Work* (1912), 485.

fish spear tines. After being softened by boiling caribou horn could be shaped into spoons with the aid of a stone knife. Several implements utilized teeth. A skin scraper consisted of four beaver teeth set in a wooden handle and secured with babiche line, while a beaver- or porcupine-tooth awl permitted drilling in wood. Men mounted two beaver teeth in a wooden frame for use as a drawknife or chisel.

The processing of animal skins constituted one of a woman's major tasks. After a preliminary smoking the worker rubbed the skin with a mixture of caribou brain and animal grease. She left the hide to soften for three days and then washed it in water. Afterwards it was kneaded with the fingers and scraped on a frame with a softening stick that carried a stone blade. Following another soaking in the brain mixture the process was repeated one or more times before smoking. Use of urine in tanning was not admitted.

Animal hides at various stages of processing, along with various vegetable products, provided materials for cordage. Types of line included sinew, rawhide, semi-tanned hide, smoked (tanned) skin, spruce root, twisted grass, and willow root. Although in a somewhat different category, the wristlets made by twisting eider-duck feathers may also be mentioned here. Fish-skin line and spruce-wood cordage are explicitly denied by contemporary informants. Strong rawhide came from bearskin and, like caribou rawhide, served for packing. Caribou and beaver (?) pelts provided babiche, while in an emergency strong packing line that remained useful for relatively limited periods could be fabricated from willow bark.[6] Grass-woven baskets had been heard about by a Dease River informant. They were manufactured in summer by women as receptacles for storing food and other materials. Grass mats met with no recognition.

Tselona. The easterly Kaksa prepared a needle with an eye from a marten bone. Although not certain of the kind of bone used, the informant would not assent to the suggestion that it might have been a penis bone.

Frances Lake Kaska. A traveler's mention of "ropes" of goat's hair among the Frances Lake Indians is evidence of the processing of goat's wool and its probable use in weaving.[7]

FOOD—ITS COLLECTION, PREPARATION, AND EATING

Upper Liard Kaska. The aboriginal Kaska community took many of its cues from the seasons, whose perpetually recurring cycle accompanied notable changes in the habits and condition of the animals on which the people depended. In late summer, when game had fattened, hunters and their families moved into the mountains in pursuit of the goat, sheep, caribou, gopher, and ground hog. People thought of the long, lean season of winter as the women busied themselves drying meat and caching it for future consumption. Meanwhile men readied snowshoes, toboggans, and walking staves. When the snow became deep and the severe cold began to set in the families gathered together around a fish lake where, a little like some of the other animals, they "hiber-

---

[6] An informant reported that among the Bear Lake Sekani line was cut from rawhide, semi-tanned skin, and smoked skin. Demonstration by another informant from this group revealed use of the bowline for splicing two ends of babiche.

[7] Hunter, *Frances Lake, Yukon* (1924), 73.

nated" in firmly built dwellings and subsisted on fish. Around the turn of the year "young fellows" set out to obtain dried meat from the caches which in some instances might be located 30 or more miles away. For most of the people winter remained a period of limited mobility and relaxed social intercourse. Sometimes, however, fishing failed and then the meat caches were quickly depleted. If fresh fishing sites proved equally unproductive the groups sought to make contact with another band, one that had been more fortunate in finding food. At such times men climbed to high places and scanned the horizons for smoke which in winter would be visible for long distances. Often it must have happened that all the neighbors in a tribal territory found themselves short of food, perhaps due to the cyclic fluctuation of the animal population. In such years, again like the other animals, the human population of the Cassiar also shrank. Thus a balance was kept between the people and the environment's resources. With the lengthening days of spring, the snow crusted and there came another favorable time to pursue game. Now beaver provided an important source of food, the people separating to travel to family-owned beaver creeks. Upon the break-up of the river ice the beaver and muskrat quit their dwellings to travel. That served as a cue for the Indians to build or recover canoes. Then once more they reassembled around a fish lake, where the hot summer was passed renewing friendships. This is a brief summary of the food quest and annual cycle, whose routines remain to be described in greater detail. The focus of the cycle was on food. One informant clearly recognized this when he remarked, "Old timers thought about nothing—just something to eat."

In the calendar of the community one sees more specifically the relationship between the people and environment, as well as the note taken of the seasonal changes. The year was divided as follows:

kliʔulaɣesa (January)—"dog burning moon." The term refers to the intense cold which caused dogs to get too close to the fire so that they sometimes burned themselves.

kaʔoɣazesa (February)—"rabbit eating moon" (0). Also taɣadasa, "cold tree moon" (X).

atasa (March)—"eagle coming moon" (0). Also called atikasa, "moon when everything [i.e., game] comes to this country" (X).

tatanasa (April)—"snow crusts moon" (0). Also tikasa, "everything here moon" (X).

A reference for the period corresponding to May could not be obtained.

ayezesa (June)—"egg moon."

akatsunzisa (July)—"game moults moon."

atosanasa (August)—"fat game moon" (0) or etdigasa, "everything ready, everything fat moon" (X).

atoditelisa (September)—"leaves color moon."

ʔustelisa (October)—"female ground hog moon."

natinitsiɬsa (November)—"little finger moon." So called because "its soft, everything is cool and yet not too cold."

tinitcosa (December)—"Christmas (?) moon."

The Indians secured food through gathering, trapping, hunting, and fishing. Girls and women did the principal collecting, although men also sought vegetable products in the course of walking through a favorable area while hunting. Berries were the main items sought by collectors and included, in approximate order of frequency, the soap berry, high- and low-bush cranberry, salmon berry, raspberry, strawberry, currant, and blueberry. Other vegetable products taken from the land included fern roots in spring; lily bulbs; mushrooms, frequently stolen from a squirrel's cache; muskeg apples, that grew up in the mountains and were described as tasting somewhat like turnips; wild onions, of which only the greens were eaten; rose petals, made into a beverage by boiling; and wild rhubarb. Both sexes chewed gum taken from a "half dead" spruce tree, a choice advised by the fact that such gum would not stick to the teeth. Jackpine and spruce fibers were also eaten but mud, birch fiber, willow buds, wild rice, and wild peas held no place in the diet. Birch sap, obtained by tapping the birch in spring, ranked as a minor delicacy but people ignored poplar sap. Children kept the camp supplied with water, securing it from the river or in the form of snow. Warmed moose milk was sometimes drunk.

Flesh food could be secured with the least expenditure of energy by setting traps, including snares, deadfalls, nets, and, perhaps, pitfalls. For bear the Indian located a snare made of braided babiche (as many as eight strands of semi-tanned skin line might be used) near a berry patch, while for moose and caribou he placed similar snares between trees and across the runways which those animals had made in the course of visiting drinking places and salt licks. Fences were sometimes extended from either side of a moose or caribou snare. At other times trappers thrust two forked poles into the ground and across them suspended a toggle pole twelve feet long and three inches in diameter. From the toggle hung a caribou snare while on either side a fence directed the animal into the trap. Men always set moose and caribou snares. "Even if a woman knew how to make a caribou snare she could not make it good enough." For lynx a semicircle of poles with a center opening for the snare was anchored in the ground. A single strand of babiche had sufficient strength to hold this animal. Such snares might be erected by women. In mountain gulches through which ran sheep trails men erected free toggle snares for sheep. Often the poles used in this work had to be packed long distances above timberline. Up to six strands of babiche were twisted together to make a snare line strong enough for that animal. For beaver, men (and also women) set snares of three-strand twisted babiche near a dam.

Ground hog snares featured a rock toggle and required two-strand twisted babiche. The family provided itself with a number of six- or seven-foot long forked poles in the fall and packed these above the timberline. The trapper firmly planted one such pole for each snare in a rock cairn near a ground hog den. On either side of the pole ran a small fence about a foot high. After forming the snare loop between these fences, the snare line was bent and knotted around a small trigger stick before continuing through the fork of the pole. Halfway below the fork the line was weighted with a 20-pound rock. The trigger stick was fitted under a convenient knob or protuberance on the upright pole, the toggle's weight serving to keep it fixed until an animal entered the snare and dislodged the stick, whereupon the rock fell to the ground. The weight of the falling toggle lifted the animal off the earth. In timbered areas lifting-pole snares like those frequently used for rabbits were also set for ground hog. In fact, the rock toggle appears to represent an adaptation of the lifting-pole principle to treeless country. Men, boys, and women built ground hog snares.

Rabbit traps were of both the lifting-pole and spring-pole types. They were mainly constructed by boys and women. With each spring-pole snare went a notched trigger stick about three-eighths of an inch in diameter and three inches long (Fig. 3, B). The person going to set snares provided himself with a supply of these before leaving camp. At a rabbit run the trapper cut a foundation pole (Fig. 3, D), which he suspended loosely in brush or snow about ten inches above the ground. Above this he bent down the willow spring-pole toggle (c) and to it fastened the doubled end of the snare line with a cow hitch. The other end was bent around the trigger stick, thereby securing it to the foundation pole below which the noose was spread, supported by twigs. Entering the snare a rabbit would dislodge the trigger stick, thus releasing it from the foundation pole and freeing the spring pole, which flew upward, drawing the rabbit, snare line, and trigger stick along. Five minutes sufficed to set such a snare.[8]

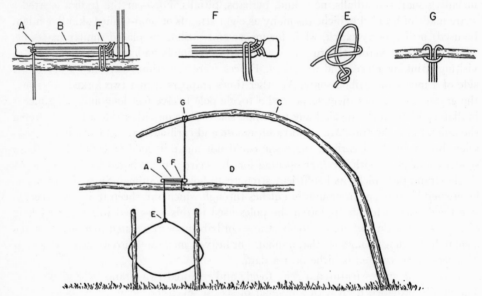

Fig. 3. Spring Pole Rabbit Snare.

The bear, marten, mink, fisher, beaver, and ground hog were also hunted with deadfalls, the construction of which varied somewhat for the different animal species. Bear deadfalls consisted of a double bed log above which a samson-post trigger stick propped up a fall log measuring a foot or more in diameter. Vertical poles driven into the ground on either side of the trap assured a direct fall for the propped-up end of the fall log, while the opposite portion rested in a short, forked stick driven into the ground. Marten and (after contact) mink deadfalls followed the same pattern but required only a two-inch diameter fall log, which rested directly on the ground. For fisher a somewhat

[8] Similar snares occurred among the Ingalik and Tanaina. See Osgood, *Ingalik Material Culture* (1940), 239 and Osgood, *Ethnography of the Tanaina* (1937), 93. The apparently greater complexity of the Kaska product may be related to the thin cotton twine with which the models were prepared.

heavier pole was employed. In winter, brush placed under the point where a fall log rested on the snow prevented this part from sinking. The pen behind the trigger stick was also provided with spruce boughs. Beaver deadfalls, erected on land behind a beaver house, were of the platform variety, the platform being secured to the samson post with spruce-root line and weighted down with rocks or earth—in winter only rocks. Ground-hog deadfalls also followed the platform pattern, the 14-inch samson post consisting of a bent alder limb or crooked spruce root. Nets of semi-tanned skin line spread under the ice also helped to catch beaver. After the net had been set the trapper broke down the animals' house, causing the inhabitants to flee toward the net. The trapped beaver were dispatched after the net was raised. The suggestion that pitfalls may have been used along the Upper Liard comes only from their mention in folktales.[9]

For hunting the Indian armed himself with the bow, arrows, spear, gaff hook, sling, or club. Black-birch wood provided the favorite material for bows and, as in toboggan construction, the wood that grew nearest the outside of the tree was thought to be best suited for bending. A small amount of (inner?) bark was often left on the bow wood in order to increase its resiliency. The size of a bow varied; a boy's reached from the ground to just above the stomach, while a man's extended to his forehead. Fitted to such large bows by means of a lashing that passed through two holes drilled in the stock, was a guard about the size of a violin bridge. It prevented the bowstring from snapping back against the fingers. A backing of tanned skin line sometimes appeared on each side of the guard. Occasionally bows were decorated with a "peppermint stick" design applied by masking the stick with widely spaced strips of spruce bark and then drying the wood over a fire. When dry the bark was pulled free, leaving an attractive black and white striped effect. Double-strand, twisted, cold-weather dried babiche supplied the bowstring. The informant objected to employing sinew, claiming that this substance would be too weak. One end of the line was knotted to an end of the bow stock, while an eye on the free end slipped into a notch at the stock's opposite end.

A light wood, such as spruce, ranked highest for arrows. A stick cut to suitable size was heated and then straightened by being worked back and forth in a forked stick split a short distance below the fork. A nock cut on the rear of the shaft fitted against the bowstring. The size of an arrow depended in part on its intended function; for game birds 24 inches was a standard size while 3 feet constituted the size of a shaft suitable for big game hunting. Points also varied according to function. Detachable points of bone barbed on only one side[10] were secured to shafts by means of line. Double bone points, the barbs facing in opposite directions, served to kill spruce hens and grouse. Blunt-tipped shafts fitted with a quarter-inch deep notch brought down rabbits and other small game. Finally, detachable stone points that remained in the animal after the shaft was withdrawn or broken off were reserved for big game. To shoot fish a detachable flint point was provided and attached to the shaft with two feet of tanned skin line.

[9] Pitfalls seem to have been absent among the Fort Nelson Slave. Honigmann, *Ethnography and Acculturation of the Fort Nelson Slave* (1946), 37.

[10] Cf., Osgood, *Ingalik Material Culture* (1940), 203; illustration *a*.

Bone for tips came from the lower hind leg of the caribou or moose. Eagle feathers, procured from the bird's nest, made the favorite vanes, although arrows for grouse and spruce hens might be tipped with feathers from owls. Crow feathers were avoided, it being said that they made too much noise. After being split, the feathers were glued to the shaft with spruce gum and secured with sinew line. Then each feather was trimmed in a graceful arc. Two- as well as three-feather vanes occurred. In the latter the vanes always lay on three sides of the shaft; never were two vanes located on top. To contain arrows, women manufactured quivers of tanned moosehide, three feet long and six inches in diameter, decorated with tassels and porcupine-quill embroidery. Shoulder straps also carried embroidery. Two compartments in the container separated bird from larger game arrows, both types being inserted into the quiver point first. A birch-bark bottom prevented the sharp points from piercing the hide. A man always wore his quiver under the left arm, shoulder quivers being unknown. When standing on land the hunter held his bow in an absolutely vertical position. In a canoe as well as when kneeling on land, he employed the weapon horizontally. The first and second fingers pulled the arrow. Use of the third finger to grasp the bowstring (i.e., the Mediterranean-type release) was not admitted.

Spears, serving as war and hunting weapons, measured from five to ten feet in length and were fitted with flint points or with sharpened, caribou-horn blades. Larger spears, used against bear and caribou, carried only flint points. Gaff hooks were of bone. Slings, employed in hunting small game, enjoyed greater use as toys than as serious weapons. From wood and caribou horn men shaped clubs used, for example, against the bear and porcupine.

Hunting techniques sometimes required the hunter to wait in ambush for an animal to come within range of his weapon. At other times a man was obliged to drive, track, or pursue game. An example of the first mentioned type of technique is seen in the erection of the "bear tipi," constructed when the people "really wanted a bear." A conical structure with an entry big enough to admit a bear was located in the bush and toward evening provided with a fire. The hunter spread animal fat around the shelter and then, armed with a heavy, caribou-horn club, crawled inside to wait. Presently, if the man's plans were realized, a bear came around, attracted by the smell of the grease. As soon as the animal put its head into the structure the man struck. The evening's success need not yet be at an end. After drawing the carcass into the shelter the Indian waited on in the hope of a second bear visiting. Sometimes cubs followed a female into the ambush.

Another kind of decoy is seen in connection with hunting caribou in winter. A hunter spying caribou on a lake might fashion a decoy by spreading a caribou skin across a willow-pole framework. With this left on the ice, the hunter hid a short distance away. The animals, their curiosity aroused, came to investigate the decoy and so entered within range of the man's weapon. Game birds were also hunted from ambush. For grouse and spruce hens an Indian selected a willow pole about 15 feet long and cleaned it of bark. At the end he provided a noose of split spruce line. With this implement he crept close to the birds, endeavoring to slip the snare over an animal's head, whereupon he pulled the noose tight. Boys sought to catch robins and other small birds with snow-shoe traps. Snowshoes were placed on their sides so that they met at an acute angle. Bait was placed under the trap, from which a line extended to a cover where the young hunters lay in concealment. As a bird entered the structure a boy pulled the line, bringing the snowshoes down on the helpless prize.

For hunting caribou, circular enclosures were built that often reached a diameter of 50 feet. Such surrounds consisted of a circle of upright poles with in-between spaces piled with brush. Various points along the fence held snares, each man who cooperated in the building of the pen also setting a few snares. Cooperative effort drove the animals into the surround, where they could be pursued and dispatched with arrows. A wounded caribou could never be clubbed to death nor might he be touched with wood. To violate these injunctions promised a quick end to a hunter's success and might bring retribu-tion in the form of illness. Men sometimes drove caribou into a ravine or against a cliff, where they could easily be speared to death. Sometimes human beings formed caribou "surrounds."

Semicircular tracking, involving a hunter pursuing an animal against the wind, figured in caribou and moose hunting. For this procedure in dry weather, a man removed his moccasins upon encountering a fresh track. Bare feet enabled him to move more quickly, it was said. In autumn caribou and moose were called with birch bark horns or with a moose scapula rubbed briefly against a tree. During the moose calling season a man exercised caution never to take a moose scapula into camp lest a woman set eyes on the bone. Should this happen, he might lose his hunting ability. Before animal traction became prevalent small dogs assisted hunters in running down moose and bear.

Other hunting techniques included breaking into a beaver house in autumn and killing the occupants with spears. The same animals were also taken with nets or with the gaff stick, an implement further employed to hook a porcupine in its den. In summer porcupine could be clubbed to death easily.

Kills of large game ended up by being shared between the hunter's and neighboring families who customarily sent representatives to pack home the meat. At the scene of a kill each man selected that part of the animal appealing to him. Sometimes, especially when meat was scarce, quarreling might occur over the food's distribution. A story is told of one man who sought to tear a caribou head from the clutch of another. The latter fiercely held on to the tongue until that organ was wrenched from the mouth. A "lazy" man, who did not choose to hunt, freely joined a party going to fetch meat from a kill. Failure to share meat aroused resentment and ridicule. As already indicated, men did the greater part of hunting, boys early accompanying fathers into the bush to learn the necessary techniques. A man who lacked sons might train his eldest daughter to hunt, but her success in such work was believed to depend largely on her chastity.

Although the Upper Liard Kaksa, like other northern Indians, regarded game as the most attractive food, actually fish provided the dietary mainstay of the population. From the lakes and rivers people took jackfish, lake pickerel, lake and brook trout, whitefish (in smaller numbers because they were also the prey of jackfish), grayling, loche, and sucker. Clubbing, spearing, shooting with bow and arrow, netting, and trapping all contributed to the accumulation of fish throughout the year. Techniques varied with the season, however. Thus only during periods of open water could the foot-long birch or poplar pole be used to club fish as they swam in shallow water. Spearing with single and double tines was limited to the same period.[11] Tines were cut from beaver and caribou bone and hafted to shafts with sinew line. A detachable point joined to its shaft with 14 feet of tanned skin line constituted a harpoon. While seine and dip nets as well as the net-like fish drag are all reported to have been lacking, the gill net ("rock sunk net") found extensive employment in summer and winter. Willow-bark line fur- nished material for the women who, using a net shuttle and measuring stick, did the netting. Small- and large-mesh nets were prepared, the latter for beaver. Large-mesh beaver nets utilized fine babiche line rather than willow bark. The measuring stick also altered its size for these various types of nets, reaching a maximum length of a foot and a width of four inches. The rock sinkers for fish nets are said to have been heavier in summer than in winter, when the net was set under the ice. Winter netting required an ice chisel, frequently a sharpened length of caribou horn, as well as an ice scoop (literally "ice spoon") made of birch. Both sexes set fish nets. Fish weirs caught mainly white- fish and grayling. The funnel-like entry was made by stitching spruce brush onto a willow-pole framework about eight feet long. Willow-bark or spruce-root line provided stitching material. The funnel led into a square trap, from which a fence extended to both banks of the stream. Spruce brush tied to willow poles with spruce-root line pro- vided fence material. Occasionally spawning fish were caught with a spruce-root snare set at the end of a seven-foot willow pole. Pike swimming close to shore could be shot with arrows containing detachable flint points. Torch fishing did not occur except to the extent that, when fish ran in lakes, people sometimes set big blazes on shore. The light showed up the fish.

The hunting and fishing techniques just described provided a variety of foodstuffs. To review, people ate caribou, moose, black and brown bear, sheep, goats (more rarely), beaver, muskrat, lynx, ground hog, gopher, and marten, the latter being described as resembling rabbit in taste. Porcupine often provided a mainstay in winter, people re- fraining from killing this animal in summer in order to insure a supply for a period when it might be sorely needed. Rabbit, as might be expected, provided a very common item of diet in all seasons. Children hunted squirrels and prepared them over small fires. Among birds the owl, goose, and duck, while not overly abundant, were relished. Ptar- migan appeared frequently in late winter while the eagle, crane, swan, loon, spruce hen, and willow grouse were welcome additions to diet. Fish may have been somewhat more important in winter than in summer for in the latter season "the hunter could approach closer to game with his bow and arrow." Fish intestines did not go neglected as food. Berries were the chief vegetable item. The Indians never ate grizzly bear, the meat being described as "too strong." The fat of the grizzly, however, rendered a much appreciated grease. Fox, dog, otter, mink, and wolverine were likewise normally re- jected.[12] Nobody thought of eating wolf, frogs, or toads. The unpleasant taste of the

[11] The single tine was called tsasi, the double tine, xɔs; they correspond roughly to lances (a) and (c) in Osgood, Ingalik Material Culture (1940), 197–198.

[12] See below, p. 108.

fish-eating ducks made them unpopular for food and the raven was deemed to be inedible. Porcupine and bear brains exercised a debilitating effect on the body and hence were not used in preparing food. In periods of severe hunger the poorer tasting foods and, perhaps, even the magically dangerous animals like mink and otter would be consumed. Under the stress of starvation selectivity broke down to a point where moosehide might be eaten. Although strong repugnance governed the consumption of human flesh,[13] unproductive periods accompanied by severe hunger sometimes led to cannibalism. Tales of confirmed cannibals occur in oral tradition. There is the story of a man widely feared for his perverted appetite, which led him to regard human beings as game. He ate anyone he came across, including his wife and several children. Three sons, however, he spared because they could work for him. Indeed, they specialized in the task of killing men for their cannibal father after the latter grew too old to hunt. Approaching a camp this man would say, "You can kill birds for me now." Then, while the boys went off he started water boiling in readiness for the meat that they would bring back. The tale ends with the old cannibal and his sons meeting death at the hands of an intended victim who possessed exceptionally strong supernatural power.

Edible foods were both prepared for immediate consumption and preserved to be eaten at a later time. Boiling constituted the primary technique of cooking. Some meats, like lynx, were double boiled, the first water being discarded. After the meat had been cooked a "soup" was customarily made, onion greens or animal blood being added to the stock. "Soup took the place of tea in the old days. When people had finished with the meat they always drank the water in which the meat had been cooked." Several methods of boiling were known. Water placed in a basket tightly woven from split spruce roots could be brought to a boil with the aid of hot stones picked from ashes with spruce brush and blown free of dirt. The meat, cut in small pieces, was dropped into the boiling liquid. These vessels sometimes rested on the ground but were also supported a foot or so above the earth on a circle of wooden pegs. Another way of bringing water to boil is reminiscent of the Plains Indians. A pit was dug in the soil and lined with semi-tanned skin or, less commonly, with grass. Hot stones constituted the source of heat and keeping the top of the pit covered with spruce bark helped to retain the steam. Caribou and moose stomachs supplied another variety of container in which food could be cooked. The organ was first carefully warmed in front of the blaze to make it dry and hard. Later it might be suspended over the fire to cook the contents. Vegetables boiled included lily bulbs, muskeg apples, and fern roots, the latter only after being stripped of their outer bark. Dried wild rose petals were "powdered" before cooking. Mashing berries during cooking was common. People sometimes broiled meat by suspending it from a broiling stick or from a bone hook that itself hung from a piece of babiche line. Pieces of fat exposed near the heat of fire provided grease, the drippings being caught in bark containers. "Sometimes, when bear fat was rendered alongside a fire, some of the melted grease was taken and mixed with a little snow. It started to foam up just like ice cream." In summer moose horn could be warmed close to the fire and the "velvet" then scraped off and eaten. Only under exceptional circumstances did the Indians eat raw meat or fat.

[13] See below, p. 91.

Autumn meant the time when caribou, moose, gopher, ground hog, and other meat, as well as fish, would be prepared for preservation. The meat of the larger animals, cut into long, thin slices, was dehydrated by hanging it in the sun over a slow fire. People avoided smoking the meat lest it acquire a bitter flavor. Sheep to be dried were gutted and boned, the carcass then being sewn together. After gutting a gopher, a person placed a stick reaching from the head to the hind quarter in the body cavity and allowed the carcass to dry in the sun. A light pounding softened dehydrated meat before it was stored in a skin bag. From dried meat came pemmican, the flesh being heavily pounded and mixed with fresh berries on a sheet of babiche. After adding melted grease the product was stored in untanned groundhog skins or in a casing of cleaned intestines. Berries could also be prepared by first boiling them and then drying the pulp on sheets of bark. After one layer of berries had dried another was added on top. Eventually an entire dry cake could be rolled up for caching. The Kaska stored food in several kinds of caches. In winter, when simple freezing proved sufficient for preservation, they placed feshly butchered meat surrounded with spruce brush in a snow pit and covered it with snow. In the mountains a cairn made by piling up rocks covered a supply of meat. A wolverine, the informant remarked, never got at food preserved in this manner. Small quantities of meat could also be suspended from a pole lashed to a tree or leaned into a fork. A pile of stones anchored the base of the pole cache. Men constructed stages up to eight feet square in trees, using poles that they lashed together with willow-bark line. The food stored on these platforms was covered with brush weighted down by poles. Men found it easier to build triangular stages set between three conveniently growing small trees. The foundation of the platform consisted of three poles lashed to the supporting trunks. Across this the builder laid a flooring of thinner poles. Four-pole shelter and four-pole platform caches could not be recalled.

Women served food on fresh poplar or birch bark as well as in birch and solid wood dishes. A hole drilled in such a wooden vessel served as a handle. People avoided using one another's dishes for fear that doing so might lead to a small otter emerging from the careless person's mouth. Utensils consisted of bone knives and sheep-horn or wooden spoons. Etiquette prescribed that a knife must never be tossed to another person blade first. Deliberately violating this rule constituted a hostile gesture. Each member of the family helped himself from the cooking pot but children shared the dishes of their parents without fear of any danger. At the end of a meal a person might wipe his fingers along the sides and bottom of the vessel to obtain even the residual film of grease. Both sexes and children ate together, mealtimes providing periods of animated conversation. In addition to the magical avoidances that governed eating[14] there existed the awareness that following a period of near starvation eating must be resumed gradually. Hospitality existed as an established virtue. A stock phrase used in gratitude for a meal was: "Brother-in-law, pretty near you killed me with this party [i.e., feast]." The host in reply would urge his guest to recall the periods of hunger that the latter had been forced to undergo. Food offered to a guest had to be "half-cool" and a serving of piping hot victuals signified an insult. The informant denied the hot-food hospitality test but

[14] See below, p. 109; also see above, p. 38.

said the custom obtained among the Fort Liard Indians. It would seem as though the "half-cool" food ritual among the Upper Liard Indians constituted a local variation of the hot-food test pattern. Unless meat was scarce, a man entertained without his family always received enough food to bring some home to his wife. Gormandizing was somewhat uncertainly denied, informants stating that a tendency to vomit could be inhibited by spitting on one's knife scabbard.

Dease River Kaska. When the environment signaled the arrival of autumn the Dease River people began their movement into the mountains in search of meat to dry and preserve for winter consumption. With the onset of cold weather several families rejoined around some "low place" to fish and here they spent the bulk of the winter. In summer too the people camped in a large body near a good fishing site along a lake or river. Previous to assembling, word traveled between the bands designating the meeting place.

The periods of the year are revealed in the following calendar:

cinsa (January)—"pretty near long day moon."
sanawsa (February)—"pretty near middle of the winter moon."
detcinsa (March)—"stick [i.e., timber] moon."
atatcosa (April)—"big eagle flies moon."
tasatsa (May)—"long day moon."
tazilesa (June)—"pretty near change to summer moon."
tanicitcosa (July)—"middle moon."
tanicicitlesa (August)—"year pretty near gone moon."
tcunuetsa (September)—"pretty soon snow coming moon."
nugecsa (October)—"snow comes moon."
tanasa (November)—"pretty near change winter moon."
makasa (December)—"pretty near short day moon."

The calendar reveals the interest with which the Indians looked forward to the long daylight of spring and early summer; how autumn warned of winter, snow, and the aging year; and how the shortest day of the year provided a landmark for reckoning time.

Food had to be secured in all seasons. In summer and fall women and girls sought blueberries, low bush cranberries, strawberries, raspberries, salmon berries, soap berries, and currants. With the aid of a digging stick women as well as men dug for wild carrots. People also collected onion greens, rose petals, spruce and birch fibers, willow buds, and spruce gum, but not wild rice or mushrooms. Goose eggs were welcomed in their season. Water, birch sap, and rose petals steeped in water furnished the main beverages.

In summer and winter traps caught wild animals for food. Bear, caribou, moose, and sheep were snared with four- or five-strand braided babiche line. In the case of caribou and moose the trapper extended fences from either side of his snare, such barriers consisting of poles lashed to trees and piled with brush. Deadfalls took bear, marten, beaver and smaller animals. Pitfalls found no place in the technology. Sometimes the Indians drove caribou and mountain sheep into surrounds where they could be shot or where they might trap themselves in snares. Sheep surrounds were built on relatively low ground and near that animal's trails. Upon completing the structure the hunters ascended the mountain and drove the sheep toward the corral. Human surrounds aided in moose hunting, a circle of men seeking to drive the animal toward a place where snares had been constructed. Great nets, 15 to 20 feet long and constructed of babiche, were planted to catch beaver, a task for summer nights when the beaver swam freely and one that invited family cooperation. Once caught in a net, the animal was clubbed to death. In winter beaver nets were sometimes suspended under the ice. Moose and caribou hunting sometimes involved semicircular tracking and in autumn a hunter called moose with a birch-bark horn or by rubbing a moose scapula against a tree. Because "moose are smart animals and run away at the smallest sound," tracking them in summer demanded that a hunter remove his moccasins. People did not hunt caribou in bare feet. Often in late winter men depended on deep and crusted snow to help them secure game. The snow impeded the travel of moose and caribou so that the lighter hunter who was also equipped with snowshoes could readily run them down.

A man's hunting equipment included the bow, arrows, spear, gaff stick, and club. Birch yielded the commonest bow wood but willow also found employment for boys. The middle of the bowstock was backed with caribou sinew, the object being to insure straight shooting. Twisted sinew or babiche furnished a bowstring. Willow and birch wood furnished material for arrows, while obsidian, flint, bone, and horn provided points. Barbed points appear to have been restricted to the latter two materials. Untipped arrows, the wood of which was sometimes sharpened, were suited for bringing down game birds. Vanes of two or three feathers made use of owl or "any other" kind of feather. Men kept their arrows in tanned skin quivers that were carried under the left shoulder and toward the front of the body. This left the weapons in easy access of the hunter's right hand. Spears, sometimes no more complex than a painted or unpainted sharpened pole, served to kill bear and beaver. Lance points of bone and caribou horn were also employed. No clear picture could be obtained of the dart thrower or "stick gun," which was frequently mentioned as having been used in the aboriginal community. The weapon apparently consisted of a piece of birchwood fitted with a hole in which was inserted a two-foot dart provided with a stone point. After aiming the dart the hunter smartly rapped the base of the dart with a stick, thereby sending the missile toward its target. Mention of this weapon also occurred in a folktale collected from an Upper Liard informant who, however, denied that the weapon had been used in his territory.[15] Gaff hooks were inserted into a beaver lodge to seize one of those animals and draw him out to where he could be clubbed to death.

Part of every successful hunter's reward came when he proudly returned to camp packing a few token pieces of meat. On the following morning other men went to the scene of the kill and selected whatever portions of the animal they pleased.

In terms of preference fish occupied an inferior dietary position compared to meat. Economically they appear to have been of far greater importance. Trout, whitefish, sucker, and jackfish were speared, netted, trapped, and angled. From the rib bones of

[15] For the tale see Honigmann, *Cultural Dynamics of Sex* (1947), 46; or, Honigmann, *Culture and Ethos of Kaska Society* (1949), 293.

the beaver men shaped double-tined points for fish spears. The Indians also relied on weirs, while gill nets were set from canoes in summer and under the ice in winter. In the latter season, before a net could be set the ice had to be broken with an ice chisel that was constructed from caribou horn. Dip nets could not be recalled. Angling occurred in summer and winter. Hooks consisted of two splinters of beaver bone crossed and lashed in the form of an x. Fish poisons do not appear to have been known.

In addition to the foods already mentioned the Dease River people readily ate brown bear, porcupine, mountain goat, rabbit, ground hog, squirrel, and gopher. Whether nutritionally important or not, the body louse, foetal animals, moose milk, and sheep milk were also consumed. The eyes of the moose and caribou provided delicacies especially reserved for children. Geese, ducks, loons, swans, ptarmigans, spruce hens, and willow grouse found a welcome part in the diet. Fish eggs did not remain neglected. Animals rarely eaten or reserved for periods of scarcity included the grizzly bear, owl, lynx, and whiskey jack. In the category of never eaten animals occurred the fox, muskrat (perhaps the pack rat is indicated?), fisher, otter, mink, wolverine, wolf, dog, frog, eagle, hawk, crow, and woodpecker. Vomiting is said to have followed any attempt to eat otter, mink, wolverine, or wolf. Mud and lily bulbs remained outside of the diet. Although consumption of human flesh rested under strong prohibition, in periods of great hunger cannibalism admittedly took place. An apprehended eater of human flesh might be isolated from his community for as long as two years. Beliefs that cannibalism led to illness or produced a craving for human flesh were denied. No evidence of ceremonial cannibalism could be obtained.

A large proportion of meat as well as eggs were boiled with the aid of hot stones, in containers of either birch bark or woven spruce root. Caribou and moose stomachs occasionally served as cooking vessels, being hung to one side of the fire. Pit cooking could not be recalled. The water in which meat had been boiled provided a soup, to which onion greens or blood might be added. People prepared animal heads, intestines, and fish on a broiling stick but did not roast food in hot ashes. Rabbits and fowl on isolated occasions might be eaten raw, as when long rain had soaked all available wood thus making it impossible to kindle fire. An informant offered two recipes for "ice cream." The first variety consisted of a mixture of grease, cranberries, and snow. In the second process cranberries or dry soap berries were added to bear or beaver grease in a kettle and the whole mixed together. Snow did not enter the compound but today sugar makes a necessary additional ingredient.

Women preserved a variety of meats, fish, and berries through sun drying. Pemmican, prepared from stone-pounded meat with grease and berries added, was stored in viscera and birch-bark baskets. Caches held the preserved food. A simple type of cache consisted of a 12-foot pole lashed onto a tree with willow-bark line. After wrapping the meat in hide or a sheet of bark, it was suspended about three-quarters of the way up the pole. A ground cache consisted of a box-like structure of poles surrounded with rocks and covered with poles weighed down by additional stones. Men also constructed four-pole shelter caches and elevated them up to 12 feet above the ground, the poles being lashed together with babiche. A double layer of poles, one running at right angles to the other, crowned such a structure. Families also utilized simpler platform caches, the food on these being covered with brush or bark held in place with heavy logs.

Women cooked on occasions when the family ate as a unit. Food was served on bark dishes or in wooden bowls. Spoons of sheep or caribou horn facilitated eating. People took meals twice a day, morning and night, both sexes as well as children eating together. An informant denied gormandizing, remarking that the people knew very well when to cease eating.

Tselona. The fat game in the high country attracted the families in autumn. With the onset of winter the bands descended to a fish lake, from which the men went out to fetch meat from caches, hauling back the food on skin toboggans. Often only two families spent the winter together at a fishing site—two brothers and their wives and children or about ten people in all. Summer sent the hunters to set snares for moose and goats. All summer the men "kept on the move," following game. The usual vegetable foods were gathered by women, including blueberries, low bush cranberries, strawberries, raspberries, currants, and soap berries. The latter berries were never mixed with grease because the berries would "smell" the grease and "settle down again, not make soap." In other words, they would not froth as they did when mashed with water.[16] People ate lily bulbs raw as well as cooked. Bark vessels served to catch birch and poplar sap for drinking. Both sexes chewed spruce gum but geophagy remained unpracticed. Spruce, birch, and jackpine fibers, peeled with a knife, were eaten raw, as was wild rhubarb which, however, people took pains to "skin." Wild onions were cooked with meat. The informant denied any use of willow buds and wild rice for food, the latter being unrecognized in this area. Two varieties of muskeg tea were sought by gatherers, the stems and leaves of both types being boiled. The species could be identified only as tas?łuse and dimasket.

Our informant confidently stated that moose had always populated the country of the Tselona but denied the presence of elk, wood buffalo, and mountain sheep. Moose were snared and also hunted with the bow, the hunter relying on semicircular tracking to approach within close range of his prey. In season the moose might be called with a dried moose scapula. No custom of removing moccasins while tracking game could be recalled. Sometimes a line of men moving forward in concerted action drove a moose toward a series of snares. Caribou were also caught in snares, and skin decoys further assisted in the hunting of that animal. A hunter who wanted to kill a bear when it was summer, sought to surprise the animal in a berry patch, shooting it first with an arrow and then finishing it off with a lance bearing a caribou-horn point. In winter men obtained bears by shooting them while in a den or by thrusting lances into the lair. Sometimes a smoke fire served to drive the animal out of its winter dwelling. Lances also aided in killing beaver in the spring. A porcupine could easily be clubbed to death but in winter had first to be smoked out of its house. No taboo forbade the clubbing of any animal. Following the introduction of dogs, people employed them to track game. Other

---

[16] Yet Pike reports the coastal tribes to pound soap berries "till a thick froth, much resembling soap bubbles, gathers. . . . this froth, with a judicious mixture of salmon oil—or, better still, seal oil—they consider one of the things worth living for." Pike, *Through the Subarctic Forest* (1896), 35–36.

animals eaten included the muskrat, lynx, rabbit, ground hog, marten, and body louse. Ground hog, the informant pointed out, furnished a far more important source of food in the aboriginal period than did the rabbit. Women preserved a large number of ground hog from the fall for winter consumption. The fox and weasel were trapped for fur alone, while the skunk remained severely left alone. Birds caught for food included the owl, goose, duck, grouse, ptarmigan, swan, crane, and spruce hen. The eagle, crow, hawk, and loon played no role in the diet. Any successful hunter of large game, after butchering his prize, returned to camp and announced his good fortune, thus stimulating men and women to set out to secure a share of the meat. In general, butchering involved first the removal of an animal's skin, severing the limbs, and removing the viscera. The carcass could then be divided further.

Techniques of fishing included spearing with bone-pointed spears (the bone coming from the ankle of a moose), angling with bone points bearing moose-meat bait, and trapping with a fish weir. In winter weirs could be set in fast creeks that never froze; there were undoubtedly a number of such creeks on the Rocky Mountain slopes in the Tselona country. People did not fish with the aid of torches nor did they employ snares. Fish eaten included the grayling, sucker, ling (loche), whitefish, and trout. Salmon did not extend into this region.

Only when fire could not be provided did the Indians venture to consume raw meat. Hot-stone boiling in bark vessels served as the standard procedure for preparing flesh food. Pit cooking as well as stomach boiling were both denied. Blood went into the preparation of soup as did additional rendered grease. Although occasionally fixed by boiling, foetal animals were generally broiled, always in their entirety without the viscera being removed. A hunter did not neglect the opportunity to drink raw milk when he had slain an animal with full mammary glands.

As elsewhere in the northern forest the group recognized late September and October as a period suitable for meat drying. Now smudge fires could be neglecting without risking the danger of blow flies spoiling the food. For preservation women cut the meat of large game animals into long thin slices but ground hogs, minus the viscera, were dried in their entirety. Berries dried as they lay spread on a flat surface and, like other dehydrated foods, might be freshened again by soaking them in water. Skin bags contained pemmican, made of chopped meat and grease and without berries. The informant denied that viscera had ever been stuffed.

An entire family ate together, taking food from birch bark dishes. (Spruce bark was avoided because it imparted a pitchy taste to the food.) Periods of starvation visited the community not infrequently and sometimes resulted from caches ransacked by grizzly bears or other animal marauders. Only by quickly locating a well-stocked source of fish could famine be avoided. Cannibalism sometimes made an appearance in periods of starvation. The sight of much food promoted the tendency to overeat, especially following a period of limited rations. At such a time friends advised a hungry man to resume eating with caution, first offering him moose blood and pointing out that death might ensue if he ate meat straight off.

Frances Lake Kaska. No data on the food quest were sought from Frances Lake informants, who were young men with records of considerable time spent in the Liard Valley. It is likely that the patterns already presented also largely obtained in the Frances Lake area.[17]

TRAVEL AND TRANSPORTATION

Upper Liard Kaska. Foodgetting among the Indians of the taiga depended thoroughly upon mobility. Although a little travel occurred for other purposes, two main patterns of mobility may be distinguished. First, groups of people moved with their belongings to various parts of the tribal territory in search of new food resources to exploit. Such travel took place, for example, in the fall when the population moved to the mountains and again in early winter when they journeyed down to fish lakes. Second, there took place a great deal of "short term" travel, required of men pursuing game or of women visiting fish nets and berry patches. The Indians remained mobile in every season but the techniques of travel differed to a considerable extent between winter and summer. With snow on the ground and bodies of water covered with ice the toboggan and snowshoe provided the basic travel aids while in the season of open water travelers relied on the canoe, paddle, and raft.

Animal skins as well as wood were utilized for toboggans. Beaver skins prepared with the hair served well for traction, the smoothness of the pelt aiding their easy passage over the snow. Three such skins sewn together constituted a good sized vehicle. A number of skins from the hind legs of moose or caribou might also be sewn together with sinew to make a toboggan six feet long and two feet wide. To hold goods securely the rear portions of skin toboggans were stitched "like a baby bag." Prepared by a woman, a skin vehicle would last a winter or even two if stored in a dry place when the snow began to melt. A man manufactured undecorated wooden toboggans, tamarack being the preferred material. After splitting the green wood with a wedge he planed the boards with his stone knife. Wood from the exterior section of the tree bent most readily, the bending process being accomplished by moistening the lumber with warm water and then forcing the board back "against a pole."[18] The running boards were sewn to cross

[17] Similar patterns are reported for the Pelly River people by Field, who says, for example, that the Pelly River people moved into "a good game country about the end of August when all game is fat, to put up a cache of dry meat for the winter months." In fall women busied themselves drying groundhog and gopher. The Indians of the Ross and Pelly valleys subsisted primarily on meat and fish. Men "used bows and arrows to hunt with, spears, snares, deadfalls also. They would make long fences when the caribou and sheep came below timberline, sometimes packing poles to make their fences up with on top of the mountains. They would leave spaces big enough for a caribou or sheep to go through in their fences and get snared in them. Whenever a herd was sighted they would try to surround them and drive them through their fences." Cordage for snares came from twisted "sinew or caribou skin raw" and the line was anchored to a movable pole toggle. "Beaver the Indian kills every way, with nets in winter, spears and shoots them . . . and kills them with a club." The gaff stick also served in hunting beaver. (Field, *Unpublished manuscript* [1913].) An Upper Liard informant (0) reported with some distaste that the Ross River Indians deliberately cultivated mold in meat that was later cooked. Such meat proved too strong for the taste of the Liard River people.

[18] The method no doubt resembled that executed by a Frances Lake Indian in 1945. See Honigmann, *Culture and Ethos of Kaska Society* (1949), 60, 73–74; also Pl. 6, A and B.

pieces with babiche line countersunk in order to avoid wear by friction At the end of the winter a careful man hung his toboggan in a tree on its upturned nose, the heavy brush protecting the vehicle from rain.

In loading a toboggan the traveler placed the heaviest load in front, this practice facilitating handling of the vehicle. Women drew toboggans when moving camp but men returning from a hunt drew meat on skin or wooden vehicles. With the introduction of dogs large and strong enough for traction, the tandem hitch came into use for traveling through bush. Toboggans were not used to transport people, with the exception of small children.

The powdery snow of the Cassiar would have hindered foot travel during a large part of the year had means not been available for adapting to this boreal forest condition. To break a trail on which the toboggan could move easily without sinking too deeply, as well as for hunting in soft snow, people employed snowshoes. An origin tale explains the introduction of these aids to travel.

In the beginning people couldn't walk as they had no snowshoes. An old man suggested taking advantage of the upraised end of a spruce branch. Wearing such brush on his feet he went up into the mountains to kill porcupine. The man's name was Kligadata, "snowshoe filling father." The people tried the idea but couldn't go far. The old man then hit upon the improved device of a snowshoe frame. He fashioned one with a stone knife and used a beaver tooth chisel to drill large holes in it. A porcupine tooth set in that animal's jawbone served to drill the holes for the fine filling. These people showed everybody how to make snowshoes and the old man became rich making snowshoes for others (X).[19]

Aboriginally the Upper Liard Indians manufactured temporary, round and pointed snowshoes. A man caught in an early winter snowfall and lacking his regular snowshoes would prepare a camp and make temporary devices. Bending and lashing a branch of willow or some other easily pliable wood into a rough circle he further provided two crosspieces consisting of short lengths of willow split at either end. The split edges were pulled fanwise in the shape of a crude y and each bar of the y was then lashed to the willow frame. Of the three panels thus formed only the center one was filled with whatever odds and ends of skin line the maker happened to have in his possession. The fronts of such snowshoes were not usually upturned. The wearer discarded temporary snowshoes once he had reached the main camp. The use of two converging willow poles in constructing temporary snowshoes was not known.

The round or Loucheux type snowshoe is said to have been in early use along the upper Liard River. The native term, however, gives no clue to relative chronology being translated as "snowshoe with pieces overlapping in front." Spruce provided the preferred material for the frames. Although birch was sometimes substituted for spruce, the former wood is said to have picked up and carried too much snow in spring, thereby increasing the weight of the shoe. One informant (O) was much impressed with the use of maple for frames. He had secured a pair of maple snowshoes in Juneau made by a Tlingit Indian and claimed the wood to be perfect for shedding snow. This tree, how-

[19] We are inclined to see the last part of the story as a late addition to the tale. A young Tahltan woman reported that her people ascribe the origin of the snowshoe to Wolf.

ever, does not grow in the Cassiar.[20] Aboriginally wood for snowshoe frames was bent after first being carefully chewed with the teeth. The forward overlap of the two parts of the frame extended for about five inches on a trail snowshoe and somewhat more on the shorter hunting variety. Two or three cross pieces resulted in three or four panels. A rounded snowshoe, it is claimed, did not sink into the snow as much in front as the pointed variety nor would it pick up as much snow.[21] While known aboriginally, the pointed snowshoe became more common following European contact.

A craftsman "tailored" the size of snowshoes to their intended function. If designed for breaking trail in front of a toboggan or for following an already broken trail the average size person could get along with snowshoes about three and a half feet long. Hunting snowshoes, designed for remaining near the surface of deep, loosely packed snow, almost equalled the height of the prospective wearer, the width being somewhat adjusted to the user's relative weight. Two varieties of babiche line served for filling, first, a heavy cordage that was woven into the center panel supporting the direct weight of the wearer, and second, a fine line for the front and rear panels. Both men and women knew how to fill snowshoes but the process generally occupied the latter. In applying the fine filling the artisan needed a bone snowshoe needle. In one type of needle the blunt end of the instrument was made concave in order to push through the line. The other end formed a slight hook, useful for pulling the line upward through filling already laid down. Another type of needle, made of wood or bone, contained a center eye in which to anchor the filling cord. Prior to lacing, loops of cordage had to be provided around the inside of the frame, to which the webbing of the front and rear panels could be anchored. Holes for these loops are said sometimes to have been drilled with a piece of hardwood heated to a glow and then pressed against the appropriate point of the frame. Several reheatings of the "awl" were necessary to complete the task. Beaver- and porcupine-tooth awls served as much more efficient drills.

The following patterns of snowshoe lacing are derived from an analysis of contemporary snowshoes. No radical differences from aboriginal practice could be discovered. When starting to fill a snowshoe the worker usually turned to the front panel, the line beginning at the right hand side (Fig. 4, UPPER LEFT, facing front end of snowshoe). One end of the line passed through the first framework loop (17) where it was tied with a double overhand knot. The other end was carried back to the crosspiece. Bending over the top of the strut (18) it came out from below and traveled up to the toe where it bent over the babiche which here held the frame together (9). (Aboriginally the Loucheux type shoes must have been provided with loops going completely around the front of the panel.) Coming out from below, the line twisted against its own part and

[20] Rocky Mountain maple "is especially used in making snowshoes and bows" among the Salishan Thompson Indians. Steedman, *Ethnobotany of the Thompson Indians of British Columbia* (1930), 499, 500; Ray, *Culture Element Distributions: XXII, Plateau* (1942), 158.

[21] At Fort Nelson an informant expressed an opposite preference when he said that rounded front snowshoes were of little use "in this country, but in the North, where the snow is packed hard, they can be used." (Honigmann, *Ethnography and Acculturation of the Fort Nelson Slave* [1946], 45.) Needless to say there is no difference in the quality of the snow between the Fort Nelson and Cassiar areas. The opinions represent diverse attitudes toward a bygone culture pattern.

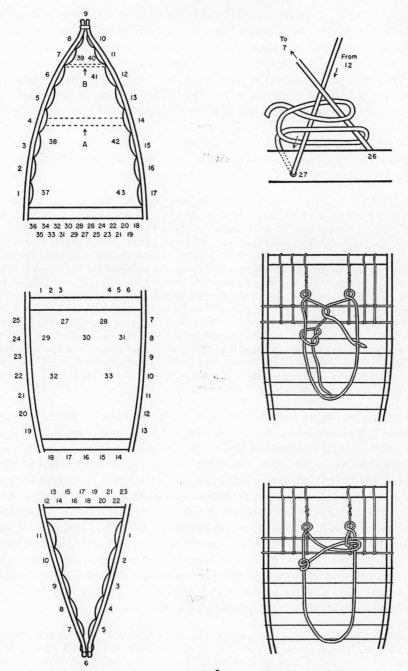

FIG. 4. Details of Snowshoe Lacing and Types of Foot Harness.

proceeded back to the forward strut at the extreme left of the shoe. Bending over the top of the strut (36) it came up from below, twisted around itself, and went to the first framework loop on the left side of the shoe (1) through which it passed from above. When pulled through this loop, the line bent against its own part enroute to the next station on the opposite side of the panel. Here, from above, it entered framework loop 16, bent against its own part, and traveled to the next station on the crosspiece (19). The same pattern was now repeated. In going forward, the line wove under the strands previously laid (1–17, etc.). All strands passed under the braces (A and B). In the snowshoes examined the foremost brace (B) consisted of several thicknesses of twisted babiche. The lacing may be followed to its conclusion by referring to the following pattern and to Figure 4.

Pattern of lacing front panel of snowshoes (Fig. 4, UPPER LEFT). 17, 18, 9, 36 (twist around 9–36), 1, 17, 19, 9, 35 (twist around 9–35), 2, 16, 21, 8, 10, 33 (twist around 10–33), 3, 16, 22, 7, 11, 32 (twist around 11–32), 3, 16, 23, 7, 11, 31 (twist around 11–31), 4, 15, 24, 6, 11, 30 (twist around 11–30), 4, 15, 25, 8. The line bent twice around the 8–10 line from above (39), twisted around its own part four times, bent twice around the 2–17 strand from above (37), twisted around its own part five times, and then proceeded to stations 5 and 14. When this crossing was completed the line traveled back to the 1–17 strand, bent around this strand from above (38), twisted around its own part six times, and then passed on to the 8–10 strand. It bent around this strand from above (40), twisted around its own part four times, and proceeded to the next station. The pattern then was: 30, 5, 14, 25, 7, 12, 29, 5, 14, 26, 7. The line next traveled to the 4–15 strand, bent around this strand from above (43), twisted around its own part four times and proceeded to stations 6 and 13. After making this crossing the line traveled to the 4–15 strand, bent around this strand from above (42), twisted around itself four times enroute to the babiche brace (B). From above the line now bent across one of the lines constituting this brace (41), twisted around its own part, and proceeded to stations 28, 6, 12, 27. The concluding knot included its own part and the 26–7 strand (see Fig. 4, UPPER RIGHT).

Lacing the rear panel departed little from the general pattern governing the front. The lacer held the shoe with the heel forward and began on her right hand side (Figure 4, LOWER LEFT). The line was tied to the rear portion of framework loop number 11 with a double overhand knot, drawn back to 12, bent across the top of the crosspiece and, coming out below, proceeded to the next station, 6. Here the line bent from above around the babiche holding the heel of the snowshoe together. Coming out below it twisted around itself twice from left to right and proceeded to the crosspiece (23). It bent around this strut from above. On emerging the line bent against itself and proceeded to framework loop 1, which it entered from above, bent against itself on emerging, and crossed to the opposite framework loop (11). In going forward (toward the heel of the shoe) the line passed under the strands previously laid while in returning to the crosspiece the line wove under the strands already put in place. The lacing may be followed to its conclusion in the following pattern:

Pattern for lacing rear panel of snowshoe (Fig. 4, LOWER LEFT): 11, 12, 6 (double twist around 12–6), 23, 1, 11, 13, 5, 7, 22, 2, 11, 14, 5, 7, 21, 2, 10, 15, 4, 8, 20, 2, 10, 16, 4, 8, 19, 3, 10, 17, 3, 9, 18, 3, 9. The line bent twice around the strut at 18, the second time being drawn under its own immediately preceding part.

The lacing of the center panel (Figure 4, CENTER LEFT) is more complicated than that of the front or rear. The worker began by tying a single overhand knot to the left hand frame just below the forward crosspiece (Fig. 4, CENTER LEFT), station 25, facing front end of the snowshoe.[22] The line then traveled three times across and back between the left and right sides of the frame (25, 7), in each case bending around the outside of the frame. This gave six thicknesses of babiche, three at the top and three at the bottom of the frame. Coming up and bending across the top of the left hand frame after the final crossing, the line was drawn back to its next station (24) and made four crossings between the left and right sides of the frame (24, 8), giving four thicknesses of babiche. This time, when the line came up to bend over the top of the left side of the frame, it bent around the four lines just laid and proceeded forward to bend over the top of the forward crosspiece (1). Coming out from below, the line twisted twice from left to right around its own part between the crosspiece and the 25-7 strand, and three times in the same direction between the 25-7 and 24-8 strands before proceeding to the rear crosspiece. It bent over the top of the strut (16), came up from below, and twisted against itself. Going forward the line went toward the right-hand side of the shoe to the forward crosspiece, across which it bent from above (6); came out from below; twisted around itself twice from left to right between the forward strut and the 25-7 strand; and twice more in the same direction between the 25-7 and 24-8 strands. Coming out from the 24-8 strand, the line bent against itself enroute to the next station on the right side of the frame. Bending across the top of the frame (9) the line came up, bent against itself, and proceeded to the opposite frame (23), bending across this from below. On emerging the line bent against itself and proceeded to station 2, above the lines previously laid. The rest of the lacing may be followed from the following pattern. Going forward the line passed over strands previously laid; going toward the rear crosspiece it wove under the already laced horizontal strands.

Pattern for lacing center panel of snowshoe (Fig. 4, CENTER LEFT): 25, 7, 24, 8, 1 (double twist between forward crosspiece and 25-7 strand; triple twist between 25-7 and 24-8 strands), 16, 6 (double twist, repeated as above), 9, 23, 2 (triple twist between forward crosspiece and 25-7 strand, double twist between 25-7 and 24-8 strands), 15, 31[23] (single twist between 24-8 and 23-9 strands, repeated between 23-9 and 22-10 strands), 10, 22, 29 (single twist, repeated as above), 11, 21, 3 (triple twist between forward crosspiece and the 25-7 strand, double twist between 25-7 and 24-8 strands), 14, 33[24] (single twist between 22-10 and 21-11 strands, repeated between 21-11 and 20-12 strands), 12, 20, 32 (single twist, repeated as above), 18, 4 (double twist between 25-7 and 24-8 strands), 13, 9, 28 (double twist between 25-7 and 24-8 strands). The line bent around the 24-8 strand from below (30), twisted around the 18-4 line once between the 25-7 strand and the forward crosspiece, passed under the crosspiece and came up to pass from right to left across the six forward running lines of the front panel (i.e., those proceeding from stations 25, 26, 27, 28, 29, 30 in Figure 4, UPPER LEFT). The line now passed under the

---

[22] In the case of one shoe made by the same worker the lacing at this point began by the line being pulled through a hole cut in the end of its own part.

[23] This station, as well as 26, represent points where the line bent across only the top two lines of the four thicknesses of babiche which had been laid between stations 24 and 8.

[24] This station, as well as 29, represents bends around the 22-10 strand.

forward crosspiece, came up from below and bent across the 25–7 strand from above (27), bent across the forward crosspiece from above (3), then twisted three times around the 3–14 strand between the forward crosspiece and the 25–7 strand, and twisted around the 25–7 strand enroute to the left hand frame, where the line knotted at station 25 with a single overhand knot that included one part of the 25–7 strand.

Two types of harness, both made from smoked-skin line, secured the snowshoe to the moccasin-covered foot. One of these is said to have been introduced into the area from Fort Liard and is currently referred to as the "Nelson type" (Fig. 4, CENTER RIGHT). The other was in use among the Liard River and "Tlingit" (probably Taku) people (Fig. 4, LOWER RIGHT).

To avoid slipping on steep inclines four bone pins were sometimes inserted into holes provided at the bottom of each snowshoe. The pins projected about an inch from the wood. The snowshoe staff further aided walking in hilly country. It consisted of a stick about four feet long with a hoop that was laced with babiche line. The hoop was located a short distance from the lower end of the staff and consisted of a short length of willow bent and lashed in the form of a circle. The filling served to keep the hoop affixed to the staff. A man prepared wood for this implement while women customarily added the filling. No distinctive staff for the snowshoe staff could be learned, informants designating it merely as "walking stick." Morice, however, has translated the Carrier name for this implement as referring to the "circular attachment which prevents it [the staff] from sinking too much in the snow."[25] Men wore snow glasses when traveling across snow made bright by the spring sun. These implements consisted of strips of tanned skin or birch bark provided with eye slits. The area around the slits was blackened with charcoal to further reduce glare.

Land travel in summer or winter generally involved men walking in advance of the women, who remained in charge of children and household goods. This pattern left men free to intercept or follow game, reduced disturbance that might drive away game, and also enabled men to prepare sufficient wood for a comfortable camp before the women arrived. Sometimes women and children did not reach a camp until midnight. In autumn, enroute to the ground-hog trapping grounds in the mountains, a number of families moved together, the men scouting for moose and the women walking in old and well-defined trails. People crossed streams on rafts as well as on log bridges constructed by felling either one, two, or three thin trees or by shifting an already fallen tree into position to serve as a span. In traveling to a game kill, as well as in other types of cross country movement, Indians sometimes indicated their route by blazes. One type of blaze consisted of a willow or other branch broken in the specified direction. In an "open place" the route might be indicated by hanging moss in trees, while up in the barren mountain tundra, which composed a sizable part of the Kaska territory, successive rock piles served as guides. River valleys were commonly referred to in giving

[25] Morice, *Carrier Language* (1932), 62. Lantis describes a similar "snowshoe stick" in use among the Nunivak Eskimo. (Lantis, *Social Culture of the Nunivak Eskimo* [1946], 167.) While informants among the Attawapiskat Cree Indians of James Bay denied the use of snowshoe pegs or the snowshoe staff the counterpart of the latter may have existed in "crutches" with a webbed lower end. These allowed lame persons to support themselves on snow. Honigmann, *Attawapiskat field notes* (1947–48).

verbal directions.[26] Separated groups of travelers who had need to communicate with each other did so by means of a limited repertory of smoke signals like these: One smoke, "we have killed game"; two smokes, "come over here"; three or four smokes, "we have had an accident (or trouble)."

Men and women packed goods but characteristically women carried the heavier loads. Only lines were utilized in packing, pack sticks being unknown. Pack lines consisted of four-ply braided babiche line. In supporting a back load the line passed along the outside of the arms below the shoulders and proceeded around the top of the head slightly in front of the vertex. If a heavy load caused pack lines to slip down the arms, a padding of moss was added. Men carried small game by tying one end of a packline around the head and the other around the rear legs of the animal. Fowl were transported in sacks of fine, netted babiche lined with babiche hide. Tanned skin bags up to three feet square held clothing and meat in transport. The colon of an animal, closed at one end by sewing, provided a handy container for small tools. Berries and meat were held for short periods in birch-bark baskets. Dogs rarely packed goods prior to European contact. In the spring a pack dog's feet could be protected from crusted snow by moose-skin dog shoes in which small holes allowed the claws to project. Horses remained unseen until 1898.

In the absence of bark-chair baby carriers a woman transported her infant in a moose-skin bag lined with deep moss, the baby facing away from the mother. The bag hung against the mother's back supported by tanned-skin line. In winter a layer of fur lined the moss bag and insulated the child from the bitter cold. Following infancy children rode pick-a-back fashion on the mother's back, supported with a baby strap that passed around the outside of the woman's arms and was tied under her chin. A shawl of animal pelts, tanned with the hair on, provided protection from low temperature.

Several early travelers have remarked on the casual use of water transportation in the early post-contact period. Thus McConnell reports that the Indians "are very inferior canoemen, and are afraid to venture on the river except in its smoothest places. They seldom ascend the river with canoes, as they prefer to carry their outfits along the shore to tracking a boat against a rapid current, and in descending use small spruce bark canoes which they build in a couple of hours and abandon without much loss.[27] Pike writes, "the Cascas and Liard Indians are poor boatmen, and do not make much use of the waterways, preferring to pack heavy loads through the woods to working a canoe upstream; while, if they wish to run down a river, they can make a bark or skin canoe in a few hours, and lose nothing by throwing it away at the end of the run. The birch on the Upper Liard does not grow to a sufficient size to supply bark suitable for canoes so much used on the lower part of the river."[28]

[26] Among the Chilkat Tlingit there were true cardinal directions that took their names from the winds. Drucker, *Culture Element Distributions: XXVI, Northwest Coast* (1950), 204.

[27] McConnell, *Report on an Exploration in the Yukon and Mackenzie Basins* (1890), 35D.

[28] Pike, *Through the Subarctic Forest* (1896), 81–82. Along the Pelly River this author "often noticed rafts tied upon the banks, evidently used by the Indians for crossing. . . . It is curious that they do not use canoes on such easily navigable streams, but prefer to pack a load on their backs and make a straight course for their hunting-grounds, crossing and recrossing the main stream to cut off a detour" (204).

Despite their reported shyness of river travel the Upper Liard Indians recall manufacturing rafts, moose-skin boats, dugouts, and bark canoes. Five or more logs provided sufficient material for the construction of a raft, the parts being lashed together with the aid of two cross poles and spruce-root line. For dryness smaller poles were sometimes laid above these crosspieces and at right angles to them, being secured to their foundation with spruce-root cordage. In the center of a traveling raft people packed mud to provide a hearth suitable for a small fire. A raft pointed at the stern sometimes served hunters in autumn for hunting fowl. These craft are said to have been faster than the square raft.

In spring and summer the people traveled downriver in moose-skin boats that sometimes contained as many as ten moose hides. Smaller craft of this type, however, comprised only one or two skins. The larger skin boats accommodated up to 20 people while the smaller vessels held one or two men going on a hunting expedition, a division corresponding to the two types of canoes to be described below. Teit suggests that among the Tahltan moose-skin boats came to supplant bark vessels, perhaps after the introduction of the gun, which facilitated hunting.[29] To construct such a boat women sewed together the hides with sinew, each skin overlapping the next by about two inches. The seams were sealed with moose grease. Spruce gum, our informant claimed, did not adhere well to moose hide. Preparation of the framework for the vessel constituted man's work and required first laying down a single spruce pole as a keel. The keel rested in the center of the sewn sheet of hides, the upturned ends being inserted into the edges of the tightly spanned skin in such a way as to arch the keel. A number of saplings provided the ribs of the vessel and were secured to the keel with babiche lashing. They also hooked into the edges of the hide. Completion of such a boat took no more than a day if both sexes cooperated. After one or two uses the hides remained useful for other purposes, but prolonged immersion in water caused them to rot. Teit advises that "these hide canoes have to be kept beyond the reach of dogs, which, when hungry, sometimes destroy them."[29] Propulsion of the skin boat was by paddling. The vessels are recalled as having been both faster and safer than rafts, largely because half-submerged driftwood did not threaten them the way it menaced the raft.

For relatively long distance travel, which required the simultaneous transportation of household goods, people used dugouts which one informant (O) referred to as the "Liard River Indian boat." The native term for the vessel meant "something floating." Relatively rare in the Northern Athapaskan area, the dugout is, of course, common among the Pacific Coast Tlingit as well as on the Plateau. Its use among the Kaska may be regarded as a trait allying these people to the two adjacent areas. Construction of the craft among the Kaska closely approximated details of manufacture reported for the Tlingit. It may logically be suspected that the building of the dugout increased following the introduction of metal tools. Teit writes, "canoes were used on the Stikine, Taku, and some other streams and lakes. They were mostly dug-outs acquired from the Tlingit, but on the upper streams were made by themselves from cottonwood-logs."[30]

[29] Teit, *Notes on the Tahltan Indians of British Columbia* (1906), 345.
[30] Teit, *Notes on the Tahltan Indians of British Columbia* (1906), 345. There is evidence that the dugout may be an old feature of circumpolar culture dating to Boreal times. (Spaulding, *Northeastern Archae-*

Material for such a boat consisted of a 20-foot (?) cottonwood tree secured in the spring "when the sap is running." The interior of the hull was hollowed out with the aid of a stone knife, the sides being thinned to a thickness of about one and one-half inches. Pins of birch, strong enough to penetrate cottonwood, kept the hollowing out process from going too deeply. Water was then poured into the excavated trunk and heated with great pile of hot stones. Rocking the hull back and forth assured even soaking and softening. Meanwhile about two dozen alder braces were forcefully inserted to spread the sides further apart. A pair of sticks always crossed each other at right angles. As a further precaution to prevent the soft wood from splitting, the craftsmen securely lashed stern and bow with babiche line.[31] Midships, the width of a dugout averaged about three and a half or four feet. When the wood had been stretched to this width, the braces and babiche lashing came away. Manufacture of the boat occupied a week or ten days and, if cared for, the vessel might last for ten years. Water, however, warped the hull so that when the vessel was not in use it was carefully placed on a boat rack. In winter a bark cover kept off snow. When navigating in a dugout the people crouched on a board placed low in the hull. Four men sometimes paddled, women sitting amidships where they could also paddle. From six to ten people could be accommodated in such a vessel.

Despite the informant's appellation of the dugout as the "Liard River Indian boat" it is reasonable to expect that the simpler construction of the spruce bark canoe made this the more common means of water transportation. In 1905 Teit reported bark canoes to have already been displaced in the Cassiar but from descriptions obtained he concluded that they appeared "to have been similar in type to those still used on the Canadian Yukon, having high, narrow, projecting prows and sterns, flat bottoms, and the bark put on in longitudinal strips."[32] Made in the spring, when the bark peeled most readily, these craft ranged in size from about 15 feet (for a hunting and fishing canoe used by one or two men or women) to about 19 feet for a boat accommodating up to 10 travelers. The latter figures correspond closely to those given for the dugout and also with information secured by Osgood among the Ingalik.[33] The canoe was constructed around a mold consisting of half-dozen or so short sticks driven into the ground. The outer surface of the bark became the interior of the hull and each gunwale was sewn between two spruce saplings. Ribs, consisting of spruce saplings, snapped in place under the gunwales and did not have to be lashed into position. The bow and stern were sewn with spruce-root line and pitched with spruce gum. Construction of a good spruce-bark canoe occupied about one and a half days. If well cared for, that is, drawn out of the water or stored on a boat rack when not in use, such a boat lasted an

ology and General Trends in the Northern Forest Zone [1946], 151.) We have also heard that the Lapps used hollowed out logs as toboggans drawn by reindeer. (Personal communication from Knute Hillgren, Lower Post.)

[31] For an exact duplication of this technique of boat building among the Tlingit see Jones, Study of the Thlingets of Alaska (1924), 79. Also Krause, Tlinkit-Indianer (1885), 170–173. Cottonwood dugouts were in use among the Chilkat. Drucker, Culture Element Distributions: XXVI, Northwest Coast (1950), 181.

[32] Teit, Notes on the Tahltan Indians of British Columbia (1906), 345.

[33] Osgood, Ingalik Material Culture (1940), 367, 372

entire summer. A cruder type of spruce-bark vessel, containing a single-pole gunwale and fewer ribs, served to cross a river and might be manufactured in an hour or two. After serving its purpose it was discarded. Spruce craft remained undecorated. When employed for hunting beaver, the hulls might be blackened with charcoal in order to make the vessels resemble sticks of driftwood. The occupants of a bark canoe sat on piles of moss about ten inches thick, legs being tucked under the body and feet flaring out in a slight angle. When he wearied of this position a man stretched his legs out in front of him but he never sat with crossed legs. Upon sighting game the Indian pointed the craft in the direction of the animal before letting his arrow fly. Shooting from the boat at an acute angle to the hull threatened capsizing. Spruce canoes constituted fragile craft. The informant recalled one that broke under the weight of a moose. While any man might try his hand at making such a vessel, a certain amount of skill was prerequisite and occasionally able men made canoes in exchange for skins and arrows. Ownership of the boat rested in the man but women freely used the smaller variety for fishing.

As we have pointed out, the scarcity of white birch in the region of the upper Liard River prohibited the manufacture of birch-bark canoes. In 1842 Campbell had to send from Fort Halkett to Fort Liard for this material in order to construct canoes for exploring the Pelly River.[34] Decked canoes and sails likewise did not exist and only rarely did travelers fasten their canoes in pairs. Sometimes this practice occurred in smooth water, when two families moved camp together. In dangerous water the boats separated.

Men constructed paddles from spruce wood, the handle being shaped with a rounded knob at the upper end.[35] A hole drilled through this knob admitted the paddler's finger and gave him a firmer grip. Blades contained a center ridge from which the wood tapered to thin edges. For bailing voyagers employed a dipper carved from birch wood but minus any handle.[36] Bailers were sometimes decorated.

Indians forded rivers by swimming in cases where an exceptionally strong current prohibited the use of rafts. The swimmers clutched a floating pole as they paddled.[37] Women crossed simultaneously with men but a short distance further downstream. Everyone in the aboriginal community knew how to swim.

Dease River Kaska. Winter land transportation in the Dease River basin depended on skin and wood toboggans as well as on snowshoes. The sled remained unknown until introduced by Euro-Canadians. The skin stripped from the leg of a caribou made a useful vehicle in which to haul meat over loose snow. Wooden toboggans utilized spruce or birch wood and lacked the sharply upturned nose characteristic of the modern-style

[34] Campbell, *Discovery and Exploration of the Pelly (Yukon) River* (1883).

[35] Crutch-handle paddles were in general use on the Northwest Coast. Drucker, *Culture Element Distributions: XXVI, Northwest Coast* (1950), 182.

[36] Bailers consisting of a wooden scoop are widespread on the Pacific Coast while bark bailers are more characteristic of the Plateau. Drucker, *Culture Element Distributions: XXVI, Northwest Coast* (1950), 182; Ray, *Culture Element Distributions: XXII, Plateau* (1942), 158.

[37] Judging from Hornell's data, swimming floats have rarely been reported for North America. Hornell, *Water Transport* (1946), 3 ff.

vehicle. Women as well as men drew the toboggans, a harness for this purpose consisting of one moose-hide line passing around the outside of the arms and around the chest while another cord passed over the top of the head.

Snowshoe types included the round or Loucheux style (said to have been preferable because of its lighter weight) as well as the pointed variety. Function determined the length of these appliances, long shoes being best adapted for a hunter's swift travel in deep snow. Small shoes served well to break trail for a toboggan. In case of emergency a man made temporary snowshoes by bending and lashing a willow pole, which he then filled with heavy babiche line. Children usually employed such crude snowshoes throughout the winter. The customary division of labor appeared, a man constructing the framework while a woman applied the filling. Bone snowshoe needles contained a concave depression at one end that served to push the line between closely laid strands of filling.

In any season the order to travel required men to walk ahead of women, a pattern that allowed them to break trail for the women and children. Blazes consisted of willow and other branches broken in the direction taken. Sometimes men hung moss in the branches of a tree, laid down stones to indicate a course, or cut the trunks of trees with a caribou-horn adz. A single tree felled by fire provided a convenient bridge. Occasionally more complex spans containing a number of poles provided safer means for crossing a stream. The tump line facilitated packing and pack sticks remained unknown. Baby packs consisted of tanned skin padded with moss. In this container the child faced away from the mother. When old enough to leave the moss bag a youngster rode facing the mother on the latter's back supported by a baby strap that was passed around the outside of the arms and tied in front of the woman's breast. Such belts were often decorated with porcupine-quill embroidery. Bark baby carriers were not made.

For communication between traveling groups, the Indians sometimes made use of smoke signals, a single smoke calling attention to a game kill. Also runners might be sent to invite people to the scene of a kill, young men being able to cover 20 miles by running in a single day. Picture writing or drum language were both lacking.

For water transportation the Dease River people relied on rafts, moose-skin boats (which occasionally reached a length of 20 feet), dugouts, and spruce-bark canoes. A raft contained the necessary number of poles lashed to crosspieces with tanned-skin line. Pointing the bow gave the craft greater speed. An earthen fireplace was often situated somewhat forward on a pointed raft, but people invariably spent nights on shore in the course of traveling. Two varieties of spruce-bark canoes may be distinguished, small vessels serving one or two hunters and larger boats for traveling. The bark was sewn to the framework with spruce root line. Decked canoes, sails, or canoes traveling in pairs could not be recalled for the pre-contact period. Men cut paddles from spruce wood. Rounded handles were denied for these implements, the informant claiming that the upper end of the shaft contained a crosspiece on which the canoer fastened his grip. Such crutch-like handles must have resembled the type in use on the Northwest Coast. A ridge was left on the center of the blade, the edges of which might be decorated with notches burned into the wood. One man believed that double paddles had been employed a very long time ago.[38]

Tselona. Babies were secured in fully tanned moose-hide bags lined with moss. In winter an inner lining of muskrat skin came to be added to these containers. Bark-chair baby carriers could not be recalled. After a year or two a baby strap supplanted the baby bag and the child now supported itself on the mother's back. In camp a baby slept in a tanned-skin hammock.

[38] A white trapper writes of bull boats consisting of "twenty-five to thirty skins" in use among the Mountain Indians. Onraet, *Sixty Below* (1949), 61.

CAMP AND CAMP LIFE

SHELTER

UPPER LIARD KASKA. The people of the Cassiar lived in structures ranging in complexity from a spruce-brush windbreak to a large, multifamily dwelling. When compared to a universal range of shelter types the housing of the Kaska Indians remains generally simple. Such simplicity nevertheless supported life in some degree of comfort when outdoor temperatures dropped to 50 or more degrees below Zero Fahrenheit.

One informant had heard that "a long time ago people dug into the side of a hill" for a place to live. The actual excavation of such a house took place in summer. Following the completion of the autumn hunt (around November) the group returned to the cave, piled brush around the walls, and blocked the entry with moss or skins. Smoke escaped through a smoke hole provided in the roof. In this setting the people passed the period of most intense winter cold.[1] Better recalled dwelling types included the conical lodge and inverted v-shaped or A-type house. Both styles provided semi-permanent winter dwellings. It must be realized, however, that their occupancy lasted only as long as a particular territory produced game and fish for food. When these resources failed or if nearby caches became exhausted, people quit a camp in a search for better stocked regions. The conical shelter consisted of a series of poles closely placed (probably on a tipi foundation) and covered with sod, bark, or moss but not usually with skins.[2] A fire laid in the center of the building served the several families. As many as 20 people could be accommodated in a conical lodge, the diameter of which reached 20 feet. One informant (O) reported that sometimes circular ground-plan dwellings were built on stone foundations. Inverted v-shaped houses may be regarded as composite structures that included two converging lean-tos.[3] Roofed with closely laid poles overlaid by brush, sod, or moss, these shelters often accommodated two, generally related, families. The front and rear ends were blocked with brush except for a narrow passage at one end closed by a tanned-skin curtain. Each family prepared its own food over a common fire laid in the center of the dwelling. Customarily each family occupied one side of the fire. Children slept toward the rear.

Simple lean-tos, occasionally covered with skins, provided temporary shelter as did various types of snow dwellings. In preparing the simplest kind of open snow camp, people cleared an area of snow, placed brush on the ground, and, after making a fire,

[1] For other data concerning cave shelters in the area see below, p. 63.

[2] The pattern corresponds closely to the conical earth lodge of the contemporary Attawapiskat Cree. Honigmann, *Attawapiskat Cree field notes* (1947–48).

[3] Tahltan "lodges were of the single and double lean-to types, mostly the latter. They were roofed with poles close together, and sometimes further covered with brush, bark, and earth or snow. No conical lodges were used, nor semiunderground dwellings." (Teit, *On Tahltan (Athapaskan) Work* [1912], 485.) Morice has termed the A-shaped house as the original shelter of the Déné and affirms that skin tipis were later acquired from the eastern Cree. Morice, *Great Déné Race* (1906–10), 583–584.

piled snow high all around the central space. The warmth of the fire caused the snow to freeze, a condition that insured better protection from wind. At other times people dug into a snowbank to fashion an overnight shelter. Snow shovels were not widely used among the Liard River Indians, so that people moved snow with the aid of snow-shoes. A snowhouse contained a fire, the smoke of which escaped through a hole in the roof.

In summer threat of an enemy attack led the people to excavate pits near the camp where young children could be secreted and covered with caribou hides (possibly camou-flaged with earth?). Birch-bark, semisubterranean, and grass-mat houses remained un-identified by informants. Log cabins commenced to enjoy popularity after the intro-duction of the steel ax following white contact. Skin-covered tipis are said to have been introduced by a Fort Liard family. It is interesting to note that while anthropological thinking might classify together the sod- and skin-covered conical lodge Indians tend to distinguish them sharply.

Appurtenances remained scarce in aboriginal dwellings. Spruce brush or grass pro-vided floor covering, the grass first being softened by rubbing between the hands. People especially favored grass for sleeping places. Raised platforms did not find a place in houses and stuffed pillows are also denied. Sleepers lay covered by robes of woven rabbit or ground-hog skins or blankets containing a number of beaver and marten pelts sewn together. Drifted snow and other debris were brushed away from dwellings with a willow broom.

Other than the cache, non-residential structures were represented only by the suda-tory, which was built over ground that had been excavated to a depth of about 12 inches. Atop the excavated space, willow poles were bent and lashed together, following which a sheathing of tanned skins went over the framework. A hole for ventilation opened in the top of the dome. Sweat houses contained no entry, the user simply lifting the lower edge of the cover when he wished to enter or leave. Hot rocks dashed with water fur-nished steam as well as a heat so intense that the bather might be driven to lift a corner of the cover to admit cool air. Ceremonial structures found no place in the Kaska settle-ment and even the brush enclosed dance or ceremonial plaza appears to have been lacking.[4]

The efficiency of any dwelling in winter depended closely on fire. Heat also consti-tuted a prerequisite for many technological operations, ranging from cooking to snow-shoe making. Two versions of a common myth explaining the origin of fire (or rather of pyrites) are given below.

One fellow [Bear?] had this rock and didn't want to give it to the Indians. He wanted to keep it. Another fellow stole the stone and gave it to Fox Man who ran away. Tsuguya [a culture hero] secured the rock and made fire with it. Then he threw the rock all around, all over the country, so that every-body could have fire (X).

Crow and Wolf held a meeting. This took place before there were any people in the world. Crow had been in the habit of flying around and when any animal killed meat he would be on hand to take some

[4] Honigmann, *Ethnography and Acculturation of the Fort Nelson Slave* (1946), 89; Osgood, *Contributions to the Ethnography of the Kutchin* (1936), 52, 122, 125.

and bring it back. Wolf, his brother-in-law, saw this and said, "What are you doing?" Crow replied, "I got this from somebody." Wolf said, "Did you ask for it?" Crow answered that he had not and Wolf pointed out that Crow had behaved wrongly.

Wolverine belonged to Crow. Together Wolverine and Crow continued to steal many things. Grizzly Bear was Wolf. Fox belonged to Crow. Grizzly Bear told Wolverine not to rob caches. Grizzly Bear had a flat stone secured under his belt. Chickadee came around in cold weather and was nearly frozen. "Grandpa," he said to Grizzly Bear, "I'm just about frozen." The latter replied, "Sit down alongside the fire." Wolf and the other animals were hiding outside of the circle of light. Grizzly Bear turned his back to the fire when Chickadee said, "You've got lots of lice on your belt." Grizzly Bear invited Chickadee to pick off the lice. Chickadee never picked the lice but worked with the belt, under which was the piece of stone. While Chickadee did this, the balls under Grizzly's tail began to twitch. As they began to move, Chickadee caressed them and urged them to be quiet. At the same time he took knot after knot out of the belt and finally seized the flint and ran off. Grizzly Bear went in pursuit but without any shoes on. That's why Grizzly has no moccasins today.

Chickadee flew a short distance with the flint and gave it to Wolf who ran half way and gave it to Lynx. Lynx went a little way and Grizzly Bear nearly got it from him. Fox got it and ran a little way and then stopped until Grizzly Bear came close. He barked, ran a short distance, and waited again. He then dashed across a gulch. Grizzly followed him and Fox ran to the next gulch and again barked. Grizzly became angry and growled. He burst the balls beneath his tail and walked off, not knowing what he would do in fall time. Fox came out on top of a mountain and smashed the flint all over and threw it around the country so that people everywhere secured fire.[5]

As these tales suggest, fire was generated by the strike-a-light method, tinder consisting of soft, dry grass; dry birch bark; or an unidentified fungus tree growth. People always built blazes on the surface of the ground, dugout fireplaces being unknown and clay-enclosed hearths remaining restricted to rafts. In conical shelters a small circle of sticks six or seven inches high sometimes surrounded the fire and prevented the floor brush from working too close to the blaze. On winter nights fires that had been fed with cottonwood were carefully banked with ashes in order to make them last until morning, when a little blowing quickly aroused a flame. During winter movement people carried fire in bark vessels that presumably contained a packing of moss. On long journeys women swung glowing sticks of rotten wood as they walked. An informant (X) reported hearing of fire drills in use, he thought, among the Babine Lake people (Carrier?).

Dease River Kaska. The Dease River people did not ordinarily construct shelters in summer, when people were content to live in open camps or under brush lean-tos when it rained. In winter two types of dwellings appeared, the inverted v-shaped structure and the conical lodge. Both contained fires in the center of the ground space. The foundation of the v-shaped shelter consisted of a ridge pole suspended between two forked sticks, the front and rear ends being closed with brush except for a single entry. Brush with snow piled on top roofed the building, in which one or two families resided. Conical lodges consisted of a circle of poles covered with spruce brush or spruce bark piled over with snow. Only a rich man could completely cover his lodge with skins but quite customarily a skin flap closed the entry of a dwelling.[6] While circular lodges oc-

---

[5] When specifically asked about Tsuguya's role in the theft of fire the informant thought that Fox must have been working for the culture hero.

[6] According to a Kechika River informant conical lodges were standard dwellings at Forts Nelson and Liard but in the Kechika basin people aboriginally built only the inverted-V type structures.

casionally reached a diameter of 30 feet and accomodated several families, smaller structures built in this style and housing only one or two families occurred more frequently.
Birch-bark and grass-mat buildings were unknown. A Kechika River man appeared
vaguely familiar with the snowhouse but would venture no description of its form or
construction. Women erected houses and were believed to construct better structures
than men. Qualities governing selection of a dwelling site included "hard" (i.e., dry)
ground and accessibility to water. Dry wood could be found nearly everyplace. People
never excavated the ground of a house site.

Within a dwelling women occupied the area nearest the entry, while a husband had
his place toward the rear. Daughters slept near the mother, sons farther back from the
entry. Infants rested in skin hammocks suspended over the mothers' sleeping places.
Along the Kechika River, at least, babies used hammocks of plaited, split spruce roots
lined with skins. Specially constructed fireplaces or sleeping platforms did not occur.
People lived on a carpet of spruce brush and at night covered themselves with robes of
sewn marten and ground-hog pelts or plaited rabbit-skin. Grizzly bear robes, because
of their size and warmth, provided especially desirable blankets. Some people used
pillows made by packing duck or partridge feathers in a smoked skin bag.

The sweat house, built for the use of both sexes, was the only type of non-residential
structure. Hemispherical in shape and about four feet high it contained a roof opening
designed to permit the escape of excess heat and steam. No ceremonial enclosures
occurred.

Both sexes showed equal skill in kindling fire by the strike-a-light method.[7] One
informant denied the use of fire drills (S) but another man constructed a bow drill
which, he claimed, had been displaced from the culture because of its poorer efficiency
compared to the use of flint and pyrites (WT). Boys and girls commonly sought fuel
with some assistance from adults. In winter when camp moved women carried fire on
glowing poles 15 or 18 inches long. Fire kept through the night if banked with earth or
ashes.

Tselona. Winter dwellings conformed to the usual two types: conical with a framework
of poles and inverted V-shaped. Roofing utilized spruce brush, moss, and sod but never
grass thatch. Occasionally a household possessed sufficient skins to cover a conical lodge.
In summer the Indians did not live in houses and only rain impelled them to put up
hasty lean-tos. Surprisingly the construction of sweat houses met with denial. In the

[7] A tale collected by Teit tells how Bear's monopoly of the fire stone was broken by a little bird who
visited Bear's lodge to warm himself. While picking lice from the Bear the bird broke the latter's belt
and flew off with the stone, passing this object to a number of waiting animals. Last to receive the prize
was Fox whose flight to a high mountain exhausted Bear. "Fox broke up the fire-stone on the top of the
mountain, and threw the fragments a piece to each tribe. Thus the many tribes all over the earth obtained fire; *and this is why there is fire in the rocks and woods everywhere now.*" As a result of losing fire
Bear made a hole in the earth to keep himself warm in winter—the origin of the bear's den! Teit, *Kaska
Tales* (1917), 443–444.

It will be recalled that the Upper Liard Indians made fire with the strike-a-light method. The Tlingit
(including the Chilkat) used fire drills, including the bow type, as well as percussion methods of fire
making. Drucker, *Culture Element Distributions: XXVI, Northwest Coast* (1950), 202.

dwelling people lived on the spruce-brush carpeted ground and slept under blankets of woven rabbit skin or stitched ground-hog pelts with tanned-skin pillows stuffed with feathers. The strike-a-light method provided fire and was used in conjunction with a fungus that grew on birch trees, from which tinder was prepared. Informants mentioned the fire drill but its use appears to have been relatively recent. Travelers in both summer and winter carried fire on glowing poles, the only type of fire carrier admitted.

Espatotena. From a trapper operating in the South Nahani drainage Godsell heard of a cave " 'cut from the rock half-way up the face of a hundred foot precipice that spans a two-thousand-foot valley. It was about eighteen feet by twelve, with a hole running straight up through the rock, which must have been a sort of chimney.' " Two additional caves were also reported, " 'chiselled from living rock by human hands.' "[8] While the construction of rock shelters by stone-tool using aborigines may be questioned, the use of cave shelters seems very plausible and is in fact corroborated by data we ourselves obtained as well as by other investigators. Dr. Wesley Bliss of the University of New Mexico entered the South Nahani country in 1938 and reports on cave habitations.[9]

DRESS AND ADORNMENT

Upper Liard Kaska. Camp provided the place where the Kaska woman manufactured clothing for her husband, children, and herself. Tanned caribou skin comprised the principal material which she sewed with the aid of sinew line and bone needles pushed with a flat piece of bone held in the palm of her hand. Women used a work board when cutting the patterns of moccasins and mittens. Small sewing implements not in use were kept in a fish-skin bag. During cold weather fur robes supplemented tanned-skin garments. These had been tanned by women workers or else been plaited from strips of rabbit, ground-hog, and gopher skins without the aid of a frame. Body parts served for measuring clothing materials.

In summer each sex wore a tanned-skin breech cloth supported from an inner belt, a tailored coat or dress with sleeves reaching to just below the elbow and girdled by a belt of tanned skin or woven porcupine quills, trousers of the same material suspended at the hips from the inner belt, and moccasins. In winter certain adjustments were made to this basic dress, notably through the use of additional garments. The breech cloth became a length of plaited rabbit skin, while over the coat both sexes slipped a parka made of smoked caribou skin or of sheep skin tanned with the hair on. The parka reached to the middle of the thigh and splits on both sides of the lower edge were provided with a lacing that could be tightened to insure a snug fit. Parka sleeves sometimes continued

[8] Godsell, *Romance of the Alaska Highway* (1945), 92.

[9] From the Pelly River country Field reports that the Indians "years ago lived in open camps sheltered on three sides by throwing up logs and brush." A fire was located in front of these lean-tos which were further covered with caribou skins. (Field, *Unpublished manuscript* [1913], 5.) In 1885 Schwatka reported for Ayan, a village below Fort Selkirk (Tutchoni area) that a few Indians had built log cabins "of the most squalid and worthless character, which they leave in winter for the better protection of the tent." There is nothing to suggest that these log houses are aboriginal. The same writer speaks of conical shelters covered with a double layer of skins and banked with snow. Schwatka, *Report on a Military Reconnaisance made in Alaska in 1883* (1900), 191.

into non-detachable mittens, in which case the sleeves of the garment were provided with a lacing located under the armpits. By undoing these ties a person could free his arm from the sleeves when he required greater freedom of movement for the performance of camp tasks. Considerable care went into the manufacture of a parka, the task being accomplished with the use of a stretching frame over which the finished article was mounted.[10] Inside the garment, next to the stomach, a pocket of caribou hide held feather duffel that contributed to warmth. Decoration consisted primarily of porcupine-quill work. Belonging perhaps to an earlier period of history than the parka was the waist-length winter coat made of skins tanned with the hair and worn with the fur innermost. Open down the front, such coats closed at the throat with "stick buttons." Another variation in winter dress consisted of coat and trouser combinations. Trouser and moccasin combinations were not limited to winter but were never donned for hunt-ing. Winter moccasins covered feet that had first been wrapped in rabbit skin. Often moose hairs or dry grass lined the bottoms of winter footgear in order to secure greater insulation from the cold. Both sexes wore leggings, those of the man reaching to the knee and those of a woman ending somewhat lower. It is not clear if leggings constituted winter garb. Around camp in winter people wore mittens of caribou hide tanned with the hair on, while the parka and mitten combination garment made satisfactory apparel for traveling.

Young children beginning to walk wore a shirt of caribou skin reaching to below the stomach. Infants who spent a great deal of time in the moss bag needed no garment other than that container. In winter baby bags were doubled and interlined with eider-down. Around the baby's feet the mother wrapped rabbit skin. In winter moss to absorb the infant's excretions was always warmed prior to being placed next to the child's body.

A variety of headgear appears characteristic of the aboriginal period. In winter men (who lacked a parka?) enjoyed hats of woven spruce roots lined with feathers and pro-vided with ear flaps of fur that tied under the chin. If a traveler grew warm from strenuous walking he could throw back the hat without undoing the chin ties, thus letting the article dangle in back of his neck. Skin from the head of the caribou furnished another type of headgear used by men. Both sexes wore hats of beaver or other skin with flaps extending below the ears to tie under the chin. Here a piece of rabbit skin might be placed for additional warmth. Bird skin, perhaps from the loon, supplied material for caps worn by men, women, and children. In winter they too reached below the ears. A strip of birch bark, an inch or two wide, sewn to form a circle and covered with smoked skin, provided a boy's hat. This item may have been a relatively recent novelty.[11]

Various techniques of clothing decoration undoubtedly enjoyed simultaneous popu-

---

[10] The sketch which the informant drew of such a frame closely resembles the frame made by the Ingalik Indians. Osgood, *Ingalik Material Culture* (1940), 253, Fig. 108.

[11] Novelty hats remain popular among the Kaska and adjoining Tahltan. A person who has worked among both the Northern Athapaskan and Northern Algonkians is quickly struck by the monotony of headgear among the latter, where almost every man and boy wears the peaked cap in every season. Professor Osgood, who pointed out to us the Northern Athapaskan's taste for varied headgear, re-marked that the Indians of the Northwest Coast also reveal a considerable variety of hat styles.

larity among the Cassiar Indians. Many garments carried porcupine-quill embroidery and quills were also woven on the bow loom to produce decorative outer belts and headbands. Besides being richly adorned with quills a woman further enhanced her dress with "the hard pellets" obtained from the tripe of moose. Skin fringes enjoyed great popularity, being strung across the shoulders of a man's coat and suspended from the lower edge of the parka. Red earth mixed with a small amount of grease or balsam pitch provided a paint applied with the fingers to clothing. The designs of such painting appeared in pairs, for example on the left and right sides of the ventral surface of the garment. Two common designs, reconstructed from memory by an informant, are indicated in Figure 5. Ground-hog skin sewn to the front of a man's winter parka probably served both for warmth and adornment. Moccasins did not carry a fur trimming. Pieces of bone, painted red and blue (blue-green color confusion obtained among the Kaska as among many American Indians) hung from coats. Blue pigment, obtainable in the vicinity of Pelly Banks, was mixed with grease or, to "really make it stick," with balsam

FIG. 5. Painted Designs for Clothing.

pitch. Black paint, the color that completed the aboriginal palette, also came from earth but appears to have been little employed for clothing decoration. Feathers did not find much place in ornament. Shamans wore a feather headdress while engaged in their professional duties and an occasional person sometimes adorned himself by sticking a feather in his hair. Feather-lined wristlets have already been mentioned.

We come now to adornment worn directly on or in the skin. Men made porcupine-quill necklaces, the quills being dyed by wives and sweethearts. Such necklaces were frequently provided with pendants hanging down in front of the body. The wrists of women carried bracelets of smoked skin decorated with porcupine-quill embroidery, while moose and caribou teeth were much fancied for necklaces. Both sexes wore quill headbands. The ear lobes of older girls and women were weighted with plugs carved from bone but no ornaments penetrated the helix. In the lower lip a woman often inserted a labret made of a small piece of fish bone.[12] A woman's brother-in-law frequently performed the operation that pierced the skin for these ornaments. In the process he pinched the soft flesh in a "wooden frame" (apparently consisting simply of two pieces of wood). The vise remained in place overnight and prevented the blood from flowing into the lip. Next morning the flesh was punctured and balsam pitch applied to forestall

[12] Among the Tlingit bone labrets in the lower lip were "a sign of womanhood" and their use was restricted to women of the upper class. The piercing of children's ears was celebrated with a potlatch. Both sexes wore nose rings. Stevenson, *Some Notes on Southeastern Alaska and its People* (1893), 82; Jones, *A Study of the Thlingets of Alaska* (1914), 66–67; Drucker, *Culture Element Distributions: XXVI, Northwest Coast* (1950), 190.

infection. Subsequently, from time to time the hole might be enlarged. Nasal rings fashioned from the wide hollow ends of sheep horns remained restricted to women but septum plugs found favor with both sexes. A man also perforated the nasal septum. In the case of boys great secrecy shrouded the operation. People believed that infection would occur if a woman chanced to see the freshly made hole. A young girl carefully concealed her unhealed septum wound from an old woman.

Men extracted their facial hair by tweezing, an old man sometimes soliciting a boy to perform the task. Rubbing the hair with rendered bone marrow probably constituted adornment, and in summer people greased their faces. To lighten dark skin a mixture of pitch and shredded bark was applied over a period of several months. Face painting marked the potlatch dancers, and youths of both sexes painted the countenance for courting, the adornment somehow signifying that the person would soon be married. Girls and young women plaited the hair in two or three braids that hung down over the back. Where the braid began a woman tied a painted band of thin, smoked sheepskin. No woman ever coiled her hair over the ears or put it up in a bun behind her head. Men let their hair hang long and unbraided.[13] Combs of jack pine or balsam brush were used and sometimes also the backbone of a fish. Death of a close relative demanded that the hair of both sexes be cut.

Boys and girls sought to be tattooed when about ten years old. The operator usually consisted of an older youth. The area to be tattooed was pierced with a porcupine quill coated with charcoal and the needle slowly drawn under the surface so that it left its color behind.[14] Only a limited quantity of tattooing went on during a single sitting, with the result that the process continued over several months. A skilled practitioner "knew the depth of the skin and didn't hurt the other fellow." Designs consisted of short parallel lines applied on the upper surfaces of both arms. Here a man would have his war record embellished. Circumcision was unknown.

Dease River Kaska. Tanned caribou skin provided the principal source of clothing, supplemented in winter by fox, marten, and other pelts. Sewing was with an awl that punched "holes through which lines were passed to keep shirts and pants together." Women also utilized thimbles of semi-tanned skin when sewing with a needle. Clothes not currently in use were stored in a two-foot long clothing bag of tanned skin.

A man's basic dress consisted of a long-sleeved coat, open in front and tied at the neck. A breech cloth, looped over an inner belt, covered the genitals. The same belt also supported trousers reaching from ankle to the middle of the thigh. Strips of tanned skin ("garters") connected the outside of these leggings to the belt. Only relatively recently, according to an informant, did the Dease River people borrow moccasin and trouser combinations from the Taku Indians. A woman did not use a coat but was attired in a dress that closed in front and extended to about the middle of the calf. She too wore leggings, fastened to an inner belt that also held up the customary breech cloth. Moccasins completed the woman's basic attire.

[13] Uncut hair was customary among the Tlingit. Drucker, *Culture Element Distributions: XXVI, Northwest Coast* (1950), 189.

[14] "Prick" tattooing is specified for the Tlingit. Drucker, *Culture Element Distributions: XXVI, Northwest Coast* (1950), 190, 261.

In winter men and women added coats of ground-hog, fox, sheep, and other skins to the previously mentioned garments. People avoided fur when traveling because they feared perspiration and dangerous chilling. Woven-skin clothes originated from the pelts of ground-hogs and squirrels, the lines cut from the skins of those animals exceeding the strength of rabbit fur. Informants seemed confused about the use of parkas. One man denied their presence in the pre-contact culture (WT). Mittens completed the winter dress and gloves (?) were donned for working around camp.

Ordinarily in summer people wore no headgear. Sometimes men appeared with "stick hats," shaped like small tambourine drums, the frame consisting of a piece of bent and sewn spruce wood. Semitanned caribou skin furnished a covering. In the same season women sometimes dressed with woven spruce-root caps or hats of birch bark which they abandoned in winter for a triangular piece of skin that covered the head and ears to tie under the chin somewhat like a modern kerchief.

Informants called attention to two moccasin types, one older than the other. The earlier pattern came to a sharp point with the stitching running from the tip of the toes back to the tongue. The second style, commonly used today, had a blunt toe, the skin being brought up around the foot and sewn to the edges of the tongue.[15] For winter use women sewed large moccasins designed to be worn with rabbit fur, feather, or dry grass duffel.

For decoration women utilized polished fragments of bone that were sewn to garments and also skin fringes, fur trimming, and dyed porcupine-quill embroidery.[16] Both sexes indulged in ornamented outer belts containing a considerable amount of quillwork. These girdles, like headbands, occasionally consisted of solid quillwork, women weaving the quills on bow looms. Tanned-skin garments were also painted with blue (or green) and red pigments. The Dease River Indians did not add feathers or hair tufts to clothing but an informant had heard that the Etca?otena of Fort Nelson utilized hair in decorating their garments.[17] Face painting enhanced personal attractiveness, red and black paints serving for this purpose. The former color came from ocher mixed with grease. White paint seems to have been used less for adornment than as protection against the strong rays of the summer sun. The object may have been to keep the face from darkening.[18] Normally people did not cut their hair, although they frequently rubbed it with rendered bone marrow or caribou grease before combing with a fish skeleton. Wristlets adorned the lower arms of girls. For good fortune men and women wore amulets of twisted eider-duck feathers around their wrists. The use of lip plugs remains in doubt.[19]

[15] A similar sequence of styles is reported for the Tahltan. "A round-toed moccasin is also made and used by the Tahltan; but they claim that this style is of comparatively recent introduction among them, being copied from moccasins worn by eastern half-breeds and whites." Teit, *Notes on the Tahltan Indians of British Columbia* (1906), 342.

[16] Among the Tahltan "porcupine quill embroidery was done on clothes and bags, and shells obtained from the Coast were much used for personal adornment and ornamentation in general." Teit, *On Tahltan (Athabaskan) Work* (1912), 485.

[17] His information is corroborated by Slave Indian informants. Honigmann, *Ethnography and Acculturation of the Fort Nelson Slave* (1946), 58.

[18] Among the Tlingit face painting furnished protection against sun and wind. Drucker, *Culture Element Distributions: XXVI, Northwest Coast* (1950), 191.

[19] It may be that labrets were of relatively late introduction and did not meet with the same reception

The nasal septum of a boy was pierced at about the age of seven, the hole being progressively enlarged with wooden plugs of various sizes. Nose ornaments continued to be worn into adulthood. A girl's mother pierced her daughter's ears around the age of ten, a porcupine quill being used for the initial operation. Some girls perforated their own ear lobes. To enlarge the hole, bone plugs of different sizes were applied. Nothing could be learned of tattooing, one informant even denying the practice.

Indians commonly washed their hands with a mixture of wood ashes and grease. Human urine contained in birch-bark vessels supplied an effective detergent for cleaning clothes. Use of urine to wash the body was denied but the pattern is said to have occurred among the adjoining Tahltan.[20] People pared fingernails and made no special effort to destroy the parings. Defecation and elimination constituted private matters, to which Indians attended in the bush. Only young children about two years old were permitted to urinate and defecate into birch bark vessels kept in the dwelling (in winter?). Following defecation the body was cleaned with moss and twigs.

Tselona. Women sewed tanned-skin clothing with both awls and true needles of bone. Rabbit-skin line was plaited for garments but no frame aided the process. Gut and fish skins found no use in clothing manufacture.

A man's basic dress consisted of an open coat reaching to the thighs and fastened with stick buttons, trousers extending upward to the thighs and attached to an inner belt by tanned-skin thongs, and the breech cloth. Women wore dresses reaching to the middle of the calf together with knee length leggings secured with line. Moccasins and decorative outer belts completed the dress of both sexes. For winter weather men wore parkas of fully tanned hide, occasionally lined with fur. No use of the parka stretcher could be recalled. Mittens packed with muskrat fur kept hands warm, while moccasin duffel of goat's hair served a similar function for the lower extremities. Dry grass found no employment as duffel. Gloves remained unknown prior to contact. Use of moccasin and trouser or coat and trouser combinations failed to be recalled. A shaman did not dress distinctively. Clothing remained unwashed as long as it was in use.

A variety of hats shared popularity. The simplest type of headgear for both sexes consisted of an approximately triangular piece of tanned skin that was lined with muskrat or ground hog fur. In wearing these, the fur rested next to the head. The lower edges tied beneath the wearer's chin thus covering the ears and cheeks. "Stick hats," made of a piece of bent and sewn birch wood covered with marten or beaver skin tanned with the hair on, were also recalled. A very decorative hat for women consisted of a loon skin. Woven spruce-root caps could not be recalled.

Clothing decoration featured skin fringes, pieces of bone, fur, paint, and porcupine quills. Fringes commonly appeared on mittens, coats, and dresses, being added to the collar as well as across the back of the latter garment. Lynx and other fur fringes contributed to the attractiveness of parka hoods and also appeared on other items of dress.

---

everywhere in the Cassiar. According to Jenness the Tahltan rejected the labret of the coastal people while the Carrier readily accepted the same ornament. Jenness, *Indians of Canada* (1932), 372.

[20] The Tlingit (including the Chilkat), like many other Pacific Coast people, used urine as a detergent. Drucker, *Culture Element Distributions: XXVI, Northwest Coast* (1950), 192.

Red appealed as the favorite color for painting skin clothing. It was applied around the neck as well as along the front of the garment, always in straight, vertical lines. Porcupine-quill embroidery adorned coats, dresses, and mittens. Men wore arm garters of plainted quills, a woman priding herself on being able to supply her husband with such "high-toned" ornaments.

Headdresses included porcupine-quill and tanned-skin headbands, the latter embroidered with quills, and headkerchiefs of tanned skin embroidered with quillwork. Women used the kerchiefs while men wore the headbands. Necklaces and wristlets could not be recalled. At about the age of seven the like-sexed parent pierced a child's nasal septum with a bone awl. In the hole the individual carried a bone plug but never a ring. Childhood also marked the time when a mother perforated her daughter's ears. In these holes the girl inserted bone ornaments carved by men. Helix ear plugs as well as face and chin labrets remained unknown. Only a woman painted her face and the use of rendered bone marrow for hair dressing likewise remained restricted to her sex. Grouard has described the appearance of women who came to Fort Liard in 1867 from the vicinity of Fort Halkett. They were attired in moose-skin (*peux d'orignaux*) garments decorated "with a kind of pommade made of goat's grease and vermillion paint with which they had daubed their cheeks, nose, and chin." When the priest told them to stop painting their faces, because the custom displeased both God and himself, they immediately began to remove the designs.[21] With a needle and length of sinew line young people of both sexes tattooed the body. Generally a companion who possessed special skill in this technique performed the initial operation. The hair normally remained uncut. Women wore braids hanging down over the back. Fish skeletons found no place as hair combing devices, the informant asserting that the people used a comb carved from birch. Facial hair was extracted by plucking but no attempt was made to get rid of pubic or armpit hair.

Frances Lake Kaska. The aboriginal moccasin pattern of the Tutcotena featured the pointed toe with the seam running lengthwise until it joined the tongue. Pike reports seeing women who wore "a large brass ring through the nose" near Frances Lake.[22]

RECREATION

Upper Liard Kaska. Sometimes in the evening when chores were done and everyone had eaten, the people played. The summer and winter gatherings around a fish lake provided opportunities for recreation but no great cooperation was required for a man to amuse himself by carving small animal images from wood or outlining figures in red paint on rocks and trees. In winter children enjoyed drawing huge scrawling designs in

[21] Grouard, *Souvenirs de mes soixante ans d'apostolat dans l'Athabaska Mackenzie* (n. d.), 105.

[22] Pike, *Through the Subarctic Forest* (1896), 138. Field reports clothing of caribou skin as well as moose calf skin among the Pelly River Indians. These materials were sometimes "tanned with the hair on, sometimes worn with the hair inside the garment, sometimes with the hair out. Some of the more stylish use beaver fur coats and hats and mitts, also in trimming garments. They use rabbit skin cut in strips and knitted for blankets, also the skins of squirrels and groundhog." Field, *Unpublished manuscript* (1913), 9.

the smooth snow of a frozen lake. Games, feasts, and potlatches involved larger scale social interaction.

The tambourine drum furnished the standard musical instrument. The best toned drumheads came from the raw skin of a young moose, caribou skin being inferior because it split too easily. The rawhide was spanned across one side of a circular wooden rim, babiche lines running from the edges of the skin to tie underneath the cover. These converging lines also made a useful handle to hold the instrument. The size of drums varied but a potlatch instrument sometimes attained three feet in diameter. To tighten the drumhead a player carefully heated it over a fire. Although the Upper Liard Indians made rattles for children, such instruments were not regarded as musical instruments. Whistles, carved from willow, also constituted toys.[23]

Repetitious, wordless chants that expressed feeling and amused or entertained listeners shared a place with true songs containing words. The repertory included potlatch songs, gambling songs for stick games, love songs to serenade a sweetheart, mourning songs, and magical war chants. A shaman sang his own song while curing, and so did a man working with a maul.

The Upper Liard Indians did not dance in a circle. Rather people ranged themselves in a row and, with the arms partly raised but not directly participating in the movement, rocked the body up and down while keeping time with the feet.[24] Potlatch dancers painted their faces grotesquely and costumed themselves in sheep and wolf skins, half-finished coats, absurd headgear, and sheep horns—all provoking considerable amusement for the spectators. Wolf's-head masks might be worn by members of that moiety.

The people liked to engage in contests of strength and skill, including throwing, arrow shooting, wrestling, and racing. Adults and children played with balls made from a mass of skin sewn into a tanned-skin container. Target shooting with a bow demanded a small stick thrust in the ground as a target. In one winter sport boys threw sticks in the snow trying to make them skip like flat stones thrown across the surface of water. Young men frequently competed to see who by using his hands alone could break the hind-quarter bone of a beaver. Occasionally a girl also joined the competition. The secret of breaking a beaver bone, according to an informant, lay in twisting it with great force rather than trying to break it in half. Riddles are said to have been told for amusement but none could be obtained.[25] Wrestling enjoyed wide popularity among young men but was specifically prohibited between two brothers-in-law. Young boys ran foot races on the snow of a frozen lake. Canoe races could not be recalled but an informant believed

[23] A Kaska informant knew the Tlingit to possess plank drums and to use rattles in dancing. According to Drucker, the Tlingit (including the Chilkat) used single-head tambourine, suspended wooden, and plank drums. Drucker, *Culture Element Distributions: XXVI, Northwest Coast* (1950), 197–198.

[24] Among the Tlingit "while dancing, the participants stand close together and scarcely move out of their tracks. . . . The dancing really consists of rhythmic movements of the hands, arms, head and entire body above the waist. . . . Time is measured by the beat of the drum. . . ." Men and women danced, painting the face with red or black pigments and also using masks. Jones, *Study of the Thlingets of Alaska* (1914), 144.

[25] "It is interesting to note the presence of riddles among the Tahltan, a feature that has not often been reported for North American Indian tribes." Teit, *On Tahltan (Athabaskan) Work* (1912), 486.

that sometimes dugouts engaged in such contests.[26] People played many games including blind man's bluff, which involved covering the eyes of a player with tanned skin while five or six other participants circled the blindfolded person, who sought to capture them. Both sexes of all ages played hide and seek. Sometimes an object was hidden and its discovery became the object of the game. With a raw skin available children initiated the game of drag-skin, jumping on the skin and trying to hold it back by their weight as it was being drawn by an older person. String figures called for a certain amount of skill to construct designs like a duck, crow, feet, and conical lodge from a length of tanned-skin line. Rope jumping and rope tug-of-war did not come into popularity until contact, and pole tug-of-war, skin-tossing, as well as snapping sticks, could not be recalled as amusement devices. Shamans may have used snapping sticks as part of the curing ritual. Story telling possessed educative value and constituted the pleasant responsibility of old men. A story teller might insist that the audience look him directly in the eyes. Should a young person shift his glance he would be reprimanded by the narrator remarking, "You won't be smart."[27] Private ownership did not extend to folk tales.

Gambling occurred in summer, when a number of family bands gathered together and the weather allowed players to assemble around an outdoor fire. The stick game, of which several alternative forms existed, furnished the most popular medium for betting.[28] Since the pattern of this game has already been described for the Kaska[29] the details will not be repeated here. Mainly the game took place at night, illumination coming from a well-tended fire located between the double line of kneeling players. A steady drumming furnished rhythm to which the gamblers moved hands and body as they challenged the opponents to guess in which hand the wooden token lay concealed. Women as well as men played the stick game but the sexes never competed in the same game. Forfeits consisted of whatever valuables a man chose to offer. Sometimes after playing most of the night a man lost all his resources. With the gambling fever still possessing him he might in the end bet his wife. Should he lose his bet the woman remained with the winner for two or three days before returning to her husband. Marriages rarely broke up as a result of this custom. Sometimes an old man, fearing that the woman would become accustomed to the other man, went to the winner's camp and urged the latter to send her back.

Feasts marked a number of points on the life cycle. Thus parents celebrated the birth

[26] The Tlingit organized three- to four-mile races, run by from three to five canoes. Jones, *Study of the Thlingets of Alaska* (1914), 81.

[27] A Tahltan informant, Beal Carlick, said that among his people a grandfather told many stories about fighting, murder, and warfare. Such deeds were explained as resulting from the evil nature of some men and the craziness of some women. "This was just like school, educate us so we don't lie, don't steal." Stories also possessed entertainment value and filled evenings when there was nothing else to do. "Sit down, listen, don't run around anymore," the informant said.

[28] Stick games were also a favorite form of gambling among the Tlingit. Swanton, *Social Condition, Beliefs and Linguistic Relationship of the Tlingit Indians* (1908), 443–444; Jones, *Study of the Thlingets of Alaska* (1914), 122–123.

[29] Honigmann, *Culture and Ethos of Kaska Society* (1949), 174–175.

of a child (first born?) with a meal to which friends were invited. The first game killed by a youth also became the occasion for a "party." A wealthy man honored his daughter in the same way when she attained menarche or married. Marriage feasts often constituted potlatches, at which the bride's mother aided by her brothers and sisters presented gifts of manufactured objects to the members of the opposite matrilineal moiety. While no elaborate death feast took place a memorial potlatch followed about a year after the death.[30] In winter people enjoyed the Biggest Cache Feast, presented by a man who owned a particularly rich meat cache. Huge quantities of cooked ground hog and gopher and birch-bark dishes filled with grease were served to the guests. Perhaps serving as a hint for someone to provide lavish entertainment, members of the Crow moiety occasionally arranged a mock feast. When the invited guests assembled they found very little food available, "just a bite for everybody." Amused, the guests exclaimed, "A Wolverine Party!" One moiety or the other would then usually announce a more satisfying repast.

The origin of the potlatch is explained in the following tale.

A girl was pregnant. When she was ready to have her baby she went into seclusion behind the dwelling. Here one day as the sun was setting her father heard her talking and laughing. The people did not know that she had given birth to a monster. The girl returned to her parents but the monster grew large and ate many people. He was almost a hundred feet long and had a great, wide mouth. Everybody wanted to kill the thing but nobody was able to do so. One day the people sent the girl away. That is when they killed the monster. When the mother returned she cried like hell because this had been her child. The girl cried so much that the old man became frightened. So the old man made a big potlatch and gave away many things. Pretty soon the girl felt better. Since then the Indians had a potlatch everytime somebody died.

To prepare a potlatch a host first had to secure sufficient quantity of manufactured goods and food that could be distributed. While some of the objects came from members of the donor's matrilineal moiety and need not be repaid, the responsibility for some of the contributions rested with the potlatcher and his family. The distribution of many fine things and large amounts of food won prestige for a man. From such behavior he won the reputation of being a "big man." But only a very capable hunter could acquire enough meat and skins to provide an elaborate give-away. Previous to the party the assembled wealth lay displayed in the dwelling on a mat of rawhide or a bear skin. The potlatcher then proceeded to invite his guests, all members of the opposite moiety. A small ceremony was attached to the invitation. The host, visiting a guest's home, planted his walking stick inside the entry and uttered the syllable, "nix!"[31] The visitors assembled in the potlatch house where brothers and sisters of the potlatcher served them food. After they had finished eating the host distributed gifts through his assistants. There occurred much joking at this stage of the proceedings. For example, a server, following the typical Athapaskan pattern of humor, would pretend to throw a visitor's present

[30] See below, p. 139, for details of a "small" death feast.

[31] Messenger sticks have been described for the Nunivak Eskimo. Here they were used by the message carrier who invited people to a social climbing feast. (Lantis, *Social Culture of the Nunivak Eskimo* [1946], 188.) The distribution of similar insignia among the Eskimo of Alaska is discussed in the same writer's *Alaskan Eskimo Ceremonialism* [1947], 69–72.) The trait is not mentioned in Drucker's check list of the Pacific Coast. Drucker, *Culture Element Distributions: XXVI, Northwest Coast* (1950).

into the fire. The recipient would cry out, "I win that!" A host gave presents with an eye to what he had already received, the more elaborate objects being presented to people who had given him good gifts in the past. A person who had given poorly received a relatively less valuable present.

When the gifts had all been allocated, a rawhide curtain was erected in the dwelling, supported from two poles held by members of the host's moiety. Members of the potlatcher's group retired behind the curtain and decorated themselves with masks, feathers, and animal skins for dancing.[32] Members of the opposite moiety painted the faces of like-sexed dancers. Costumes did not include ceremonial wigs or aprons. When they were ready the dancers called for the curtain to be removed and began dancing to the rhythm of drums and potlatch songs. After one moiety had performed the guests allowed their faces to be painted and in turn also danced. Crow dancers sometimes ran their hands upward along the faces of the Wolf people, brushing the latter's hair away from the face. Celebrations lasted as long as four days, large meals being served every evening. In the night people gambled far into the morning. Competitive grease-drinking contests were also featured at potlatches, winners receiving their rewards in arrows and other useful prizes. Besides marking puberty, marriage, and anniversaries of death, potlatches constituted a ritual means of reducing hostility between moieties. Thus if a member of the Crow side had killed a Wolf he might avoid the open resentment of the other moiety by assembling wealth and inviting members of the offended side to attend his potlatch. The exchange of ceremonial civilities between the two parties erased all memory of the offense.

Dease River Kaska. Averaging about 15 or 16 inches in diameter, the tambourine drum of semi-tanned moose hide furnished the chief musical instrument of the Kistagotena. Only shamans decorated these objects with symbols representing the sky, moon, and stars. Along with the drum people provided rhythm with bells, made from hollowed caribou horn, or moose hooves threaded on a piece of line from which they could be swung. For amusement youths made willow whistles in the spring. Apart from potlatch chants and songs for gambling, love, and mourning, people sang to secure good weather and favorable hunting and fishing. Hunters knew specific, and presumably lucky, moose, ground hog, caribou, and beaver songs. All chants were generally wordless and in essence consisted of a few syllables repeated over and over in a minor key. The refrain of a potlatch song follows:

ha·ʔe ha·ʔe i·ʔe
ha·ʔe hi·i· ho·ho·ʔo
ha we hi· e·ʔe

Songs might be revealed in dreams or learned from one's father. People did not sing war songs.

Dancing provided a popular source of amusement. Sometimes the son of a headman led dancers in a circle while pounding a drum. During the potlatch people performed and clowned while covered with bark masks, the features of which were outlined with char-

---

[32] At the Tlingit potlatch animal masks and skins were worn to represent the crest animals. Swanton, *Social Condition, Beliefs and Linguistic Relationship of the Tlingit Indians* (1908), 435.

coal. Other masks came from the head skins of black and grizzly bears, the goat, and sheep.

Potlatches were accompanied by games and sports, some of which included competitions between teams recruited from opposite moieties. Popular sports including racing, tugs-of-war, blind-man's bluff, wrestling, target shooting, throwing, and gambling. Races took place between men, the end of a course sometimes being marked by the prize that would become the property of the winner. Thus an arrow thrust into a tree would be pulled out by the first contestant to reach the objective. Two spruce bark traveling canoes also raced, each containing a team selected on moiety lines. The winning team claimed the rival vessel as their prize. Three or four men engaged in swimming races, often to see who could cross a river quickest. Tugs-of-war also occurred between moieties. Customarily some boiled meat piled on one side of the playing ground constituted the prize of the winning side. The Kaska, one concludes, did not enjoy sport for its own sake but preferred to compete for some tangible reward. Men and women engaged in tugs-of-war, the sport being played with lines as well as with poles. Poles in turn were both pushed and pulled. Blind-man's-bluff found favor with children and adults. In this game one of the contestants had his eyes bound with caribou hide. Moving with outstretched arms toward the sound cues of the other participants he sought to grasp somebody's coat or arm. In a variety of this game a blindfolded individual sought to secure a marten skin hung in a tree. Success earned him the right to keep the prize. Wrestling matches endured for several hours, for as one contestant was overcome another stepped from the circle of onlookers to challenge the victor. Each defeated challenger paid the victor in moccasins, a bow, or an arrow. Wrestling for women was denied but the informant, in typical fashion, remarked having heard of the practice among the Espatotena and "Mackenzie River Indians." Shooting with bow and arrows for a mark on a tree or toward some other target rarely involved a prize. Sticks were also flung across snow (snow scaling?) to see how far one could hit. Skin tossing and drag-skin games could not be recalled. People keenly relished gambling in the form of the stick game. Teams consisted of from five to ten men each. Instead of playing with the hands under a robe the contestants held their arms behind the back while they shuffled the pointed wooden token. Two drummers accompanied the players and simultaneously chanted "hö, hö, hö, hö." Should drums be unavailable the players themselves chanted in a moderately fast, double rhythm, six-eights time: "ha-ha, hu-hi, hi-ha, hu-hi."

Through feasts the Indians celebrated a youth's first successful hunt for large game, a girl's return from her initial menstrual seclusion, and a youth's completion of his dream quest. Sometimes the feasts became potlatches. No mortuary feast took place but a "remembrance" potlatch occurred about one year after death. Potlatches were exchanged between moieties and followed a period of gift solicitation. Objects given to a potlatcher constituted outright gifts for the festival from which, in turn, all the givers derived prestige. The contributors received gifts when the opposite moiety repaid the potlatch. Only rich men provided a potlatch, their poorer fellows being unable to accumulate sufficient food or objects for such an undertaking. Clowning and masked dancing enlivened the give-away but nobody recalled the use of ceremonial wigs.

SOCIAL ORGANIZATION

FAMILY AND KIN

UPPER LIARD KASKA. While the nuclear or conjugal family certainly served important functions in the life of the aboriginal Kaska Indians, this unit was normally incorporated in a larger extended family that linked a woman and her daughters. Typically such an extended family included a man, his wife, perhaps her sisters and their husbands, married daughters and their husbands, unmarried sons, and the unmarried children of the married daughters. An extended family often constituted the microcosmic band, to which additional unrelated individuals of either sex attached themselves. In winter the band or extended family sometimes shared a large conical house, although households containing two sisters and their families of procreation were also common. The distinction between nuclear family, extended family, and household is illustrated in Figure 6. Here the broken lines (enclosing individuals A, B, C, D, G, H, and I) indicate a household in which A, B, and G are members of one nuclear family and C, D, H, and I belong to another. In this diagram E, F, J, and K constitute another and adjacent household. While the children, J and K, would probably spend most of their time in their parent's dwelling they would be equally at home in the household of the maternal grandparents. Daughters tended to establish households quite soon after marriage, perhaps because of the strong avoidance governing the relations of a man and his mother-in-law. Not all microcosmic bands conformed to the matrilocal extended family here outlined. Sometimes a band formed around the nucleus of two brothers and their wives. Daughters on occasion also left their parents' band after marriage to take up residence with their husbands' kin. Bands tended to be fluid among most Arctic-drainage Athapaskan groups and few pressures could be relied upon to maintain any particular type of organization. A man lacking skill in hunting might join with his wife's family, expecting the latter's brother or father to furnish a dependable source of meat. Should his unproductive presence come to be resented, friction might send him to rejoin his own parental group. If his skill or "luck" improved he would be able to fulfill the ideal expectations of a son-in-law or might decide to go off with his wife to shift for himself. Adoption, which was widely practiced, also complicated the composition of Indian groupings. Orphans as well as children whose parents still lived were adopted, the latter being somewhat better treated than parentless children. It is interesting to note that a parent who subsequently wanted an adopted child returned had to offer payment except in cases when the foster parents were guilty of mistreatment.

Following are relationship terms employed by the Upper Liard Indians:

(e)stsii'e: my MoFa, FaFa, FaSiSo (m.s.), WiFa (m.s.), HuFa (w.s.).
(e)stsuu': my MoMo, FaMo, FaSi, FaSiDa (m.s.), WiMo (m.s.), HuMo (w.s.).
eta': my Fa.
ena': my Mo, MoSi.
(e)sta': my FaBr.
seze': my MoBr, SiSo.

75

(e)stcuu′e: my So, BrSo.

(e)stuu′e: my Da, BrDa, SiDa, also stepdaughter.

gutii′e: my eBr; also, if older than ego, FaBrSo, MoSiSo, WiSiHu.

(e)tcit′le: my yBr; also, if younger than ego, FaBrSo, MoSiSo, WiSiHu.

(e)taa′te: my eSi; also, if older than ego, FaBrDa, MoSiDa, HuBrWi.

(e)ta′tze: my ySi; also, if younger than ego, FaBrDa, MoSiDa, HuBrWi.

(a)sla′: my MoBrSo, FaSiSo (w.s.), HuBr (w.s.), WiBr (m.s.), SiHu (m.s.), WiSi (m.s.).

ekle′: my MoBrDa, FaSiDa (w.s.), HuSi (w.s.) SiHu(w.s.), BrWi (w.s.).

(e)sii′on: my Wi.

se′lige: my Hu.

(e)spa′: my WiSi (m.s.), BrWi (m.s.).

(e)stca′: my SoSo, DaSo, SoDa, DaDa, SoWi.

senaze′: my DaHu.

(e)syaˀe: my stepson.

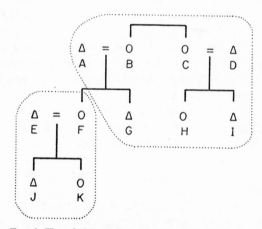

FIG. 6. Household and Extended Family Patterns.

The outstanding features of this kin-term system, which will be compared with kinship usages obtaining among adjacent Athapaskan tribes, may be briefly summarized. The present tense is used as a matter of preference.

1. Cousin terminology is of the Crow type with parallel and cross cousins called by different terms. MoBrSo and FaSiSo are called by different terms (man speaking) as well as MoBrDa and FaSiDa. A man classifies his FaSiSo with his grandfather, his FaSiDa with his grandmother. A woman classifies these cousins with her siblings-in-law, a feature consistent with asymmetrical cross-cousin marriage.[1]

2. Bifurcate merging terminology identifies Mo and MoSi, So and BrSo.

3. Generation-type terminology results in the identification of Da, BrDa, and SiDa.

4. A reciprocal term applies between the MoBr and his SiSo.

5. The wife's and husband's parents are classified with grandparents. FaSi and FaSiDa are also grouped with the latter relatives. These failures to recognize collaterality represent further instances of bifurcate merging terminology.

[1] See below, p. 131.

6. While no term for DaHu was obtained, SoWi is designated by a distinctive term, which elsewhere in the intermontane area designates granddaughter.

7. There is a single grandchild term.

Turning to kinship behavior, joking obtained between grandparents and grandchildren. The former sometimes resented being teased and reprimanded junior relatives with some such remark as, "You'll be old too when your time comes. Look after yourself." Circumspect behavior obtained between siblings of opposite sex. An older boy avoided directly addressing his sister (real or classificatory) and limited his interpersonal relations with her.[2] Any reference to the sexual organs in the presence of siblings of like or opposite sex brought severe scolding. Some degree of familiarity obtained with father's siblings, although marriage with a paternal uncle or aunt was prohibited. Nevertheless sexual relations with the father's sister were countenanced. Following such intimacy the aunt is said to have "wanted me more." Respect governed behavior toward the mother's siblings. Part of a man's shyness with his mother's brother stemmed from the fact that the latter was regarded as a prospective father-in-law, to whom respect was also enjoined.[3] A man sometimes jokingly referred to his sister's children as "slaves." Strong reserve also marked relations between a man and his mother-in-law while a warm camaraderie linked brothers-in-law. However no undue familiarity entered their conversation. A man enjoyed teasing his brother's wife and sexual allusions were a prominent topic in their relations. For example, a married man might inform his sister-in-law that he would quit his wife in order to pursue her. Close friends addressed one another with the brother-in-law term, asla. No ritual acts marked the initiation of such friendships. Asymmetrical cross-cousin marriage with the MoBrDa or FaSiSo has already been mentioned.

Dease River Kaska. Below is a list of kinship terms employed among the Indians of the Dease River basin.

estsii: my MoFa, FaFa, WiFa (m.s.), HuFa (w.s.).
estsuu: my MoMo, FaMo (m.s.), WiMo (m.s.), HuMo (w.s.).
ete: my Fa.
ene: my Mo, MoSi.
esta: my FaBr.
seze: my MoBr, SiSo, SiDa.
(e)stcuume: my So, BrSo.
estue: my Da, BrDa.
gutdiie: my eBr; also, if older than ego, FaBrSo, MoSiSo.
itcitle: my yBr; also, if younger than ego, FaBrSo, MoSiSo.
etare: my eSi; also, if older than ego, FaBrDa, MoSiDa.
etaze: my ySi; also, if younger than ego, FaBrDa, MoSiDa.
esla: my MoBrSo, WiFa (m.s.), SiHu (m.s.).
espa: my MoBrDa (m.s.), HuBr (w.s.), SiHu (w.s.), WiSi (m.s.), BrWi (m.s.).
ekle: my MoBrDa (w.s.), HuSi (w.s.), BrWi (w.s.).
esiiuu: my Wi.

---

[2] Among the Tlingit brother and sister taboos also obtained, those relatives not speaking to each other. Jones, *Study of the Thlingets of Alaska* (1914), 145.

[3] See below, p. 132.

esɫitiʔa: my Hu.
estsuwa: my SoSo, DaSo, FaSiSo (m.s.), FaSiDa (m.s.).
senuza: DaHu.

The following are some characteristics to be observed in these terms:[4]

1. Cousin terminology is of the Crow type, with parallel and cross cousins differentiated. MoBrSo and FaSiSo are terminologically distinguished by speakers of each sex, as are MoBrDa and FaSiDa. While among the Upper Liard Kaska a male speaker classifies the FaSiDa and FaSiSo with grandparents, the Dease River speaker of either sex groups these cousins with grandchildren.

2. In addition to the bifurcate merging indicated in cousin terminology, the Mo and MoSi are terminologically identified.

3. The pairs, Da and BrDa, So and BrSo, are also merged.

4. A reciprocal term applies between MoBr on the one hand and SiSo and SiDa on the other.

[4] Compare these terms with the system of the adjacent Tahltan which follows:
estsi̱ïa: my MoFa, FaFa, WiFa, HuFa.
estci̱ï(n): my MoMo, FaMo, WiMo, HuMo.
etȩ: my Fa.
eła (or eʔɫii): my Mo.
ista: my FaBr, FaSiSo.
eda: my FaSi, MoSi.
edeθe (edeze): my MoBr.
istciima: my So.
istuua: my Da.
etdiia: my eBr; also, if older than ego, FaBrSo, MoSiSo, WiSiHu.
istcitla: my yBr; also, if younger than ego, FaBrSo, MoSiSo, WiSiHu.
adaade: my eSi; also, if older than ego, FaBrDa, MoSiDa, HuBrWi.
isdadze: my ySi; also, if younger than ego, FaBrDa, MoSiDa, HuBrWi.
esiiya: my MoBrSo, BrSo.
estsiʔa: my MoBrDa, BrDa.
ispa: my FaSiDa.
saze: my SiSo, SiDa.
istiiyane: my Wi.
iskaliine: my Hu.
esla: my HuBr, WiBr, SiHu.
istca: my SoSo, SoDa, DaSo, DaDa.
iscdii: my sweetheart.

The following features may be pointed out: (1) Cousin terminology is of the Crow type. (2) Lineal terminology results in the grouping together of MoSi and FaSi while Mo is terminologically differentiated from these aunts. Bifurcate collateral terminology manifests itself in the distinctive terms for Fa, FaBr, and MoBr. (3) Bifurcate collateral terminology results in terminological distinctions being made between ego's children, nieces, and nephews. (4) There is no reciprocal usage between MoBr and SiSo or SiDa. However, SiSo and SiDa are classified together. (5) The parents-in-law are merged with grandparents. (6) Terms for children's spouses could not be obtained. (7) There is a single grandchild term. Note that the tendency to bifurcate collateral terminology in (2) and (3) may represent survival of a social organization based on non-sororal polygyny with patrilineal descent or it may be consistent with patrilineal emphases such as have appeared among the Northwest Coast people. The Tlingit and Haida Avuncu-Crow systems reflect such a shift.

5. A wife's or husband's parents are merged with grandparents.

6. SoWi is classified with granddaughter but DaHu is terminologically differentiated.

7. There are two grandchildren terms applied according to sex and extended as indicated in (1) and (6) above.

The extension of bifurcate merging terminology to group Da and BrDa represents a difference between Dease River and Upper Liard River kinship usage that may indicate longer matrilocal residence and matrilineal descent in the former area.[5]

Clear evidence of joking between grandparents and grandchildren could not be obtained for the Kistagotena. The informant, himself an elderly man, stressed that grandparents exercised an educative and disciplinary role over grandchildren. A boy avoided his real or classificatory sisters after he as well as they had reached puberty. Prior to that time they played together freely. A sister continued to sew moccasins and other clothing for her brother as long as he remained in his parents' household. Following marriage she exchanged gifts with her brother's wife. Two Dease River informants manifested inexplicable reluctance to speak of cross-cousin marriage but asymmetrical cross-cousin marriage was finally admitted, together with the fact that these relatives remained on terms of easy familiarity even if they did not wed. A man's mother-in-law demanded respect and avoidance of undue intimacy. However the pair of relatives were permitted to engage in necessary conversation and could freely eat together. A son-in-law was expected to "feed" his father-in-law, especially when the latter became too old to hunt. A man joked freely with his wife's sister and brother's wife. The treatment of orphans and, perhaps, the fantasies of these unhappy children are reflected in "The Story of the Water-Man" related by Teit.[6] In this folk tale an orphaned boy who had been harshly treated succeeds in doing what nobody else had managed to achieve, breaking the Water Man's penis. The youth allows his uncle to gain credit for the feat. Eventually the uncle is killed, whereupon the boy overcomes Water Man, is made "chief" by the people, and takes his uncle's elder wife as his own. He refuses to have anything to do with her younger co-wife. Psychoanalytically minded readers will readily discern the Oedipus situation in this folktale.

Friendship patterns remain to be discussed. Two men might informally institute a close friendship, in which they would hunt and travel together. They addressed each other sexliʔate ("just like one"), undoubtedly a cognate of the husband term.

Kechika River. Although informants showed no readiness to classify the Kechika (Muddy) people apart from the Dease River Indians, a number of differences in kin terminology between the two areas suggest that we isolate the former region at this point for special consideration. The differences are particularly interesting because they reflect a social structure which has not fully assimilated matrilineal, exogamous moiety organization. Such an interpretation coincides with the fact that the Muddy River is relatively peripheral to the area of intensive unilinear organization, the Northwest Coast. The kin terms collected from Mark Margout, our Muddy River informant, follow.

[5] Murdock, *Social Structure* (1949), 149.
[6] Teit, *Kaska Tales* (1917), 460–461.

estsii: my MoFa, FaFa, WiFa (m.s.), HuFa (w.s.).
estsuu(n): my MoMo, FaMo, FaSi, WiMo (m.s.), HuMo (w.s.).
atę: my Fa.
anę: my Mo.
esta: my FaBr.
suze: my MoBr, MoBrSo.
soo²e: my MoSi.
setcue: my So, BrSo.
setua: my Da, BrDa.
gutdiie: my eBr; also, if older than ego, FaBrSo, MoSiSo, FaSiSo.
estcitle: my yBr; also, if younger than ego, FaBrSo, MoSiSo, FaSiSo.
atdade: my eSi; also, if older than ego, FaBrDa, MoSiDa, MoBrDa.
astada: my ySi; also, if younger than ego, FaBrDa, MoSiDa, MoBrDa.
estsiie: my FaSiDa.
samaγu: my Wi.
setawhu: my Hu.
estca: my SoSo, DaSo, SoDa, DaDa, SiSo, SiDa, SoWi.
esla: my HuBr (w.s.), WiBr (m.s.), SiHu.
espe: my HuSi (w.s.), WiSi (m.s.), BrWi.
sunaze: my DaHu.
sagahe: my sweetheart.

Analysis reveals the following features:[7]

[7] Bear Lake Sekani terms, representing usages at Whitewater, B. C., are given for comparative purposes. In some respects the system which follows differs from that reported by Jenness and based on Fort Grahame data. (Jenness, *The Sekani Indians of British Columbia* [1937], 51–52.)

istsiia: my MoFa, FaFa.
etsuun: my MoMo, FaMo, MoSi, WiMo (m.s.), HuMo (w.s.).
aba: my Fa.
ana: my Mo, MoSi (also called sowe).
isda: my FaBr, MoHu.
saze: my MoBr, WiBrDa (m.s.).
sowe: my MoSi (also called ana), FaWi.
setcua: my So, BrSo (m.s.), WiSiSo (m.s.), HuBrSo (w.s.).
setuue: my Da, BrDa (m.s.), WiSiDa (m.s.), HuBrDa (w.s.), SiDa (w.s., also called sedaze).
γudiiga: my eBr; also, if older than ego, FaBrSo, MoSiSo, FaSiSo, MoBrSo, BrSo (w.s.).
istitla: my yBr; also, if younger than ego, FaBrSo, MoSiSo, FaSiSo, MoBrSo, BrSo (w.s.). Also HuSiSo (w.s.).
sedade: my eSi; also, if older than ego, FaBrDa, MoSiDa, FaSiDa, MoBrDa, BrDa (w.s.).
isd(ii)e: my ySi; also, if younger than ego, FaBrDa, MoSiDa, FaSiDa, MoBrDa, BrDa (w.s.). Also HuSiDa (w.s.).
(s)edaze: my SiSo, SiDa (also called setue), WiBrSo (m.s.).
senawu: my Wi.
setawu: my Hu.
atse: my WiFa (m.s.), HuFa (w.s.).
klaze: my SiHu.
isla: my HuBr, WiBr, SiHu (also called klaze).
abęa: my WiSi (m.s.), BrWi (m.s.).
ekla: my HuSi (w.s.), BrWi (w.s.).
sinaze: my DaHu.

1. Crow-type cousin terminology is confused by the extension of sibling terms to FaSiSo and MoBrDa, as well as to parallel cousins. FaSiDa and MoBrSo are, however, distinguished from other cousins, the last being terminologically identified with the MoBr.

2. Bifurcate collateral terminology distinguishes between Mo, MoSi, and FaSi, as well as between Fa, FaBr, and MoBr. However, FaSi is merged with the grandmother.

3. Bifurcate merging terminology identifies the following pairs: Da, BrDa and So, BrSo. However, SiDa and SiSo are classified as grandchildren.

4. No reciprocal term operates between MoBr and SiSo. The maternal uncle term, as already indicated, is extended to include the MoBrSo.

5. Parents-in-law are classified with grandparents.

6. As in the Dease River basin the son's spouse is classified like a grandchild; DaHu is terminologically isolated.

7. There is only a single grandchild term, extended to include SiSo, SiDa, and SoWi.

Tselona. A common social unit among the Tselona was the dual family household, which according to the informant usually consisted of "two brothers," their wives, and children. Kinship terms of the Tselona Indians are given below.

asta: my MoFa, FaFa, FaBr.
(i)sųų(e): my MoMo, FaMo, WiMo (m.s.).
ete: my Fa.
ane: my Mo.
sade: my FaSi, MoSi.
saze: my MoBr, SiSo, SiDa.
setcua: my So, BrSo.

---

setca: my SoWi (term also applied to grandchildren?).
seda: my sweetheart.

We did not obtain terms for grandchildren.

The following features may be pointed out: (1) Cousin terms are of the Hawaiian type, with all cross and parallel cousins called by the same terms as those used for siblings. This is the pattern among the Sekani studied by Jenness and also obtains among the Fort Nelson Slave. Sibling terms are extended to BrDa and BrSo by woman speakers. (2) Bifurcate merging results in the terminological identification of Mo and MoSi. (3) Bifurcate merging results in the classification together of the following pairs: Da, BrDa (m.s.) and So, BrSo (m.s.). However, SiSo and SiDa are distinguished from lineal descendants and classed together. One informant said that a woman calls her SiDa "daughter." In distinction to male usage a woman addresses her BrDa and BrSo by sibling terms. (4) There is no reciprocal usage between MoBr and SiSo or SiDa. (5) A mother-in-law is grouped with the grandmother but the father-in-law is terminologically isolated. (6) DaHu is isolated and perhaps so is SoWi. (7) Grandchildren terms were not secured from the Whitewater speaker but at Fort Grahame, according to Jenness, there is only one grandchild term. It is not extended to SoWi. Note that children of a wife's sister are merged with lineal descendants, as are the children of a husband's brother. These usages are congenial with sororal polygyny and the levirate respectively. A man calls WiBrSo "sister's child." This is a pattern correlating high with exchange of sisters as a form of marriage. The same form of marriage can explain why the WiBrDa is called MoBr if one assumes (in view of a lack of factual data) that she in turn calls her FaSiHu by the term of MoBr. Under sister exchange the FaSiHu would be the MoBr. The terminological identity of brother's children (woman speaking) and husband's sister's children can also be explained as following from the pattern of marriage by exchange of sisters. Along with such a pattern a husband's sister's children would correspond to brother's children.

setue: my Da, BrDa.
hutdiie: my eBr; also, if older than ego, FaBrSo, MoSiSo.
acitle: my yBr; also, if younger than ego, FaBrSo, MoSiSo.
(i)sade: my eSi; also, if older than ego, FaBrDa, MoSiDa.
astiie: my ySi; also, if younger than ego, FaBrDa, MoSiDa.
sitsiiyo: my Wi.
sakahe: my Hu.
ase: my WiFa (m.s.), HuFa (w.s.).
aca: my SoSo, SoDa, DaSo, DaDa, SoWi.
asla: my FaSiSo, MoBrSo, WiBr (m.s.), HuBr (w.s.).
eklę: my FaSiDa, MoBrDa.
espe: my WiSi (m.s.), HuSi (w.s.).

The following features may be pointed out in these kin usages:

1. Iroquois cousin terminology results in FaSiDa and MoBrDa being classified by the same term, and MoBrSo and FaSiSo are also terminologically identified. Cross cousins are distinguished from parallel cousins, the latter being grouped with siblings.

2. Lineal terminology results in the classification together of FaSi and MoSi.

3. Bifurcate merging terminology groups together ego's children and brother's children but SiSo and SiDa are not so identified.

4. As among the Dease River people reciprocal terms apply between the maternal uncle and his SiSo and SiDa.

5. The WiMo and HuMo are classified as grandmothers but WiFa and HuFa, while grouped in a single category, are not classed in the grandparent generation. FaBr is merged with grandfather.

6. DaHu could not be reliably identified. SoWi is classed as a grandchild.

7. There is but a single term for grandchildren and it is extended to include the SoWi.

Iroquois cousin terminology in the absence of matrilineal organization identifies the Tselona as a normal Yuman-type social organization, which is presumably in transition toward a unilinear organization, perhaps like that found in the west.

Frances Lake Kaska. The circuit of the Cassiar is completed when we have moved north to the Frances Lake region. The kinship terms reported for this country follow.

istsiie: MoFa, FaFa, WiFa (m.s.), HuFa (w.s.).
istsuu: MoMo, FaMo, FaSi, WiMo (m.s.), HuMo (w.s.).
itę: my Fa.
inę: my Mo, MoSi.
ista: my FaBr.
seze: my MoBr, SiSo.
istcuę: my So, BrSo.
istuę: my Da, BrDa, SiDa, SoWi.
gutdiia: my eBr; also, if older than ego, FaBrSo, MoSiSo.
itcitle: my yBr; also, if younger than ego, FaBrSo, MoSiSo.
idade: my eSi; also, if younger than ego, FaBrDa, MoSiDa.
itaze: my ySi; also, if younger than ego, FaBrDa, MoSiDa.
isla: my MoBrSo, HuBr, WiBr, SiHu.
ispe: my MoBrDa (m.s.), WiSi (m.s.), BrWi (m.s.).
ikle: my MoBrDa (w.s.), HuSi (w.s.), BrWi (w.s.).

sełii: my Wi.
seeon: my Hu.
istsuue: my SoSo, DaSo, SoDa, DaDa.
sinaze: my Da Hu.

Terms for FaSiSo and FaSiDa could not be secured. The following features are readily apparent:

1. Indications are that Frances Lake cousin terminology, like that of the adjacent Upper Liard River Indians, is Crow in type.

2. Bifurcate merging results in the classification together of Mo and MoSi.

3. Generation terminology leads to the grouping together of Da, BrDa, and SiDa. One's son is classed with BrSo but SiSo is terminologically identified with MoBr.

4. Reciprocal terms apply between MoBr and SiSo. However, SiDa is classified with daughter, as already indicated.

5. Parents-in-law are identified with grandparents; FaSi is also merged with the latter lineal relative.

6. SoWi is classed with Da. The DaHu is terminologically isolated by the son-in-law term, which is the one common to the whole intermontane area.

7. There is only a single grandchild term.

Striking is the almost perfect correspondence between the Frances Lake and Upper Liard kinship systems. A word of caution is suggested in the fact that the informant was married to an Upper Liard Indian woman.

Summary. What common features link the intermontane kin term systems? Some generalizations emerge from a study of the data and may be summarized as follows:[8]

1. Crow-type cousin terminology gives way in the eastern part of the Cassiar to Iroquois terms. Here there is also an absence of unilinear organization.

2. Bifurcate merging is manifested in the identification of Mo and MoSi. The merging of these terms fails to appear in the Muddy River basin and among the Tselona.

3. Bifurcate merging is manifested in a tendency to identify terminologically So and BrSo, Da and BrDa. Children of a sister are frequently distinguished from own and brother's children. Thus SiSo is classed with MoBr among the Upper Liard, Dease River, Tselona, and Frances Lake Indians. SiDa is merged with Da in the Upper Liard and Frances Lake tribes, with MoBr among the Dease River and Tselona people, and with grandchild along the Kechika (or Muddy) River.

4. A term is frequently used reciprocally between MoBr and SiSo.

5. Bifurcate merging results in the identification of grandparents and parents-in-law.

6. Bifurcate merging results in the frequent classification together of SoWi and granddaughter. DaHu is consistently designated by a son-in-law term.

[8] It is well to remain aware of the fact that the kin-term systems presented are those which informants knew through use. That is, they were current in 1944 and 1945. There is no certainty that the terms correspond to those used aboriginally although a considerable degree of agreement can be assumed. It is likely that careful research in the Cassiar will reveal a number of errors in the present writer's material, partly because the genealogical method was *not* used. Experience has demonstrated to us the value of this method and today we would not try to collect kinship data without this tool.

Two grandparent and four sibling terms (generally extended to parallel cousins) are found throughout the area. In general the kin terms are consistent with a system that includes matrilocal residence, matrilineal moieties, sororal polygyny, sororate, and asymmetrical cross-cousin marriage with the MoBrDa or FaSiSo.[9]

SOCIAL UNITS LARGER THAN THE FAMILY

Two permanent social groupings larger than the family or kin group may be distinguished in the Cassiar, the band and the moiety. It is scarcely possible to discern fixed economic or social classes, the latter term referring here simply to a distinction between rich and poor families. The term "band" designates the microcosmic extended family group with its unrelated hangers-on or adopted children. Several such units occupying contiguous districts constituted the unorganized and highly amorphous macrocosmic band for which we have used the word "tribe."[10] Beyond speaking a similar dialect and intermarrying, the component units of a macrocosmic band experienced little feeling of solidarity. Vague shifting boundaries further reduced the integration of these groups. As already pointed out, relatively large aggregates of people remained in temporary association around a fish lake in summer and winter. Such transitory villages, however, probably did not usually include an entire macrocosmic band, although the pattern of living and playing together, like marriage, must have counteracted feuding and thus strengthened the integration of the people in a territory.

Upper Liard Kaska. Bordering the twisting valley of the upper Liard River lay the territory exploited by the extended-family bands of the Natitu?agotena. Little could be recalled about these units except that on occasion, in winter and summer, many of them camped in one place (tenanat?klone, "lots of people stay together"). Each of the migratory bands recognized a headman. As one informant said, "Before the arrival of the white men there were many bosses" (X). These leaders were primarily family heads so that, according to Chapple and Coon's system of analysis, true (i.e., interfamily) political organization remained only incipiently realized in aboriginal Kaska society.[11] The headman's ability as a hunter, a quality that attracted people to join his band, also helped him to accumulate wealth. When need required, his food resources were freely distributed among the band members. A leader held authority as long as he lived. Upon death a son succeeded to the position of family chief. Should the youth be a poor or indifferent hunter, any other man in the band might be called upon to assume leadership. The death of a headman probably caused a redistribution of the band's personnel around one or more new leaders. Leaders who lost competence found themselves ignored, the people adhering to a more intelligent man. The headman's functions transcended mere food getting. His wisdom derived from experience, and the ability to speak convincingly reinforced his authority in moral matters. When food resources ran low the

[9] See below, pp. 131, 135.

[10] This terminology was first employed to describe the social organization of the Fort Nelson Slave. Honigmann, *Ethnography and Acculturation of the Fort Nelson Slave* (1946), 64–65.

[11] These writers have defined true political authority as arising when one individual or group originates action to persons other than his kin. Chapple and Coon, *Principles of Anthropology* (1942), 330.

headman encouraged men to hunt. He urged his followers to maintain peaceful relations and reprimanded the lazy, with good reason for a chronically non-productive man represented a drain on the capacity of others.[12] The chief did not often try to punish adult members of his band but could expel a person for certain crimes. Any man might express disagreement with the headman although he would be urged to "watch" his words. The informant appeared to recognize the description of a council and described such meetings at which discussion centered on important hunting plans or on an outbreak of ingroup aggression. Men and women attended such deliberations but women never tried to speak.

The dwellers on the upper Liard River were divided into two exogamous matrilineal moieties, the Wolf and Crow. Slightly greater prestige appears to have attached to the Wolf section. According to one old man (X), who had come to the Cassiar as a boy from Espatotena country, the Kaska lacked moiety division prior to the time when Tahltan Indians penetrated the area. When the latter encountered a Kaska Indian they said, "You're a Wolf" or "You're a Crow," thus classifying the population. At first the Kaska did not understand such talk. Eventually they adopted the dual division of the Tahltan.[13] A myth gives a more exotic account of the origin of moiety organization. The tale has been reported for the Pelly River Tutchone by Poole Field and was known to our chief informant (O). The man previously referred to (X), who came from the east, did not know the account. Following is the unedited version of the tale taken from Field's manuscript.[14]

The animals were the first people and the smartest of all the animals, and the wisest were the wolves and ravens, the next was the wolverine. All the animals could talk and understand each other and can yet. The wolves and ravens intermarried and their children were Indians. They called the wolverine their brother-in-law and were very friendly with him.

The wolves and ravens held a meeting and made a law that they would not marry any other animal, but a wolf was to marry a raven and a raven a wolf. The children would take their name from the mother, and their mother would own the country. Sisters and brothers, after they became of age, should not speak or play with each other; when a wolf died the other wolves should make a big feast for the ravens to eat and would find the raven presents but would eat nothing themselves. When a raven died he was to do the same for the wolves and so the world was started.

---

[12] Hallowell's figures, which show that in hunting bands one male hunter supports about three persons including himself, appear to be borne out when other groups are examined. Hallowell, *Size of Algonkian Hunting Territories: Function of Ecological Adjustment* (1949); Honigmann, *Intercultural Relations at Great Whale River, P. Q.* (1952), 510.

[13] The question of the relationship of dual organization among the Kaska to the social organization of the Tlingit has still to be settled. Although social organization was more complexly developed on the Northwest Coast, the basic feature of moiety organization is similar between the two regions. Tlingit moieties, which were matrilineal and exogamous, are designated Raven (sometimes Eagle) and Wolf. The Kaska fire origin myth given above (see p. 61) suggests that certain animals were somehow closely "related." Thus the wolverine, fox, and black bear "belonged" to the crow; the grizzly bear and lynx were allied to the wolf. Swanton's evidence suggests a similar identification of grizzly bear with wolf among the Tlingit while Krause includes the (black?) bear here too. See Swanton, *Social Condition, Beliefs and Linguistic Relationship of the Tlingit Indians* (1908), 398, 415–417, 422–423; Krause, *Tlinkit Indianer* (1885), 112, 122; Jones, *Study of the Thlingets of Alaska* (1914), 25, 44, 170–171.

[14] Field, *Unpublished manuscript* (1913), 10–11.

These laws are followed to the present day amongst all the Indians on the Yukon, Pelly, Teslin Lake, and Upper Liard, but the Mountain Indians do not.

Exogamous moieties regulated marriage. Members of one division also prepared the opposite group's dead for burial. The sides tendered potlatches to one another. On such occasions the members of each group adorned their faces with a particular colored paint, blue for the Crows and red for the Wolves. The designs, however, did not differ. When a large number of people camped together each moiety "rustled" wood for the fire, stacking poles in a single heap. Then they would slide the fuel into the fire, each side in succession adding one piece after the other. Afterwards the brothers-in-law (i.e., the men belonging to opposite moieties) sat around and talked. The practice of fire tending may be regarded as a simple rite of intensification,[15] serving to promote inter-action between the segments and thus to contribute to the solidarity of the larger ag-gregate.

Three social levels were distinguished in the pre-contact Kaska community, the rich, poor, and slaves. Social stratification on the basis of wealth is a prominent feature in the culture of the Pacific Drainage Athapaskans and is even more extensively de-veloped among the Indians of the Northwest Coast. One informant (O) knew about an hereditary nobility among the Tlingit but stated flatly that the system of social stratifi-cation found there had no counterpart in the Cassiar. Such a statement is not unex-pected in terms of the association to be anticipated between class structure and surplus-wealth production.

A rich man, tenatiia (the same word today is used to designate the Supreme Being), stood out among his fellows because he could support four or five wives, wore finer clothes, enjoyed more possessions, and employed occasional servants. His word received ready attention. "People always listened to a rich man." Wealth derived from skillful hunting and trapping. The poor man, tenaɣteɣxeʔitʔa, lived with a single wife and often found it difficult to provide even for her and their children. Poorer clothes distinguished the poor man and in group affairs his word carried little weight. Ideally, cordial relations existed between the rich and poor. If a rich man spoke harshly to his less fortunate peer the former's supernatural power might desert him and all his ability to kill game would be reduced. Under such circumstances helping a poor man would assist him to recoup his luck. Poor men who received assistance from wealthier people repaid such help by working for their patrons, for example, visiting the latters' deadfalls. In this way the rich came to enjoy the labor of servants. A slave, xiina (this is said to be a Tlingit word adopted into the Liard River vocabulary), represented a war captive. Inasmuch as the Kaska generally killed enemy male captives, slaves were usually women. A man some-times referred in fun to his sister's children as slaves.[16]

Dease River Kaska. As late as 1928 Father Allard, an Oblate missionary stationed at McDame Creek, wrote, "All members of the tribe are free to hunt and fish over all the tribal territory. They hunt and fish in little bands of one, two or three families,—each family consisting of father, mother and children, with sometimes other members,

---

[15] Chapple and Coon, *Principles of Anthropology* (1942), 485–486.
[16] See above, p. 77.

married or single.[17] Such a description represents the aboriginal pattern of Dease River social organization. Each band recognized a "chief,"[18] or leader, who guided the people in hunting. Outstanding in his ability to secure game, a headman was also always a rich man. Sometimes as many as seven families comprised his following. As a headman aged and became incapacitated, he relinquished his role in favor of a son or brother whose duties included caring for the retired leader.

All the Dease River Indians were divided into two moieties, tsinii ("sides"), the Wolf and Crow. The two sections represented exogamous units in which membership followed the matrilineal line. Potlaches promoted interaction between the divisions, the members of which also prepared each other's dead for burial and competed in sports.[19]

Rich and poor men tended to stand out in the pre-contact community. The former represented able hunters who managed to secure large quantities of meat and skins. Such abundance attracted followers and dependents who accepted their patron's authority. Thus rich men also held positions of band leadership. The poor depended on the wealthy for food and skins. They made no return for such assistance. Sometimes a man became temporarily impoverished as a result of losing his hunting "luck." Help to such a man was advantageous because he would certainly remember the generosity when his fortunes turned. Poverty, as long as it did not stem from laziness, provided no bar to marriage, but a lazy man merited only laughter and jeers.[20]

[17] Allard, *Notes on the Kaska and Upper Liard Indians* (1928), 24–25.

[18] When the Hudson's Bay Company entered the Cassiar, they appointed local chiefs to develop trapping. The word is derived from this period. The "company chief" was provided with a certain amount of regalia and received flour and tobacco to distribute to his "boys." Upon the Indians' arrival at the post the manager fired a gun to salute the executive. Prior to this period, informants agreed, no comparable leader existed among the Dease River people.

[19] Teit reports a more complex social system for the adjoining Tahltan. "Their social organization appears to be based largely on that obtaining among the Tlingit. Like the latter, they are divided into two exogamous phratries called Wolf and Raven (as in the case of the Kaska, the former is more important and is said to represent the original Tahltan people). Children belong to the phratry and clan of their mother. Each phratry consists of three clans or gentes, each of which has a hereditary chief and a territory of its own. These six chiefs form the governing body of the tribe. The clans do not have special totems, nor traditions deriving their origin from mythological ancestors. Crests and totems usually belong to the phratry. A seventh clan exists at the present day, having originated about 150 years ago through immigration of and intermarriage with the Tlingit. It belongs to the Wolf phratry, but has no recognized territory nor chief within the country of the Tahltans; it is called by its Tlingit name. There is an aristocracy of rank and wealth, but these nobles have no special rights in hunting grounds, fisheries, etc. Methods of obtaining rank, the potlatch, and many of the social and ceremonial customs of the tribe are closely adopted from the Tlingit." (Teit, *On Tahltan (Athabaskan) Work* [1912], 484–485. See also Jenness, *Indians of Canada* [1932], 373.) Mrs. William Strong, of Vancouver and Telegraph Creek, B. C., loaned the present writer several photographs of a Tahltan potlatch held in relatively recent times. These showed men wearing dark cloth robes embroidered with what appeared to be crest figures and very similar to the robes often illustrated for the Northwest Coast.

In Lower Post we learned of only two exogamous moieties among the Tahltan, the Wolf and Crow. Teit's description of clans with territorial rights does not sound convincing and may refer to local divisions in the Tahltan nation.

[20] Slaves were reported for the Tahltan where one "chief," Makuske, is said to have held 22 captive workers. These hunted and fished for their master and were well treated. (Personal communication from

Tselona. Dichotomous social organization appears to have been absent among the Tselona or Nelson Indians and even today most of these people cannot identify with either exogamous division, except as they adopt a conventional designation following marriage with a woman from one of the western tribes. The fact that one informant from this group affirmed the presence of moieties may indicate his familiarity with the pattern rather than its adoption by the easterly people.

Espatotena. Jenness reports absence of dual organization on the South Nahani and Beaver rivers.[21]

Frances Lake Kaska. Two moieties, the Wolf and Crow, were probably present aboriginally in the Frances Lake area as they are today.[22]

SOCIAL PRESSURE—LAW AND WAR

In this section we propose to discuss the social pressure exerted upon members of the community who departed from expected norms of behavior as well as the pressure exercised upon or by outsiders. The first type of pressure includes behavior usually called customary law, while the second corresponds to war. Norms governing property relations and interpersonal conduct will be presented along with the description of the sanctions available for enforcing those norms.

Upper Liard Kaska. With the exception of beaver creeks, the microcosmic band did not enjoy exclusive ownership rights to any territory. In other words no family-hunting-ground system existed in the aboriginal period. Indians felt free to hunt or fish anywhere within "their own country," i.e., the territory customarily inhabited by the macrocosmic band. Generally a man avoided those regions which he knew another family to be currently exploiting. Each family (it is not clear if extended family is implied) controlled its own beaver streams, ownership of these residing in the man, although the entire family shared in the resources. Marriages did not secure new beaver grounds for the husband, who had the choice of returning to his parents' creek to hunt or of taking the animals on his father-in-law's territory. The former pattern seems unlikely because it would result in bilocal residence, a pattern to which informants did not allude. The informant (O) maintained strongly that family control of beaver streams antedated white contact. Ownership was symbolically expressed in the custom of naming such creeks.[23] Other property marks were denied. The development of possessory rights with

---

George Adsit.) Jenness echos Teit in speaking of a tripartite class structure featuring nobles, commoners, and slaves for the Tahltan. Children of the slaves retained the status of their parents but commoners could raise their rank by potlatching. Jenness, *Indians of Canada* (1932), 373.

[21] Jenness, *Indians of Canada* (1932), 399.

[22] For information of dichotomous grouping north of Frances Lake see above, p. 85.

[23] McLean reports that among the Mackenzie River Slave "the hunter who first finds a beaver lodge claims it as his property, but his claim is not always respected." (McLean, *Notes of a Twenty-Five Years' Service in the Hudson's Bay Territory* [1932], 343). Among the Pelly River people "each Indian has his own beaver country where he can go at any time and get his dinner, as the beaver, if not disturbed, will stay for years in one place or close in that neighborhood. He arrives at his beaver country to find some one has been before him and not only taken his dinner but also his money in the shape of the beaver skins, and if he catches the man that did it as a rule there is trouble of some kind. This is how

respect to beaver is partly explicable in terms of the animal's habit of remaining and reproducing within a relatively circumscribed district unless population pressure forces migration of the excess stock. Thus in most years Indians could depend upon being able to find food wherever beaver lodges were known to exist.

Of movable goods a man owned the bark and wood dishes, as well as the eating utensils which he made for his family, his own tools, caches (but not the food upon them), personal clothing, canoe, weapons, toboggan, personal snowshoes, and masks. A woman owned the bark- and spruce-root vessels that she manufactured, personal tools, the dwelling, food, prepared skins, personal clothing, all lines except those which she had given to her husband, and paints. Meat on a cache or freshly killed game cannot be considered the exclusive property of either the hunter or his family because the community felt and exercised a claim on such food. Failure to meet this expectation in the case of large game animals aroused resentment. In a sense children owned their toys as well as personal clothing and snowshoes. The mother controlled a child's possessions but they could not be disposed of outside the family, even by lending without the child's permission. By virtue of the control which parents claimed over a young person's nominal possessions they were able to use the latter freely. Although death might be followed by the destruction of some goods belonging to the deceased the custom did not have as its purpose transmission of wealth to the ghost. In the absence of grave goods people did not conceive of the ghost as owning anything. Even the burial clothes worn by the corpse "belonged to nobody."

Aside from one's name, ownership did not attach toward intangible goods. Nobody exercised individual control over songs or folk tales but it is likely that every man enjoyed some exclusive rights over the magical songs which he had dreamed on the vision quest.

Inheritance norms pertained to names and material goods alone.[24] Following death one half of a man's possessions went to his brother while the children divided the other half. Personal items were destroyed. A son usually acquired the scalps taken in battle. The widow might receive a share of the goods to which her brother-in-law enjoyed paramount rights, but her inclusion in inheritance does not appear to have been rigorously enforced. A man could marry his widowed sister-in-law or else could dispose of her to another husband but it is probably incorrect to list this pattern in a discussion of chattels. A woman's wealth fell to the widower, who customarily gave all or most of it to his brother's wife. The knife employed to sever the umbilical cord became the property of a woman's daughter.

---

a lot of trouble between different tribes is started, also amongst the tribe itself." (Field, *Unpublished manuscript* [1913], 9.) Among the Tsapagotena (Beaver Indians of Fort Liard, perhaps the same group to which McLean refers), "when an Indian discovers one or more beaver lodges, if not already appropriated, he immediately puts his mark upon them, and no one dares to intrude upon his property without his permission, although I know of no punishment inflicted upon the guilty party unless it be the infamy attached to the action, which is considered as very mean and heinous." Keith, *Letters to Mr. Roderic McKenzie* (1890), 69.

[24] For the inheritance of names see below, p. 141.

Sanctions invoked to enforce property conceptions failed to be made explicit by informants. Probably they included the application of individual force, expressed verbally or physically, with the consent of the community. That is to say, if a man could not claim that to which he felt a right he might seize the goods and in the process perhaps inflict punishment on his rival. Property offenses also earned offenders an unfavorable public opinion. No force was used to compel a person to share meat but "We had a cache too. We could do the same thing. We won't give him much." Reciprocity therefore constituted one device serving to maintain the pattern of food sharing.

The aboriginal community found itself compelled to deal with lying, assault, manslaughter, infanticide, murder, cannibalism, sorcery, incest, unwed motherhood, adultery, and treason. A common form of lying consisted of a person returning from a hunt and telling exaggerated stories of the amount of game that he had seen. Not many such accounts were needed before the liar found himself regularly disbelieved. Against slander a quick tempered man reacted by killing his calumniator. Injuries inflicted due to assault were settled by payment, a distinction apparently being made between wounds deliberately inflicted and those resulting accidentally. At least, no payment followed in the case of hurts secured from children's play. Likewise the people distinguished manslaughter from murder. In event of the former no vengeance followed but a payment, considerably lower than that obtaining in the case of murder, was expected. An Indian who committed manslaughter might be adopted in place of the deceased.[25] People would drive out of the community a woman whose neglect caused her child to starve. "Let her starve," the people said in the hope that other people would thereby learn the necessity of treating each other more kindly. Infanticide of either a girl or boy infant merited severe scolding. The temptation to kill a baby appears to have been limited to cases where offspring resulted from incestuous unions. Such a child was sometimes killed in the birth camp, the mother stuffing its mouth with moss. The informant recalled no instance of abortion but he thought the deed would have been classified as murder.

Murder might be settled through a large payment, made in installments running over a year or more, or by blood revenge. Weregild required the cooperation of all the members of the murderer's family. Vengeance constituted the duty of the victim's brother or uncle (father's brother?) and was never undertaken by a father. Retaliatory action always went against the actual killer and not against members of his family.[26] It is not

[25] Among the Tlingit "any crime may be paid for on a money basis." (Jones, *Study of the Thlingets of Alaska* [1914], 193.) Weregild is stated to follow in restitution for murder and manslaughter among certain Kwakiutl tribes, the Tsimshian, Haida, and Tlingit Chilkat. Drucker, *Culture Element Distributions: XXVI, Northwest Coast* (1950), 221.

[26] "The original Indians claiming the country of the Upper Pelly and its tributaries have completely disappeared with the exception of one old woman.... The main causes for this is quarreling amongst themselves.... generally started by two men fighting and one killing the other, when the relations and friends would take the quarrel up and kill the first man or some of his relatives to get even and so they would keep the quarrel going until one party were all dead or so weakened that for a time they were satisfied to stop. Secondly, by stronger tribes making raids on them and killing the men and taking their women away with them ...." Field, *Unpublished manuscript* (1913), 1.

clear at this point whether the informant meant to describe an ideal or manifest pattern. The murderer's escape from the area brought about an at least temporary halt in proceedings. Instead of seeking retaliation the family of the slain man might, through a kindly disposed headman, press for the adoption of the murderer in place of the victim. This may have occurred when the two were both young and of about the same age. The murderer's family always put pressure upon its member to accede to such a request. He then grew up as the son in the other family, and appropriate kinship terms defined his position (X). No punishment existed for attempted suicide. Cannibalism, a practice apparently regarded as habit-forming, earned banishment and, as a further consequence, death by starvation. People were dissuaded from sorcery by the logical argument that the deed would result in insanity. Interpersonal punishment for sorcery was not mentioned by informants. Similar magical retaliation followed incest, but public opinion dealt very harshly with those members of the community who committed incestuous offenses. Overwhelmed by shame and guilt in such circumstances, an unhappy man might tear off his penis or leap into the fire. Most grievous of all was incest between brother and sister.

A brother wanted his married sister but couldn't get her. He went one day to hunt beaver with the girl's husband. This man had a premonition that he was going to be attacked and the sister dreamed of her brother assaulting her husband. The brother succeeded in wounding his brother-in-law after which he returned to the dwelling with a beaver. The girl refused to eat the meat until her husband would return. When he didn't come back soon, she started out to look for him. She found him lying wounded at the beaver house. After treating his wounds she asked him to kill her brother, which he did.

An unwed mother felt ashamed when she brought forth a child. Sometimes, especially in summer, the community further punished the offense by forcing the girl into a month's exile, during which she subsisted mainly by clubbing porcupines. People intended the punishment to teach her sense and prevent repetition of such behavior. If they knew the baby's father, pressure might be placed on him to marry the mother. Such a marriage would not long endure, it was believed, because a girl who became impregnated outside of marriage was too wild to make a good wife. The lover might also give a small gift to the girl's father, thus acknowledging his offense. An illegitimate baby was fairly well treated if it survived the mother's banishment.[27] People recalled its status, however, and in later years a man might be taunted with the appelation xiina ("slave"). Such jeers rankled and sometimes led a man to fight his detractors.

An unfaithful wife and her paramour ideally shared in the condemnation of adultery. Generally, direct punishment fell on the woman alone. In the presence of an economy that forced men to leave their wives in camp while they hunted, plenty of opportunity for adultery existed. Chronic jealousy and suspicion haunted husbands. Returning to camp some men closely inspected the spruce brush in the dwelling. Should they find it "tipped over" or upset, evidence of the woman's unfaithfulness was presumed. Punishment for adultery consisted in beating the guilty wife or divorcing her, with resultant

[27] Among the Tlingit the killing of an illegitimate baby by stuffing its mouth with moss or grass had magical repercussions. If neglected "very bad luck will follow the family, or clan." Jones, *Study of the Thlingets of Alaska* (1914), 45.

shame for both the woman and her family. A husband did not challenge his wife's lover but a woman who knew of her husband's infidelity attacked the other woman both verbally and physically. Folktales, such as the one describing a jealous husband cutting off an adulterous woman's leg below the thigh, highlighted the seriousness of the offense. Mention of a chastity belt crops up in an anecdote which the informant did not believe to be true. It concerns a husband who prior to leaving for a hunt secured a rawhide line between his wife's legs to prevent her from having sexual relations during his absence.

Treason met with no punishment except that a traitor was not allowed to fight the enemy. He could, however, pack for the military expedition.

Violation of food and other avoidances did not so much result in the application of direct punishment as they led to fear of magical retribution. Reasoned arguments following from culturally standardized premises dissuaded people from breaking these taboos, and hence exemplify a particular type of social pressure.[28] Fear of punishment by ghosts for injuries done to people in their lives also represents a sentiment limiting conduct.[29]

In summary we can say that socially approved punishment in pre-contact Kaska life consisted chiefly of unfavorable public opinion, exile, fines, and blood revenge. The latter two sanctions were reserved for offenses against life. Nobody explicitly enjoyed the power to impose punishment on behalf of the total community. Hence most social pressure was informal or individualized. It should be clear that negative pressures did not exhaust the techniques for maintaining equilibrium in the social system. Potlatching, affinal ties, games, and minor rituals undoubtedly played their parts in preserving harmonious social relations.

War represented group retaliation for offenses committed by relative strangers upon members of the community. Since military revenge in turn promoted the desire for fresh vengeance on the opposite side antagonism between the Upper Liard Kaska and their neighbors tended to be chronic. The prevalent state of intertribal mistrust is well illustrated in the discomfort and frank suspicion aroused by any stranger. The Nakani and Nahani complexes, with their initial bound form indicating "enemy" or "hostile," reflect these states of anxiety and hostility. Informants refused to regard the Nakani as supernatural but applied the term to Indians with whom the Kaska had little contact, that is, "strange" Indians who raided people and stole women. The term Nakani applied particularly to the Cree (teciina, a word deriving from the root for "tree") who hid in the bush with rifles waiting for an opportunity to abduct women.

Fighting occurred between the Upper Liard Indians and the people of Teslin Lake (probably the Taku), Pelly River, Espatotena, and, of course, the Cree Indians. Warfare with the Tahltan was denied by one man (O), who stated that prior to contact the Kaska had traded with the Tahltan, so how could they have fought as enemies? His argument holds only for the relatively recent prehistoric period. It is not applicable to an earlier period, when the Tahltan were not yet middlemen in the trade originating west of the

[28] Wilson, *The Analysis of Social Change* (1945), 53–55. For further information about avoidances see below, pp. 108–110.
[29] See below,. pp. 136–137.

Coast Range. Even in 1945 mild hostility characterized Tahltan-Kaska relations and young men of the former group boasted of their ancestors successfully fighting the Kaska. Other informants corroborated the fact of war between the two groups. Nobody recalled trouble with the Bear Lake Sekani. The upper Liard River people regarded the Etca?otena of the Fort Nelson River as stupid and almost inhuman but fighting with them could not be recalled.[30]

Large-scale aggression did not occur frequently and there existed no value on fighting for its own sake. War was defensive in theory, a means of subduing bad or potentially dangerous people. Woman felt dismay when preparations for hostility began and some sought, with only rare success, to keep their men from battle. Both sexes equally welcomed the resumption of peace. Typically a war party originated in a situation like the following: A man, visiting the camp of a stranger, saw a scalp which he suspected belonged to one of his relatives. The traveler returned to his own country and discovered who was missing. If several people had not been heard of for a long time the original surmise became fact. Driven by anger, the man began hostilities by killing a woman who had originally belonged to the enemy group. In front of his companions he displayed a knife, blade uppermost, and moved it in a semicircle as a gesture of hostility. "I'm still hungry," he would say. Then those people prepared to attack the enemy. The desire to steal women took its place alongside revenge as an auxiliary motive for aggression. The wish for prestige played little part in promoting aboriginal warfare.

A war leader was not identical with the band's headman. Sometimes the expedition also included a shaman who worked sorcery against the enemy. While the war chief acted as "boss" of the war party he had no power to inflict corporal punishment. At most he could order a disobedient member to quit the group. Several microcosmic groups probably provided recruits for a military expedition, so that the leader assumed the proportions of a true political authority. The expedition itself contained two divisions, young men about 19 or 20 years old, who packed the goods, and warriors, averaging about 30 years of age, who did the actual fighting. Women never directly participated in aggressive warfare but they sometimes visited the enemy camp to act as spies. Such an envoy might return to tearfully beg that the intended victims be spared.

Preparatory to fighting men made new knives, lances, fitted with stone or caribou horn blades, and many arrows. Each warrior provided himself with two bows in the event that one should break. In addition the men donned bear skin armor in the form of a sleeveless coat that reached to the knees. This was made from hides tanned with the hair on and worn with the hair out. Magical significance is probable, since among the Indians the bear enjoyed a reputation for his fierceness. Over his head the warrior carried, fur exposed, a caribou-skin helmet lined with birch bark. Sometimes headgear included a vizor covering the whole face and provided with holes for vision.[31] Helmets

[30] For counter attitudes among the Slave, see Honigmann, *Ethnography and Acculturation of the Fort Nelson Slave* (1946), 73–75.

[31] Tlingit armor consisted of long tunics made with two or three thicknesses of hide or hide reinforced with wooden slats. Twined-rod jackets were used by the Chilkat and helmets of solid wood with vizors held in the teeth. Jenness, *Indians of Canada* (1932), 330; Drucker, *Culture Element Distributions: XXVI, Northwest Coast* (1950), 187.

furnished disguise because they prevented the enemy from recognizing the attackers. Painting the whole face with a mixture of charcoal, spruce gum, and grease served the same end.[32] After the fighting this paint was removed with the aid of grease. Birch-wood shields, designed to deflect arrows, consisted of two or three pieces of wood, each about three feet long and sewn together. Grease layered the forward surface of the shield. In warding off an arrow by this device the warrior spoke a one-word charm, ?uk ("swan"). Menstruation on the part of a man's wife did not prevent him from joining a fighting party but following his departure this woman was bound to avoid crossing the warrior's trail lest danger befall him. Prior to setting out a man abstained from coitus for four days. "If you stay with your wife you will be killed, you weaken yourself."[33] Winter or summer each member of a war expedition toughened himself by plunging into cold water.

After the men had departed the women left in camp constructed a number of human images, using robes and skins stuffed with brush. Human features were added with red paint. The dummies stood in the camp and each morning women attacked them with ceremonial wooden knives. The ritual gave additional strength to the warriors.[34] Women also girdled themselves in fancy outer belts which dared not be removed until the party had returned. Untying the knot promised death to the fighters. This belt undoubtedly symbolizes the chastity of the women during the husbands' absence.[35] At the same time the rite no doubt allayed the jealous temperament of the men and allowed them to focus on the business at hand without distraction. It may well be that such belts possessed indirect survival value.

The warriors traveled quickly. In advance went two or three scouts, intelligent men about 40 years old. At night young men remained posted around the camp, acting as sentries. The expedition camped in brush-banked lean-tos enclosed on three sides and sharing a common rear wall. Usually two lines of such shelters faced each other and a fire burned in the space between. Moccasins dared never be removed while sleeping lest the wearer imperil his life. No effort was made to conceal the light of campfires. Frequently during the course of travel the shaman performed rites designed to prevent bow strings from snapping or to break the enemy's snowshoes when the latter sought to escape. At night the fighting party sang songs magically designed to weaken the enemy.

All military action took place on land. The Kaska did not fight from canoes, although the informant had heard that the Tlingit fought from boats. Fighting started as soon as

[32] The same means of disguise accompanied war among the Kutchin. Osgood, *Contributions to the Ethnography of the Kutchin* (1936), 87.

[33] Tlingit men expecting to join a war party "were not allowed to see or go to any woman. This tabu depended on the length of time they expected to be gone. 'Sometimes they did not see a woman for a year.'" Swanton, *Social Condition, Beliefs and Linguistic Relationship of the Tlingit Indians* (1908), 449.

[34] Tlingit warriors constructed such dummies before leaving camp. "All the men and their wives had such images." Swanton, *Social Condition, Beliefs and Linguistic Relationship of the Tlingit Indians* (1908), 449.

[35] "While the warriors were away the leader's wife had to have stones tied about her blanket just as did her husband on the expedition. . . ." Swanton, *Social Condition, Beliefs and Linguistic Relationship of the Tlingit Indians* (1908), 450.

enemies were encountered and continued until one or the other side weakened to the point where it sued for peace or fled. Men were not spared for capture. As victims fell warriors wielding stone knives detached scalps by cutting above the ears and along the brow. Then the hair was seized and the scalp torn free from the flesh. Decapitation was not practiced.[36] To sue for an armistice one side might raise a slab of wood on which were painted figures of animals and fish. Lasting peace was promised when an enemy surrendered or when all potential avengers were killed. However fear and mistrust often prevented both sides from immediately negotiating friendly relations on a verbal basis. When peace negotiations were conducted on the spot, the victors usually demanded a number of women by way of indemnity. Unwilling as the latter might be, they were always forced to go. At other times fighting lasted until the enemy had lost many men or had been completely routed. The victors then displayed an orgy of sadism and hate. The bodies of the dead received obscene treatment, a woman's legs being spread apart to expose her naked genitals. Necrophilia, however, was never practiced. Live children were spiked on sharp stakes set around a fire. Live men might be suspended from trees by the feet, a separate line securing each limb. A heavy pole would then be dropped into the crotch of the helpless victim. Neither side troubled to dispose of the dead. Ceremonial cannibalism also followed fighting, but instead of flesh only the raw "belly fat" was eaten. This ritual meal strengthened the victors and enabled them, should necessity demand, to eat raw meat in the future. Young men serving the expedition as porters did not join in the rite.[37] Instead of partaking in the cannibalistic meal a man could fast for four days, eating only a very little food and drinking small quantities of water. Women and children formed the bulk of the prisoners. Mostly the children were killed during the homeward journey, the custom being to strangle or knife one child at each camp made by the returning expedition. Each night a moiety took its turn in executing a child. In winter, for every youngster killed a marker of spruce brush was thrust into the ice at the center of some lake where the group happened to be camping. Still other young prisoners might be killed after the expedition had returned to camp. Women captives became wives who initially had to be carefully watched or tied lest they seek to escape.[38] If any men had been taken they were permitted to marry daughters of the captors. Upon begetting a child the man received his freedom. Exchange of prisoners was unknown. Following a battle every man who had shed enemy blood ritually tore his sleeve. "To kill a man puts human blood in the killer's sleeve," the informant explained metaphorically. Such blood now received the opportunity of flowing out. (A man performed the same rite when his brothers first killed game.[39]) The victors "did

[36] Heads were taken by the Tlingit and scalped as the expedition neared home "unless they had had time to do so on the spot." Scalping is specifically stated to have been done in such a way as to exclude the ears. Swanton, *Social Condition, Beliefs and Linguistic Relationship of the Tlingit Indians* (1908), 450.

[37] A similar custom is restricted to novices among the Kutchin with the intention of preventing "a sickness which inevitably follows a first killing, as well as general bad luck." Osgood, *Contributions to the Ethnography of the Kutchin* (1936), 87.

[38] For the distribution of captive women within the community see below, p. 131.

[39] See below, p. 110.

not think of another war," a statement which suggests that fighting brought about rather full release of suppressed anger and strain.[40]

On the return journey scouts were dispatched in advance to learn about conditions at the home camp. They reported back to the expedition. Nobody who had been left behind dared come forward to meet the warriors. To do so would have been an omen of misfortune. Upon returning to camp each man went directly to his own dwelling. Then the women prepared a steam bath for those men who had been wounded. This sudatory possessed especially strong properties because it included a specimen of every tree that the expedition had encountered on its homeward trip. Weekly for a month or so after the return the men danced with the combed enemy scalps on their heads. This helped them "to forget the fighting." Contact between a woman and a scalp had to be avoided lest the warrior lose his strength. Only the man who had detached the trophy wore it in ritual. At other times the scalp remained in a smoked-skin container. A tattooed line crossing the upper arm just below the shoulder designated a man's participation in a war party. The number of such stripes revealed his war record.[41] While prestige did not constitute a primary motivation for fighting, a record of successful war participation enhanced a man's standing. For a year or two (?) the warrior received gifts of food, not to honor him but because hunting remained a dangerous occupation for a man who had killed human beings. If "game blood" became mixed with human blood that he had shed, it would make the man "heavy." It remains problematical whether such avoidances constituted disabilities for the man. More likely, it may be argued, refraining from hunting focused attention on the individual that rewarded him for his war effort. It may also be questioned whether a group living close to the level of subsistence could support even one nonproductive male per band for one or two years. Warfare or, more specifically, contact with killing, rendered a man unfit for sexual intercourse. Hence a two-month avoidance of cohabitation followed his return. Violation of this taboo might mean the death of his children. The hunting and cohabitation avoidances reveal the antithesis felt to exist between enemy killing on the one hand and sex or hunting on the other. In this connection it may be significant that the contemporary Kaska unconsciously perceive coitus as akin to hunting.[42]

Dease River Kaska. Neither primary family nor microcosmic band exercised exclusive ownership rights over hunting or fishing sites. Generally, however, a band sought permission before moving into an area which another group was currently exploiting. Consent always followed, but the pattern nevertheless reveals a conception of usufruct probably coupled with an awareness that a given area could support only a limited number of persons.

The community dealt harshly with theft, behavior that made a man comparable to a dog. Depending on the gravity of his offense the punishment of a detected thief ranged

[40] This parallels Lantis' interpretation. Lantis, *Social Culture of the Nunivak Eskimo* (1946), 168.
[41] Among the Peel River Kutchin a line was tattooed from the corner of the eyes or mouth for each enemy killed. The Crow people, however, made their lines on the top of the bicep of the right arm. Osgood, *Contributions to the Ethnography of the Kutchin* (1936), 87, 88.
[42] Honigmann, *Culture and Ethos of Kaska Society* (1949), 255, 296.

from beating to killing. Injuries inflicted in quarrels demanded settlement by payment. To avoid blood vengeance in the event of murder the murder's family might accumulate many valuables, like skins, robes, and clothing, for presentation to the victim's kin. Even intertribal wars with the Tahltan could sometimes be avoided by offering valuables. A cannibal found himself banished from the community for as long as two years. Ostracism also greeted a couple guilty of incest, an offense covering sexual relations between members of a common moiety. Magical retribution further promised to hasten the death of such people.[43] A folk tale explains that men were likely to find their sisters sexually attractive because of an incident that had occurred very long ago. There once lived a man who left his two wives (they were sisters) and his children, killed his brother-in-law, and copulated with his widowed sister. The deserted wives killed the incestuous couple with the approval of the husband's brother, who said, "My brother did evil and acted like a dog."[44] An adulterous wife suffered a beating but a man had to be careful not to inflict serious injury or his behavior would constitute a crime punishable by the parents-in-law, who might demand an indemnity. A woman could divorce a philandering husband. The extent to which marital jealousy was developed is suggested in the tale of "The Deserted Woman."[45] A woman became suspected of infidelity because she offered her husband grease that she had found. The man, believing that the grease represented payment from a lover, burned his wife's clothing and tools and deserted her, expecting that she would die of cold and starvation. She managed to survive until two brothers discovered and married her. Subsequently she refused to return to her cruel husband. Illegitimacy disgraced both a mother and, later, the child.

Intergroup attitudes are reflected in the Nakani fear. The term designates a "bad Indian," who is given to lurking in the bush as he waits for an opportunity to steal girls. Victims of such an attack were never recovered but were taken to the abductor's tribe to become his wives. Dease River informants asserted as confidently as upper Liard River speakers that a Nakani represented a flesh and blood Indian rather than a supernatural being. The chronic insecurity marking intertribal relations sometimes exploded into war, resentment over encroachment of territories by foreigners being a common motive for fighting.[46] Many engagements were recalled between the Kaska and Tahltan. Ideally the fighting began when an enemy party raided a Kaska encampment, stealing women and killing the men. Inevitably relatives or friends discovered the crime and

---

[43] George Adsit reported that the Tahltan punished incest by death. On one occasion a guilty couple fled from their band and ascended a small salmon creek. Here, surrounded by an abundance of food, they raised two children before their people discovered them and killed the whole family.

[44] Teit, *Kaska Tales* (1917), 459–460.

[45] Teit, *Kaska Tales* (1917), 455–457.

[46] Morice speaks of feuds over hunting grounds dividing the Tahltan and Kaska. (Morice, *Nah-ane and Their Language* [1900–1903], 520.) The entry of white trappers into the Cassiar also met with resentment. "The Casca Indians have the greatest objection to white men trapping on their own account in their country; gold dust they can take as much as they like, but the fur is the Indian's equivalent for gold and must be left for the Indian. They are very firm on this point—so much so that a couple of white men who were trapping on the Liard some years ago were killed by the Indians because they refused to let the fur alone." Pike, *Through the Subarctic Forest* (1898), 112.

set out to avenge the deaths. The retaliatory party also captured women, children, and occasionally robes and arrows. Children were never killed. Shields and armor could not be recalled.[47] Weapons included clubs, bows, and arrows. Sometimes both sides agreed to the cessation of hostilities by raising both hands over the head and then bringing them together again in front of the body as in prayer. Wars were followed by feasts and dancing.

Tselona. At Fort Nelson in 1943 an old Kaska woman, Widow Matoit, gave a somewhat ethnocentric account of fighting between Kaska and Cree Indians. It seems likely that she belonged to the Tselona division and, because her story has not previously been printed, it is given here.[48]

This fellow was alone in the bush. It was spring. While he was alone, the Cree Indians captured him and his wife together. They took both of them away to the Cree people's country in the south. They never fed the man but only the woman and they also kept them apart. Each chance she had the woman slipped a little food to her husband, the little she could lay her hands on. Whenever the party pulled out of a camp they gave the man the big heavy packs to carry. He had to do it or be killed. Finally, when they arrived in a strange country, they turned the woman's husband loose. His wife said, "You don't have to go back where you came from. Just stay here but keep off the trail. I'll always have some food and I'll leave some. In that way you'll have food." He kept off the trail but followed the group through the brush. When they made camp he hid. Always when he came to the camp after they had left he found that his wife had left some food for him. Finally these people came to their own country. Now this man had some good moose-hide clothes heavily decorated with fancy quill-work and fur trimmed. These people had never seen such clothes. When the party arrived at the Cree camp the husband hid a distance away from the settlement. There was a fellow who was cutting poles for the trading post. The husband was afraid to move, even when he saw the man with a big ax coming toward him. He was sure that these were not the people who had captured his wife because the woodcutter was a white man. The white man began to cut down a tree near where the Grand Laker was hiding. The latter was afraid to move, not knowing who this man might be. The tree promised to fall straight down toward where the husband was hiding. If it fell on him, he decided, he would run away. The tree began to fall on the Indian so he jumped up. Now the white man saw him. He saw the good clothes and he wondered where they had come from, knowing that such things were lacking in this country. He talked to the Indian. "Where did you come from?" The Grand Laker understood. "You are not from this country. Those clothes are too good for this country. I never saw anything like that before. You stay here. I'll go and tell the boss that I found somebody with good clothes. Don't move."

The man remained where he was while the other fellow told the boss. The boss came out and asked the stranger, "Where are you from?" The man told him. The boss invited him to stay and offered tobacco. The Grand Laker had never tasted tobacco but now he learned how to smoke. At first he did not like the taste. Then the white man gave him a gun and taught him how to shoot. The husband stayed for a while but finally returned to his own country with gun, ammunition, and tobacco. But he lost his wife.

He came to his own country knowing where the people would be in the late fall. The last night it snowed a little. The husband was looking for his brother and father. The brother was out hunting and

[47] The adjoining Tahltan fought with the Tlingit, Upper Nass, Taku, and Stikine Indians using skin armor and helmets of thick goat skin. They sought scalps as well as women prisoners. The Tahltan sometimes released captives in return for a ransom. (Jenness, *Indians of Canada* [1932], 372; Teit, *On Tahltan (Athabaskan) Work* [1912], 485). A local informant corroborated the information that the Tahltan scalped their enemies. According to George Adsit these Indians also recognized war leaders.

[48] For a thumbnail sketch of the informant see Honigmann, *Ethnography and Acculturation of the Fort Nelson Slave* (1946), 16.

happened to strike a track. He thought a stranger had made the trail but he followed it. All the people had been looking for this man and his wife. Soon the brother saw the man packing something. The brother circled and crept up. Meanwhile the husband saw the creeping man. He saw where the latter had dropped by a short spruce. As the brother lay quietly the husband shouted. The fellow by the spruce looked up at him. It was his missing brother! "What are you doing here?" He cried. "We have been looking for you all summer. Are you really my brother?" Then they recognized each other and went home together.

That's the way the story goes. The husband told all about the way the Cree Indians had treated him. He would have died if it had not been for his wife. The storekeeper had saved his life by giving him the rifle.

BELIEF AND THOUGHT

COSMOGONY AND THEOGONY

U PPER LIARD KASKA. Cosmological speculation remained unelaborated in aboriginal Kaska culture. Also, the limited material we collected on this topic makes it impossible to iron out inconsistencies and contradictions. A distinction between the sky and the earth obtained in pre-contact times,[1] and recognition of at least two periods of terrestrial habitation is implicitly revealed in cosmogonical narratives. The earlier period of the world antedates "true Indians." Perhaps it is then that "the animals were like people." At any rate, animals constituted the original earthly population. While they were still powerful (but not necessarily prior to human creation), there came a great flood that killed the monsters who threatened already existing people. Informants ascribed the flood to God who designed it to punish the people because they fought "all the time." Some Indians secured themselves by building a raft which the rising waters lifted until it came to rest on a mountain top. "You can still see the place where the raft came down. Here you can find big elephant [mammoth?] teeth" (X).[2] Following the flood Crow restored the world, the myth describing that event being the familiar Earth Diver tale. Today original creation is attributed to God, Tenatiia, a word probably designating a "rich and powerful person." Nobody regards God and Crow as identical. Informants could not say whether the idea of an anthropomorphic supreme being antedated European penetration of the Cassiar. They implied that Tenatiia had always existed but not as a supreme god. This, of course, does not mean that the ancestors of the present day Kaska recognized Tenatiia as a deity. The evidence strongly suggests that the name was syncretized to designate the God of the Hebraic-Christian tradition.

Apparently not all the animals can be traced back to a prediluvian golden age. Beaver, for example, had to be created from human stock!

Originally there were no beaver in this country. A couple had one girl. These three were traveling but did not know how they would cross the creeks. At every creek except the last they found a bridge. The last creek they couldn't cross. They camped for the night and when they started the next day found that the girl was missing. But there was a beaver dam across the creek. Just as the father came up to it he saw a beaver swimming away and recognized his daughter. This was the first beaver (X).

---

[1] In Tlingit belief ". . . the earth was conceived of as flat and the sky as a solid vault. Inside of and between these everything was alive with spirits . . . and some also resided upon the sky itself." Swanton, *Social Condition, Beliefs and Linguistic Relationship of the Tlingit Indians* (1908), 451.

[2] Field reports that the Pelly River Indians "have lots of old legends of the country being flooded, also of being covered with ice, another of the country being covered with ashes, and the trouble the people had at that time to live." (Field, *Unpublished manuscript* [1913], 16.) The flood tradition also is found among the Tlingit where a mountain top on Prince of Wales Island is pointed out as the resting place of the Indians who survived. (Jones, *Study of the Thlingets of Alaska* [1914], 188.) Swanton, also apparently perplexed by conflicting traditions, says, "Raven was the creator, or rather the organizor, of the present state of things." Swanton, *Social Condition, Beliefs and Linguistic Relationship of the Tlingit Indians* (1908), 451.

Like most people the Kaska Indians postulated the existence of certain normally unseen and unsensed entities, including counterparts or souls of the empirically sensed animals.[3] Other sensed events, like stones or clouds, also possessed a transcendental character such that they perhaps warrant designation of Kaska thinking as animistic. The normally unseen world included Gusłii'na ("devil"), who dwelt at the last point of a long river.[4] He lived in the company of a woman, ɔ'ɣa, who became the first sheep after she had been killed by the culture hero, Tsu'guya. The attribution of horns to the devil may well represent the influence of biblical mythology. Informants denied the notion of a cold being operating as the devil's helper. Apparently the words gusłii, "cold," and Gusłiina are not related. The Indians were cognizant of the North Wind Man (itsiipaʔotena) who brought suffering. "If I am mean he will make a big wind to make me suffer. He doesn't want an evil man to follow his track, so he covers it with snow."[5] Cannibalistic giants, like Teɣutsiia and Etceɣus'tala, inspired considerable fear. Tsitaɣitsatse, another giant, befriended men. Weaker than Etceɣustela he nevertheless killed the latter with the aid of Indians. When Tsitaɣitsatse defecated, his feces became hard as rock the moment that they struck the earth. Helpful to man and powerful in his behalf were the dwarfs, who, however, were constantly menaced by animals. In warfare these small beings helped to bring up wind and cold that paralyzed the enemy. In size a dwarf reached about the height of a caribou jaw. One such being could pack only about half a pound. Despite the tendency of the dwarfs to steal women, people laughed when they spoke of the antics of the little people.[6] Nobody ever secured shamanistic power from a dwarf. Informants could not recall a practice of making offerings to rocks.

Long ago monstrous animals roamed the world. Although similar beliefs are widespread in North America, in the Cassiar traditions of such animals cannot be discussed without reference to the fossil evidence of mammoths and dinosaurs encountered in the region. The following tale illustrates the kinds of narratives that perpetuated beliefs in monsters.

Once when a group of people were camping a big monster, like an elephant, came close to the camp. A shaman who had six fingers (lasłoona, "many fingers") went out to meet the animal and addressed it like a person. The monster exclaimed, "I saw young game track. I was going to have a good meal,

---

[3] "It is believed that all animals understand human speech. For this reason natives are careful what they say about them. . . ." Jones, *Study of the Thlingets of Alaska* (1914), 164.

[4] Along the Mackenzie the Indians recognized a cognate "devil, 'Ha is linee,' or, 'the sorcerer.'" McLean, *Notes of a Twenty-Five Years' Service in the Hudson's Bay Territory* (1932), 342.

[5] Among the Swampy Cree the oldest of four brothers was the North Wind who sent cold and punished evil doers. Skinner, *Notes on the Eastern Cree and Northern Saulteaux* (1911), 59; Speck, *Naskapi* (1935), 56–57.

[6] Among the Pelly Indians "there are the little men of the Mountain that are supposed to be about four feet high at the most and have fine living places in the heart of the mountains and are exceptionally strong and wise who come out occasionally and capture their women for wives in some cases making the father of the girl they have taken a medicineman in return for the girl." (Field, *Unpublished manuscript* [1913], 5.) The Attawapiskat Cree were also not afraid of the dwarf people who inhabited the rocky cliffs along rivers. Honigmann, *Attawapiskat Cree field notes* (1947–48).

having come a long way." The shaman turned back and flew over the camp. He told the people, "The animal is coming close to the camp. I can't stop it. You boys better move." All the people fled, traveling about 20 miles over the mountains. When they grew tired they made camp. The shaman caught up with them and said, "I've fixed him. When daylight comes you'll hear the animal. He'll go back where he came from."

With daylight they heard a howling and saw two bars of light in the mountains. All the people became afraid. The shaman went out to meet the animal, who said, "You're going to make a trip with me." The shaman advised the people that he would stay with the animal ten days. Then he disappeared. In ten days he returned reeking so strongly that the people could smell him a mile off. He explained that when he had reached the monster the latter had swallowed him. "I went all through the guts and came out the other end. That's why I smell so strong." He then directed the people to smoke him in a fire of rotten wood. The shaman circled the fire singing.

Several culture heros were assumed to have existed at an earlier time. Kli?atata ("filling snowshoe father") invented the bow, the snowshoe, and taught the people to make fish nets from willow-bark line. The informant ranked him "pretty near as good as Tsuguya," suggesting in addition that Kli?atata might have been the latter's son. Tsuguya's adventures with the devil made good narrative material.

Tsuguya was a smart man who could make anything. One day he went down [up?] a long river. He heard a dog barking and saw a camp at the bottom of a hill. Here there was a woman who looked like a dog. Everybody who came by and saw this dog thought that its owner must be living there and so decided to visit. The dog was ɔɣa, a devil's girl. When Tsuguya got out of the canoe he fell and the woman took an ax and struck him. She skinned him and put him in the pot. After boiling the contents a long time she uncovered the vessel but found Tsuguya still alive. Then she fried [broiled?] him. Finally she realized that this man could not be killed.

Tsuguya went hunting. He met a bear who also had a girl. This woman, too, was a helper of the devil. The girl said that there was a bear across the lake. She hoped to trap the man. Tsuguya went over and killed the bear. The devil now chased Tsuguya, who went into a hole and turned into a beaver. The devil told his girl to set a net. They set the net but when they hauled it in found that it had caught nothing. The beaver just kept swimming around. The devil now drank all the water in that place. The smart man went into the mud and caused the water to reappear again (X).

Many other adventures and narrow escapes befell Tsuguya. In one of these he outwitted the anthropomorphic moon plus the latter's animal helpers in order to win the moon's daughter for a wife. The moon is also identified with the devil (O). Tsuguya appears to be the Athapaskan counterpart of the Algonkian Gluskabe and Tcikapis. The remaining Kaska culture hero, Gatco ("big rabbit"), bore no relationship to Tsuguya. Although nothing was learned of his activities it is not improbable that he is cognatic to Nanabozho, identified by Ojibwa and Menomini as the Great Hare.[7]

Dease River Kaska. Contemporary informants speak readily of the Supreme Being who "made everything." Another version of creation has been recorded in this area by Teit.[8]

[7] Fisher, *The Mythology of the Northern and Northeastern Algonkians in Reference to Algonkian Mythology as a Whole* (1946), 230.

[8] Teit, *Kaska Tales* (1917), 441–442. Speaking of Tahltan cosmogony the same writer says: "Some of the Tahltan beliefs are very interesting. The earth is thought to be circular, and to be surrounded by salt water lakes. The sky is dome-shaped, and hangs over the earth like an umbrella, the edges touching the waters all around. The sky revolves sunwise, while the earth is considered stationary. At

ORIGIN OF THE EARTH

Once there was no earth. Water was where the earth is now. The world was a great lake. The animals and birds wanted to have an earth, and proposed to dive for it. The earth was very deep under the water. Beaver and Muskrat, and all the animals and birds, dived, but none of them reached the bottom. None of them stayed under water longer than half a day. At last Diver (a bird) went down. After six days he came up quite exhausted and speechless. His friends examined his toenails, and found mud or earth under them. From this they formed on top of the water a new earth, which grew until it formed the present earth. At first it was merely mud and very soft. Later it became firm, and trees and vegetation began to grow on it. Now the earth is old and dry. Perhaps it is drying up.

Perhaps there came a second flood. At any rate Teit collected a tradition of a great inundation.[9]

THE GREAT FLOOD

Once there came a great flood which covered the earth. Most of the people made rafts, and some escaped in canoes. Great darkness came on, and high winds which drove the vessels hither and thither. The people became separated. Some were driven far away. When the flood subsided, people landed wherever they found the nearest land. When the earth became dry, they lived in the places near where they had landed. People were now widely scattered over the world. They did not know where other people lived, and probably thought themselves the only survivors. Long afterwards, when in their wanderings they met people from another place, they spoke different languages, and could not understand one another. *This is why there are now many different centres of population, many tribes, and many languages.* Before the flood, there was but one centre; for all the people lived together in one country, and spoke one language.

Looking beyond the everyday world of the senses the Indians postulated a variety of entities or beings. The cannibalistic Big Man (Tenatco), who used no dwelling but sometimes dug a hole in the ground, inspired fear because of his predilection for stealing adults and children. Bald Man constituted a beneficent giant, who subsisted on fish and always walked stooped until one day by straightening up he raised the sky. Bald Man continues to live on earth but is never seen. The Little Men, Klunetene, who lived on

---

the edges of the earth the weather is always chilly. Some think that above or beyond the sky there is another earth, which is inhabited by birds. Possibly the sky is the floor of this other world. There is also a belief that the sky is animated and the same as the mother of the people, while the sun is masculine and the same as the father. The sun was formerly prayed to, and traces of sun worship abound. The earth we tread is like a crust, or skin, or blanket, which is held up by the earth-mother, who is like a post that supports it. When she gets tired, she moves her position, which causes an earthquake. She is becoming older and weaker all the time, therefore the earth is not so high as formerly, and is sagging down into the waters. Some day she will be unable to hold it up any longer. She will fall like a rotten post, and the earth will drop down and be submerged. There is also a belief in the meat-mother, who gave birth to all the animals and still controls them. The moon and stars are transformed beings. Wind is the breath of people, viz., a cold people who live in the far north, and a warm people who live in the south. When they speak, cold and warm winds blow over the earth. Thunder is a bird, and the noise of thunder is caused by the flapping of its wings. Its armpits are red, and when these are exposed by the extending of its wings, the red is seen as lightning." (Teit, *On Tahltan (Athabaskan) Work* [1912], 485–486.) Our upper Liard River informant (O) reported that Tahltan believed in the Nadanke (also, Nadanii), who wore large patched moccasins and sometimes caused people to faint upon his sudden appearance. To pacify him people left large moccasins in the bush but they were never taken.

[9] Teit, *Kaska Tales* (1917), 442–443.

mice which they secured with small bows and arrows in the tall grass, sometimes befriended men. They also enjoyed a reputation for their fun making. Information about
Fire Man (Kondiklutc or Kotc) came to the Kaska from the Taku Indians, who called
him Tciskiiʔe. An evil being, he spoke in the fire's cracking and to him the people then
threw small bits of meat. The devil sent cold and controlled other evil beings
like Tenatco. Long ago Tiɣutsiia, a cannibal, prowled the earth for unsuspecting victims
whom he clubbed to death and then prepared like game for eating. The track of this
being struck great terror when encountered but he perished long ago in the flood. Water
beings were unknown. Thunder originated from a great "fly" (bird? insect?) with a
large mouth.[10]

Tselona. No idea of a Supreme Being obtained in aboriginal times. Something called
a devil (Liiap) entered into the aboriginal belief system but details could not be recalled.

SHAMANISM

Upper Liard Kaska. An informant told us that a shaman was always a fat person
because he constantly dreamed that he was eating. Such a characterization may be
derived from one or two renowned shamans about whom the informant had knowledge.
Every young man received the opportunity to acquire power that would enhance his
personal capacities. Hence every man was a potential shaman (meta or nudita; the
latter word appears to designate the curing status of the person). Women too could be
visited by extraordinary dreams through which they, like men, acquired shamanistic
power. By working harder at shamanism some men and a few women acquired a wide
reputation as curers, prophets, and conjurers.

The power to perform shamanistic functions came from "dreaming of animals in a
lonely place" (O). A young person would spend time in the bush. At night he might
hear ɔɣa singing like a human being or he might hear a moose or bear singing. "You go
in bush. Pretty soon get dark. You hear somebody sing. Bye and bye get light. Fellow
goes and just moose there when you wake up. Bye and bye get dark and that man come
back" (X). When a boy reached about 14 or 15 years in age his father directed him to
sleep in the forest. Before leaving camp the youth would sometimes suck his mother's
breast "just like a little baby." Generally the aspirant traveled about ten miles from his
parents' camp, stopping at a place where he saw porcupine tracks. Arriving at such a
site the boy painted his chest with a pigment made from rotten wood. Always he camped
alone, accompanying his one or two days of isolation with sparse eating and little drinking.[11] It was forbidden to take a bow and arrows along on a vision quest. Every night

[10] Thunder birds have been reported for the Tahltan (see footnote 8) and Tlingit. Swanton, *Social
Condition, Beliefs and Linguistic Relationship of the Tlingit Indians* (1908), 455; Jones, *Study of the
Thlingets of Alaska* (1914), 186.

[11] Among the Tlingit would-be shamans "spent long periods in the forest in absolute solitude, sup-
posedly in communication with evil spirits. They also had periods of fasting and their diet differed in
many respects from that of others." (Jones, *Study of the Thlingets* of Alaska [1914], 155–156.) Drucker
is more explicit in listing the following traits for the Tlingit power quest: shaman's power from animal
spirits; bathing and "medicines" used preparatory to novice's vision quest; fasting and continence
enjoined during the quest; bathing and fasting after first encounter as well as a four-day period of singing

that he lay down to sleep the youth wished that a source of auxiliary power would that night be revealed to him. Communications from animals or other symbols constituted the marks of a successful vision quest. Sometimes the animals encouraged the boy to emulate them. "Don't stay with a bunch of people. Stay alone and you'll have strong power," might be their advice. Or the youth might be advised to avoid sleeping with women "for a little while" in order to obtain lasting good fortune. Some animals assured the aspirant that when he was hungry an animal patron would always provide assistance. Such a dream must never (?) be revealed to another person. Following his initial experience a boy usually sought additional helpers, subsequently spending longer periods in solitude. Sometimes an aspirant passed a month alone in the bush. In his dreams the youth might be advised that his power had now been secured and that he could freely "bother" women again.[12]

A successful vision quest apparently represented a portion of the animal's wind (or soul) passing into the dreamer to enhance the latter's natural ability. Upon returning from a dream quest a boy would always contrive to enter camp by a trail different from the one along which he had started forth. In the period of seeking visions a young man felt sensitive about his sister (or other women?) staring at his mouth. According to the informant, only "nice" people encouraged their sons to dream for power. A father who feared the hardships associated with life in the winter wisely insisted on the vision quest, thus insuring that the boy would be able to predict the location of game and save the people from starvation. Should a man's son show fear of sleeping in isolation he would not be forced into the ritual. A man might falsely pretend to have secured power. Eventually the lie revealed itself in the person's ineffectual attempts to cure or to locate game. The story is told of one Indian who reported an exceptional vision to his friends. A grizzly bear with a cub had come to sing to him. Nobody believed him. The shaman said, "Come down with me and you'll see the bear and the kid play with me." Somebody accepted the invitation and witnessed the grizzly harmlessly play with the man. The "kid" played with them both. Perhaps this tale is more related to the wonder working undertaken by powerful shamans than it is to the dream quest.

The successful solicitation of power brought a man into relation with one or more animal helpers upon whose aid he now counted in performing curing and other ceremonies. In addition curers might dream of natural objects (like leaves or bark) that possessed medicinal properties. A shaman collected such materials and kept them in a small pouch. Ordinarily no particular dress distinguished a shaman. When called upon

---

and dancing; further power sought; shamans possessed several spirits; most shamans were men. The Tlingit patterns of obtaining an animal sponsor differ substantially from those followed further south on the Pacific Coast but resemble closely shamanistic patterns of the Cassiar. Drucker, *Culture Element Distributions: XXVI, Northwest Coast* (1950), 223–225.

[12] The English word "bother" is used by the Kaska to designate a variety of experiences, including sexual intercourse. (Honigmann, *Culture and Ethos of Kaska Society* [1949], 138.) Navaho interpreters also use the same English word to translate what is probably the same Athapaskan verb. "For example, when the sense is that a person ought to avoid persons, animals, or objects, the preferred English verb is 'bother.' 'Don't bother your wife.' (Usually with the meaning: 'don't have sexual intercourse with your wife.')" Kluckhohn, *Patterning as Exemplified in Navaho Culture* (1941), 110.

to practice, however, he might represent his power source by donning the skin of a moose, bear, sheep, or other animal.[13] "New" clothing belonged to shamanistic performances. When not in use these garments remained in a bag that a man kept outside of the dwelling. How they were then kept dry cannot be answered.[14] Drums played no role in curing but some men employed clappers made of two or three pieces of wood that were probably held between the fingers. Practitioners at work carefully avoided exposing their mouths to women and concealed their features beneath a piece of skin (in post-contact time underneath a handkerchief). The association between the breath and shamanistic efficacy no doubt determined in part such attention to the mouth. Payment for curing constituted a voluntary gift that varied depending on the shaman's degree of success or on the economic status of the patient. A mere token gift rewarded a curing rite that failed. Large payments were exceptional. Should a shaman fail twice to effect a cure then a more powerful practitioner would be asked to exercise his power.

Shamans assisted war parties, using their power to weaken the enemy. Probably the commonest function of a shaman was divination or clairvoyance.[15] With or without the aid of external oracles[16] the shaman "dreamed" the location of game, the number of days that would elapse before a patient recovered, or somebody's imminent death. One man predicted the arrival of many white men in the Cassiar and announced that the visitors would find "all the Indians dead." "That's what happened," the informant added. Judging from folk tales, a shaman also protected his people from monsters and cannibalistic giants whom he usually contrived to kill.[17] Finally, some shamans enhanced their prestige by public wonder working or conjuring. The feats such men are said to have performed include walking on the surface of water "so that everybody

[13] Tlingit shamans symbolized their powers on marks or in articles of apparel. Swanton, *Social Condition, Beliefs and Linguistic Relationship of the Tlingit Indians* (1908), 463–464.

[14] Jones reports that Tlingit shamans began their work "in perfect nudity" wearing "a girdle composed of bones, claw-nails and talons . . . about their loins, then a necklace of such about their necks, and last of all they were given rattles especially made for their use." Jones, *Study of the Thlingets of Alaska* (1914), 155–156.

[15] Clairvoyance by shamans occurred along the length of the Northwest Coast with a special class of clairvoyants appearing among the Haida. (Drucker, *Culture Element Distributions: XXVI, Northwest Coast* [1950], 228.) Among the Tlingit "besides curing the sick a shaman had many other functions, such, for instance, as the location of supplies of food and assistance against enemies in war." (Swanton, *Social Condition, Beliefs and Linguistic Relationships of the Tlingit Indians* [1908], 465.) As a diviner the Tlingit shaman "was often consulted as to weather, the proper time to start on a hunt, whether a certain venture would meet with success or failure and about other things." (Jones, *Study of the Thlingets of Alaska* [1914], 159.) Among the Pelly River people "the medicine man has the power of a kind of second sight either in dreams, or when he or she whoever the doctor is starts singing, they will be able to foretell the future also cure the sick, and so forth, which gives them considerable influence with the tribe." Field, *Unpublished manuscript* (1913), 5.

[16] See below, p. 113.

[17] "They have tales of enormous animals such as the mammoth and spiders as large as a full-sized grizzly bear and long worms that are supposed to be alive today and nobody can save them from these animals but their doctors" (Field, *Unpublished manuscript* [1913], 5.) Among the Attawapiskat (Swampy) Cree it was not unusual for the shaman to retire into the bush to kill a cannibalistic wiitiko. Honigmann, *Attawapiskat Cree field notes* (1947–48).

could see it" and sleight of hand. Thus a performer caused a decorated foot-long staff to disappear. Two shamans might compete in public conjuring, the object of each being to prove himself the more powerful. The loser in such a contest might die.[18]

Dease River Kaska. Both men and women became shamans among the people in the Dease River valley. A girl sometimes acquired her power (nɔtzut, "strength") while undergoing menstrual seclusion. Generally in summer when a boy reached 16 he was directed to go a short distance into the bush to dream. Here he remained for about a month, living in an open camp made by clearing a patch of willows. Occasionally more adequate shelters housed the vision searcher. The youth painted his face in either red or black. While a woman was forbidden to visit the aspirant, the latter was freely visited by his father who brought food. Generally, however, a youth seeking a dream consumed little food and drank water sparingly. According to one informant a boy used the drinking tube during his seclusion but not the scratching stick, which was associated with a girl's puberty sequestration.[19] Sometimes three or four boys passed their vision quest together. Power came from dreaming of a "strong" animal, mythological being, sun, or moon. Girls often dreamed about otters. Power dreams were never revealed. Boys whose experiences seemed particularly efficacious—for example, if they received communications from animals like the bear or mountain goat—might become successful curers. No formal instruction in shamanism followed the dream quest—"a man taught himself." While almost every man enjoyed some power, each microcosmic group customarily recognized one individual who stood out by virtue of such ability. Indirect revelation of a power source occurred when a shaman wore in his hair the feathers of a bird patron or, if his helper was a bear, carried a bear-skin headband or necklace of that animal's claws. Indians desiring to be cured either visited the practitioner or summoned him. Curers customarily performed with rattles. Payment consisted of skins, snowshoes, or articles of wearing apparel. Sometimes a successful man received his patient's daughter as a wife, but only with the girl's explicit consent. Age enhanced a man's supernatural powers while longevity in turn proved that a man enjoyed particularly strong helpers. Such men acquired widespread reputations. Conjuring, mainly by sleight-of-hand, constituted a firm part of the shaman complex and served to spread a man's ability far afield. Shamans also engaged in competitive performances.

Tselona. An informant clearly described the source of shamanistic ability. "All kinds of game, they help," he said. "Moose, beaver, lynx, marten, otter, sheep, goat, caribou—all make people doctor. When they want to hunt they catch anything. Somebody get sick, make all right the people. The water too make somebody doctor. Water he talk, he

---

[18] Widespread in the northern Athapaskan area, public conjuring is also related for the Tlingit. ". . . shamans of hostile towns were in the habit of dressing up to fight each other by means of their spirits. Sometimes they performed for no other reason than to show their power." (Swanton, *Social Condition, Beliefs and Linguistic Relationship of the Tlingit Indians* [1908], 465.) Sleight-of-hand among the Tlingit is mentioned by Drucker. (Drucker, *Culture Element Distributions: XXVI, Northwest Coast* [1950], 226.) From an upper Liard River informant we heard that Ross River shamans made objects disappear and also caused ptarmigan to walk "straight into camp."

[19] In this connection see also the statement of another informant in reference to puberty rites for boys, p. 125 below.

know. Poplar, willow, any kind stick [i.e., tree] make doctor." Thunder, too, could confer power and gave a man the ability to control weather. A man's power helped him to attain old age but when he died his acquired ability "died" with him.

The vision quest among the Tselona involved the aspirant's seclusion in the forest, where he saw animals or other sponsors who sang to him. As a rule only a boy undertook searching for a vision but occasionally a girl also slept in the bush and secured shamanistic power. Only when engaged in curing did the shaman wear a distinctive garb, for example carrying a fur scarf around his neck. The skin represented his power source. Neither drum nor rattle played a part in curing. According to our informant only Cree shamans drummed. Conjuring could not be recalled but the informant had heard of a similar practice among other Indian groups.

MAGIC

The term magic is used in this section to include not only behavior but also a manner of thinking or state of mind. The major characteristic of magic is that it holds material things or behavioral events "to be the unfailing residence of certain intrinsic qualities."[20] Magic as a term thus includes ideas as well as manifest avoidances and other rites, like amulet wearing, removing illness by sucking, and various forms of divination. Not all of the magical observances in Kaska culture have been incorporated in this section. A number have been introduced previously (for example in connection with warfare) while others will be included with the life cycle.

Upper Liard Kaska. In pre-contact times the Indians of the Cassiar recognized several species of animals as magically dangerous. Holding first place in this category we find the otter, a creature that in this region occupies the focal point of ideology which among other Mackenzie drainage people is reserved for the wolf.[21] Like the mink, the otter could drive persons insane, subject them to fainting, nosebleed, and produce more serious illness such as "twisting up." Both animals were avoided as food. A mink inadvertently caught in a deadfall had its carcass thrown into the fire and covered with feathers. This "put them [i.e., mink] in good mind." To take a live mink from a trap was particularly dangerous. An otter taken in a beaver deadfall was returned to the stream or lake with instructions to one's children not to drink water near the place. Dreaming of the otter made people fearful and such dreams were regarded as originating with the animal itself. Otters possessed power to transform themselves into human beings.[22] Attitudes of profound respect and avoidance were not lacking for the wolf. A hunter who wounded this animal always let it go free with the expectation that the creature would again present itself to the hunter. Should it then be killed, a depletion of game would follow within two or three years.[23] Thus the cyclic fluctuation of game animals appears

[20] Wilson, *Analysis of Social Change* (1945), 93.

[21] Honigmann, *Ethnography and Acculturation of the Fort Nelson Slave* (1946), 76.

[22] ". . . the land otter was dreaded more than any other creature. This was on account of his supposed supernatural power, fondness for stealing people away, depriving them of their senses, and turning them into otter men. . . . Years ago the Tlingit would not use them for fur." Swanton, *Social Condition, Beliefs and Linguistic Relationship of the Tlingit Indians* (1908), 456.

[23] ". . . the wolf was also supposed to possess great power." Swanton, *Social Condition, Beliefs and Linguistic Relationship of the Tlingit Indians* (1908), 455.

to have been recognized by the Indians, who regarded such variation as magically induced. The killing of wolves and crows was also avoided in deference to the members of the moieties named after those animals.

Contemporary informants still categorize the mink, otter, and wolf as "devil's helpers." Also allied with Gusɫiina are the snake, toad,[24] elephant (nuʔuti), shark, wolverine, flying squirrel, and grizzly bear.[25] Some of the items in this list were undoubtedly known only by hear-say, if they were known at all in aboriginal times. Of the wolverine it was said that he stole on behalf of the devil.[26] The flying squirrel sought to remove people from this world but to kill the animal promised illness and its meat was never eaten. The grizzly occupied himself with trying to kill men for the devil and manifested extraordinary sensitivity to ridicule. When slighted he might harbor resentment for several years until finally taking his revenge by killing the person who had laughed at him.[27] Magical power of another quality was ascribed to the beaver, moose, and caribou. Beaver bones had always to be discarded in the fire, while the bones of the other two species were thrown far away from camp in an effort to attract fresh game to the locale. People burned the hair scraped from a moose hide. If a woman stepped on this material her husband would become powerless to kill moose, while if a dog ate moose meat then the owner would never again be able to track the moose successfully. To club wounded caribou caused illness. It was very foolish to make pets of large game animals. Raising a young moose, beaver, or bear in captivity would promote the deaths of many poeple. The children of the captor would die off as the species of animal multiplied, the deaths of one balancing increase of the other.

Young men took water, grease, and bone marrow in measured quantities both in order to preserve their health and to enhance their hunting ability. Too much water interfered with digestion and hence undermined a man's capacity for sustained effort. Grease was "too heavy" for a youth. Leg tendons also remained taboo for young men; to eat them invited the danger of leg cramps at a time when unhampered movement was essential. The hind quarters of an animal were best avoided in favor of the forward portions that contained "strength." Boys ate lightly and not until a man's marriage had produced four or five children should he begin to eat as much as he cared to of whatever he liked. Such avoidances did not apply to girls, because women were not hunters and their work was not as exhausting as men's.

The relationship entered into between a man and his animal sponsor did not result in a complete avoidance of that animal for food in those cases where the species was

[24] "The slime exuding from a frog's skin was thought to be very poisonous and fatal to smaller creatures." Swanton, *Social Condition, Beliefs and Linguistic Relationship of the Tlingit Indians* (1908), 458.

[25] Old World folklore also accounts for the evil dispositions of certain animals by classifying them as creations of the devil. Thompson, *Folktale* (1946), 236.

[26] "The wolverine . . . was also held in great respect." Christianized Tlingit regarded him "next to the devil for badness." Swanton, *Social Condition, Beliefs and Linguistic Relationship of the Tlingit Indians* (1908), 456.

[27] Special respect for the grizzly has been reported for the Tlingit. Swanton, *Social Condition, Beliefs and Linguistic Relationship of the Tlingit Indians* (1908), 455.

commonly exploited. Some parts of the meat would be avoided. Often the animal helper itself prescribed the avoidance to be followed. Thus a moose might tell the dreamer, "Eat only my ribs," "Don't eat my head," or "Don't eat my guts."

Cohabitation promised to be magically dangerous under some circumstances and therefore had to be avoided.[28] For example a man held off from coitus in the night before he started on a hunt. Following his return the hunter remained continent for about six days.[29] Miscellaneous avoidances included the taboo on making snowshoes before snow lay on the ground and a reluctance to deposit parts of the human body on or in the earth. Apparently because of the disgust associated with rotten things like teeth, the umbilicus, the afterbirth, and perhaps the corpse were rather cached or burned than buried. Whistling met with special precautions, but use of the willow whistle does not seem to have been affected.

By far the largest amount of magical ritual concerned itself with hunting and the cure of illness. Not only could a shaman through divination learn the location of game but he could then perform rites to guarantee the successful killing of food. Singing the songs which had been learned from one's animal sponsors secured hunting luck; a "moose doctor" for example sang his "moose song." Men with inadequate power frequently asked a stronger shaman to perform rites in their behalf. Seated alongside the practitioner the hunter might accompany the shaman by singing. On other occasions a man with strong power etched the image of an animal on a small piece of caribou bone. The hunter took this amulet on his journey and returned it when it had served its purpose. Other amulets, like a piece of weasel or loon skin worn in the hat, assured all-around good luck. Any man might be fortunate in finding substances that assured successful hunting. Such "medicines" (perhaps earths?) were shaped like pills and carried on the hunter's person. In early post-contact times a man who struck a moose trail would smoke one of these pellets in his pipe, at the same time singing and wishing to encounter that animal. Another form of hunting ritual involved an older brother tearing open the left sleeve of his coat when a younger sibling killed his first large game animal. The ritual insured a lasting abundance of game. Instead of remaining hidden the animals would fall out of the sleeve, metaphorically speaking. Scapulimancy performed by a shaman sometimes preceded hunting for moose, caribou, and bear. The following account probably indicates that the informant had forgotten the details of this technique. The shaman is said to have begun by singing, at the same time placing the scapula of a moose or caribou near the fire. Heat, the informant explained, caused a moose or other animal to appear on the surface of the bone. This indicated that the hunter would have good luck whereas if an image failed to materialize then he would kill nothing. At the end of the performance the shaman blew on the bone, flipped his fingers, and caused the design to vanish. As elsewhere in the northern forest it is likely that cracks in the scapula were interpreted.[30]

[28] See also pp. 94, 96, 117, 118, 124–126, and 140.

[29] Continence as a preparatory observance for luck is widespread among Pacific Coast tribes, including the Tlingit and Chilkat. Drucker, *Culture Element Distributions: XXVI, Northwest Coast* (1950), 223.

[30] ". . . people used to talk to a piece of bone that comes out of a seal's shoulder blade, saying, 'Will

Whether following from sorcery or the breaking of some avoidance, illness represented the alienation of a life-giving property (which informants referred to as "wind") from the body or the instrusion of a malevolent substance into the organism.[31] Many but not all illnesses were treated through shamans. For example, any person could alleviate headache by placing a toad on the painful part leaving it there until the animal jumped free. Then the pain would also disappear. A shaman, however, effected cures with the aid of the power that resided in his soul or wind. He did not paint his face while curing but sang and utilized a variety of ritual objects to promote recovery of health. Among the upper Liard River people each shaman freely composed (or dreamed) his own chants. In turn they were heard (and, may it be assumed, imitated?) by persons in the group of relatives who gathered to watch the performance and, as the night wore on, joined in the singing. Sometimes the practitioner "blew" water from his mouth on the sore part of a patient's anatomy or he might drive the illness into a foreign object, like a rock or a small doll that had been prepared by his wife. He pushed the image into the patient's body, causing it to disappear. Then object as well as illness were extracted and quickly stuffed into the curer's pouch. Sucking blood from the head of an ailing person (never for some reason from the hand or arm) also constituted a recognized pattern of doctoring. Sometimes small gophers or weasels were extracted during sucking and these represented the causes of the particular malady. If a person had been rendered sick as the result of killing mink or otter, the shaman occupied himself in extracting one of these animals' "three spirits."[32] Should two souls have penetrated the victim, then death was almost inevitable while all three resulted in severe mental illness. Every shaman carried amulets or "medicines" in his pouch to aid him in his work. Moose excrement and various roots provided effective antidotes which, however, were never taken internally. The selection of these materials probably stemmed from dreams. Remaining unexplained is the custom of planting several sticks, two or three feet high, in front of a patient and filling the spaces between them with moose-hide line.[33] Tattooing never served as a cure.

---

you tell me what I am going to kill? Am I going to kill a seal or a bear?' Then the speaker spit upon it and threw it up into the air. If it remained in a certain position after it fell the man would kill something; otherwise he might as well stay at home." (Swanton, *Social Condition, Beliefs and Linguistic Relationship of the Tlingit Indians* [1908], 457.) Bone tossing is widely distributed in northern North America but was not inquired into among the Kaska.

[31] Tlingit shamans sometimes cured "by passing over the affected parts carved objects supposed to have power." Swanton, *Social Condition, Beliefs and Linguistic Relationship of the Tlingit Indians* (1908), 464.

[32] The Tlingit attributed sickness to "witchcraft" and "after pretending to draw a spear or some other foreign object from the sick man, the shaman designated who had sent it into him." Swanton, *Social Condition, Beliefs and Linguistic Relationship of the Tlingit Indians* (1908), 464.

[33] One of our informants (O) revealed a little about curing ceremonies among the Ross River Tutchoni. As many as four shamans sometimes sang over a patient, persisting until they collapsed (in a trance?), "just like they're dead." As they lay unconscious an assistant flexed their legs to prevent stiffening. During their unconsciousness the shamans went "under the ground" to retrieve the sick man's wind.

Certain therapeutic rites required silence in order to be effective. These a shaman performed at a considerable distance from the sick camp, never within range of the sound of barking dogs. Probably under such circumstances a healer caused a sorcerer's evil to recoil on the latter. Detection of a sorcerer was easy if it happened that somebody remained conspicuously absent from a curing ceremony. Against the absent one the shaman directed the finger of guilt.

Confession helped to diagnose illness resulting from broken avoidances and apparently also possessed curative value in itself. The shaman asked, "You ever bother your sister?" "You ever kill an otter?" "How you kill mink?" "You ever steal?" When the patient had admitted an offense the confessor warned him not to repeat the deed upon recovery.

Following contact with Europeans a hunter came to perform a ritual to alleviate intense cold. He fired a dry root ("wolverine medicine") from a shotgun. Informants did not recognize the reference to "lucky number." The preceding material, however, suggests strongly that the number "four" possessed special significance. Apart from love songs, which may have been used with the idea of magically attracting a member of the opposite sex, love magic occupied little attention.[34]

As already indicated people sometimes used their magical power against other people. For example a reputed shaman who felt slighted or ridiculed might use sorcery in vengeance against his real or fancied detractors. People took care not to annoy a shaman. He should be "only pleased," said an informant. A man whose temperament favored sorcery sought to increase his power by dreaming of animals like the mink and otter but not all persons were sorcerers whose power emanated from these species. A sorcerer tried to "steal" his victim's wind, perhaps first securing a piece of the latter's clothing. Burial of such a possession in the ground brought about death. (Note the use of burial in this context.) A person suspecting sorcery might pay to have his wind returned. In this way really malevolent practitioners extorted women. Sorcerers meted out not only death but also illness, physical and mental, and also "troubled" a man by ruining his hunting ability. A good hunter knew that he had been sorcerized when, seeing a moose, he failed to strike the animal with his weapon. Black magic held a danger of mental illness for the evil magician, who in some cases was also executed with the community's consent. Sorcerers, however, could evade execution by slipping through their enemies' hands. An informant related a story about two Tlingit shamans, one of whom was evil. They both flew through the air. The good man disappeared after a time but his

---

The wind had gone so far away that the patient was close to death. During the interval of unconsciousness nobody might leave the dwelling. After perhaps four hours the men simultaneously returned to awareness and renewed their singing. Part of the paraphernalia used in the rite consisted of a line strung with feathers. This the practitioner lashed around the patient's wrists and used to pull the latter from his bed. In that way he was pulled back to life, the informant explained. The pattern of going into a trance to retrieve an errant soul is close to the Eskimo pattern of shamanism. The line fastened to the patient recalls Eskimo divination customs.

[34] Love magic has been reported for the Tahltan. In one particular variety a white root was obtained from the ground and rolled into pellets. The woman's image was then drawn on a piece of skin and encircled with the pellets. If the charm was to be successful the pellets moved and at the same time the woman found herself attracted to the magician.

partner continued to fly, indicating that power for evil exceeded in strength power for good.[35] The following tale is about an upper Liard River shaman who was still alive in early post-contact times:

> Squeaky Dick was an evil shaman. Once the people lined up in front of his camp to kill him. He knew this. They had a muzzle loader to shoot him. The gun couldn't fire; all the parts refused to work. The people then started to kill him with a knife. Dick threw himself down and disappeared—blanket and all. The people poked through the brush with a knife hoping to kill him. Later Squeaky Dick returned and boasted of his escape.[36]

People consulted a variety of omens. Crackling of the fire represented a communication from the dead and portended another death in a short time. Indians commonly threw a small offering of food into the flames when they heard this sound.[37] Smoke from a campfire drifting and hanging across a river instead of rising promised that there would soon be meat. The following formula is self explanatory: "If you expect your partner back and he doesn't come, tie a knot in a moccasin lace and put it near the fire. It it jumps a little he'll be back quick." To learn if one would soon travel a person held the broken-off wing of a spruce hen with tendons attached over heat. The tendons were first twisted. If the exposed tendon jerked, then one would soon travel in the direction indicated by the movement.[38] Belief in the revelatory power of dreams was common and a body of lore existed for interpreting common dreams. To dream of eating with a deceased person indicated that the dreamer would die the next autumn. A dream of joking about or with a deceased acquaintance showed that a hunt undertaken on the following morning would be successful. Erotic dreams portended the killing of female animals. To dream of arriving swans meant snow; a flock of approaching ducks in a dream spelled rain within a few days. A sick person sometimes dreamed of the individual who had sorcerized him.

A few common weather omens follow:

> Rainbow: The end of rain.
> Ringed moon: Rain or snow in two days time.
> Ringed winter sun: North wind soon with snow.
> Ringed summer sun: Rain in two days.
> Red sunrise: Rain at night.
> Red sunset: Bad weather in about three days.
> Red northern sky at sunset: Warm wind and mild weather.
> Red southern sky at sunset: North wind coming.

[35] The informant reported hearing that Tlingit (?) sorcerers of the Teslin and Nisutlin rivers took an animal bladder, filled it with air, and then inscribed it with the image of a man. By piercing this image with pins "all over" the victim could be brought to illness and death (O).

[36] For the description and interpretation of a witch-fear epidemic that gripped the post-contact Kaska, see Honigmann, *Witch-Fear in Post-Contact Kaska Society* (1947).

[37] "When the fire crackles, spirits are hungry and calling for food. Then food must be put into the fire." (Jones, *Study of the Thlingets of Alaska* [1914], 235. See also Swanton, *Social Condition, Beliefs and Linguistic Relationship of the Tlingit Indians* [1908], 461.) Kaska Indians vouched for similar beliefs among the Tahltan.

[38] For an oracle operated with a piece of line and witnessed in contemporary Kaska society see Honigmann, *Kaska String Oracle* (1947).

Dease River Kaska. Many of the animal avoidances common among the Upper Liard people were shared by the Dease River Indians. Danger came from the mink and otter, while the killing of a toad always produced illness. People fed moose, caribou, and beaver flesh to dogs, and informants did not admit to having been careful in disposing of moose hairs. Women ate any part of an animal that a man used for food. Dream animals, from whom power had been obtained, were avoided for food but whether completely or only in part we did not learn. Illness followed violation of such taboos. Young men and women drank lightly of water, apparently in order to maintain their strength.[39] No restrictions on youths' drinking grease were admitted. A man avoided coitus with his wife for one night before going to hunt.

Shamans made hunting magic by singing magical animal songs accompanied by other men. Singing also operated in curing ceremonies. Any person with some power, even a youth, might perform healing magic. Should the disease not be relieved, increasingly more powerful (reputed?) shamans would be solicited. Successful cures enhanced a practitioner's reputation. In addition to confession, techniques of doctoring included blowing into the person to restore the latter's soul when it was believed to have been stolen through sorcery. A shaman also sucked intrusive disease from the body, revealing stones or very little animals that had caused the ailment. Sometimes a practitioner blew his breath into a vessel containing water for the sick man to drink.

Sorcery involved the capture of another person's wind. This produced illness. Any man with sufficient power could succeed with malevolent magic, or else the services of a stronger shaman guaranteed successful completion of the deed. Only evilly disposed men accepted such employment, indicating that in-group sorcery met with disapproval. The man who produced illness could also cure it and sometimes offered to do so in exchange for a payment of skins. Suspected black magicians inspired fear and respect. No physical sanctions appear to have been directed against their activities.

Scapulimancy was practiced. The bull-roarer possessed magical power and a man swung it for magical assistance, to chip stone successfully and also to bring about milder weather.

Tselona. Certain animals aroused great fear and were never trapped. These included the flying squirrel, toad, mink, and otter.[40] To kill one of these creatures promised that one's children would sicken and die. The wolf and wolverine were also avoided for fur

---

[39] Before marriage a Tlingit boy's uncle told him: "Do not drink too much water or it will make you lazy." Swanton, *Social Condition, Beliefs and Linguistic Relationship of the Tlingit Indians* (1908), 428. See also above, p. 107.

[40] For the Bear Lake Sekani attitudes of respect have been reported regarding the wolf, toad, salamander, and otter. "The Indians around us had many superstitions regarding wolves; a rifle that killed a wolf would soon kill a human; or a person born at a certain time must never kill a wolf, because if he did, his nearest female relative was certain to become insane." Children were startled when shown toads. "It was quite taboo for them to touch or get near 'frogs.' Such an action meant death or illness and all sorts of horrible things." To touch salamanders "might mean that a man would lose all his worldly possessions." Otter skulls were preserved by the youngsters and would not be surrendered to the naturalists lest the "mother would be possessed by the spirits of the three departed otters and eventually become insane." Stanwell-Fletcher, *Naturalists in the Wilds of British Columbia* (1940), 131, 137, 221.

and food but they do not seem to have possessed the same dangerous potency as the mink, for example. The informant denied any general avoidance of the otter. Rather some people paid more regard to him than others. Clarification of this statement could not be secured. Perhaps a man who enjoyed otter power felt less fear for that animal. Following their introduction in numbers, dogs came to eat the meat of any animal but not the leg tendons or intestines of the moose. Avoidance of these foods preserved the dog's endurance.

A young man observed a number of food avoidances designed to develop capacities for hunting. He drank water lightly, since many animals disliked water. Avoidance of the beverage magically helped a man to obtain greater power over game. He also ate sparingly of leg tendons, moose intestines, and moose brains lest his quickness and resistance to fatigue become impaired. The successful tracking of large game depended on speed. No grease taboos were known. Except during menstruation when a woman avoided fresh meat, women ate the same foods eaten by men. Avoidances designed to develop hunting power did not apply to women. As the informant explained, "Game don't want him, that woman." Dream animals played no part in the diet, not being eaten in whole or part. Some shamans never ate porcupine or beaver and others rejected the head of moose. These observances would seem to be auxiliary to the taboo on the meat of the animal sponsor or may represent a partial contradiction of that statement. Cohabitation taboos prior to hunting were denied.

Frances Lake Kaska. Attitudes toward the otter are described by Pike.[41]

A curious superstition prevails that if you kill an otter it is capable of causing much trouble by coming to life again in your stomach. Only three winters ago a Frances Lake woman lay at death's door with this malady, but she was saved by the timely arrival of the only medicine man left in the tribe. He seems to have diagnosed the case correctly at once, and holding a sheep's horn spoon to the patient's mouth, he proceeded to repeat a long incantation suitable to the occasion. As soon as he had finished, to the great joy of all the relatives who had gathered to see the death, three little otters dropped out into the spoon. The old lady recovered rapidly, and afterwards confessed to having stolen and eaten an otter that she had found in somebody else's beaver trap during a long period of starvation in the early summer.

Hunting rites included depositing an unidentified "medicine" on a moose track, either to attract the animal back to that spot or to make him more vulnerable to the hunter's arrow. After spreading other substances around a beaver house the hunter would sit down to await the appearance of the game. Scapulimancy could not be recalled. The wearing of animal figurines cut from bone insured success in hunting.

Sucking provided the commonest means of curing but other conceptions of illness coexisted with the notion of intrusion that sucking suggests. A young man carefully

41 Pike, *Through the Subarctic Forest* (1896), 145. Field reports that "The Pellys and Little Salmons believe that very near all sickness comes from the otter and mink and if anybody kills one, they or some of their near relatives will get sick and die. If any should happen to kill an otter or mink and skin it, he generally will use some old knife and throw the knife away when he is finished. He believes by doing this he guards against getting sick as the sickness is in the knife. Also if you touch or kill a frog your limbs will lose their strength, and you will get poor. Your flesh will gradually waste away till you die." Field, *Unpublished manuscript* (1913), 6.

pointed out that in illness all the wind did not leave the body—this would have caused death. To cure, a shaman blew some of his wind into the patient's body. No recollection of confession was admitted but Field's anecdote above suggests that practice. Sorcery sometimes resulted in death, or was believed to have that power. The avoidance on making snowshoes before snow lay on the ground obtained among the Frances Lake people as it did in the upper Liard Valley.

MEDICINE AND SURGERY

It appears that, compared to the magical rites discussed above, relatively less dog-matic attitudes governed the methods of therapy to be described in this section. Some of the techniques to be discussed may even have been supported by an awareness of their empirically verifiable relationship to the desired end.

Upper Liard Kaska. Charcoal rubbed under the eyes prevented snow blindness. To cure the affliction the sore eyes were bathed in infusions of alder or tamarack bark. No help for snow blindness came from the application of spruce gum nor was bleeding ever used for this purpose. Spruce gum helped to treat blisters, while the young flowers of the fireweed boiled in water provided a drink that relieved muscular pains. An unidenti-fied white root (negata), with an odor as penetrating as horse-radish, growing in moun-tainous country cleared up head congestion resulting from colds. After grinding it and mixing it with grease, a sufferer breathed the root through each nostril in turn. Sweat baths afforded protection from colds. Both sexes took such baths regularly from about the age of ten. Men preceded women in the sweat lodge. Bathing in the sulphurous hot springs of the Cassiar possessed no therapeutic value.[42]

Dease River Kaska. People used balsam gum to staunch the flow of blood from a cut and then bound the wound with dry grass. The same substance applied to the inner corners of each eye relieved snow blindness without bandaging. Snow blindness was caused by small "white bugs" springing from the snow into the victim's eyes. Snow also harbored small black insects (ta?uctetla?) that had no injurious effects on human beings.[43] A tourniquet prevented fatal bleeding in case of a severed artery. Animal grease or brains relieved the pain of burns. Broken bones were set by shamans, the limb being stretched and tightly bound with a layer of grass wrapped around with tanned-skin line. The casing remained in place for several months or until the break healed. Snowshoe "sickness," manifested by aching in the toes and insteps, could be relieved overnight by wrapping and binding the feet with grass. To thaw frozen parts of the body people gently rubbed snow on the affected part. Also the frozen organ might be immersed in extremely cold water. Remedies for toothache were denied. Emetics are probable but their nature could not be recalled precisely. To treat colds, urine in a vessel was heated with a hot pole. The patient then crouched over the liquid, his head covered with a skin, and inhaled the fumes. Presumably human urine is indicated.

[42] For some contemporary remedies, a few of which, like the inhalation of urine fumes, probably have roots in the aboriginal period, see Honigmann, *Culture and Ethos of Kaska Society* (1949), 247.

[43] "Small black worms" were thought by the Fort Nelson Slave to cause snow blindness. Honigmann, *Ethnography and Acculturation of the Fort Nelson Slave* (1946), 132.

LIFE CYCLE

FROM BIRTH THROUGH CHILDHOOD

UPPER LIARD KASKA. A girl announced her initial pregnancy by telling her mother that she had missed one or more menstrual periods. The older woman explained that the girl would have a baby and both then preserved the secret from other people. Even a husband realized the fact only when his wife's condition became indisputably apparent and even then people avoided the subject in conversation. A gossip was reprimanded with the words, "People don't want to know." In spite of these attitudes men, excluding the prospective father, sometimes bet on the probable sex of an expected child.

Pregnancy frequently produced nausea and weakness, whose only known remedy was rest. An expectant mother also developed preferences for certain foods, like intestines and soft meat. Foods advised for pregnancy included ribs, brisket, the meat around the backbone, roast moose head, marrow, fat, rabbit, spruce hen, porcupine (but not the intestines nor the head), and beaver (all parts except the feet). Enjoined were moose blood, stomach, porcupine intestines and feet, and beaver feet. The pregnant woman also avoided chewing on bones, and in order to develop a strong child her husband ate no kidney until the expected baby had made its appearance. An older woman advised the woman with child not to lift heavy weights and to care for herself. When the girl felt life stir in her womb she reported the fact to her mother who warned that from now on sexual relations must be discontinued. To reinforce the avoidance and for the baby's safety a woman advised her daughter not to sleep facing her husband and to use her own blankets. Informants failed to recognize the custom of wearing a special skin belt in pregnancy.

An infant entered the world sheltered by a simple windbreak, which had been erected for the event about 10 or 15 feet from the family dwelling. A girl's mother prepared the birth camp because of the danger associated with delivering in the family dwelling. The aura of magical danger associated with birth (comparable, as will be seen, to attitudes connected with menstruation) also required the new mother to use personal dishes and utensils and to eat food that had been specially prepared for her by mother or sisters. The same women assisted in delivery, supporting the parturient below the arms. A woman never supported herself on a pole but informants thought the custom may have occurred in the Fort Liard area. A male shaman performed rituals in the event of a difficult delivery but remained standing a distance from the birth camp and in direct line with the woman's head. From that position he handed over water for the parturient that contained his power. An old woman cut the umbilicus with a stone knife which, because of the use that it had been put to, henceforth remained dangerous for any other purpose. To leave less than half an inch of cord projecting from the infant's body might cause the latter's death. With the woman remaining only slightly elevated, the afterbirth was allowed to deliver itself. Then, wrapped in birch bark, the placenta was cached in a tree some distance from camp, where no young man would be likely to encounter it. A rich man might follow the birth of a child with a lavish feast.

People possessed a theory to explain the reproductive process. Conception, they thought, resulted from sexual intercourse, in the act of which the spermal fluid (klaga) entered the woman's body to mix there with the fluids discharged during her orgasm. The mixture of these substances produced the baby whose soul or wind entered through reincarnation.[1] Repeated copulation developed the embryo but great frequency might produce twins. Contraceptive techniques remained scarcely suited to attain their intended end. To prevent herself from conceiving a woman might draw back an inch or so when she sensed that her partner was on the point of ejaculating. Coitus interruptus and continence were not practiced with the end of reducing pregnancies. According to one informant, if a husband and wife desisted from sexual relations the marriage would very likely break up and the man take up with another woman. One ritual designed to forestall conception involved a woman's mother filling the expelled placenta of her daughter's last pregnancy with porcupine quills and then caching it in a tree. To burn the clothing worn during delivery also helped to avoid future impregnation. A girl who suffered extremely during parturition would beg her mother to perform that rite in spite of the fact that magic of this kind sometimes led to injury or illness. Barrenness shamed a woman as well as her parents and the cause always resided in the woman. To cure the condition a shaman might give her a strip of fur representing his animal sponsor and this she wore as an outer belt. The husband of a barren woman also took a second wife without, however, quitting his barren spouse.

The Indians blamed falls and other mishaps for miscarriages but sorcery remained an always possible explanation for a spontaneous abortion that could not be linked with an accident. The aborted foetus, contained in a hollow log, was either cached in a tree or inhumed between two poles. According to an informant's suggestion, premature babies represented reincarnated souls impatient for rebirth. Generally such infants died but without being neglected or killed. A stillbirth received the same treatment as an aborted foetus. Congenital deformations had their inception when the mother turned in her sleep; hence women in pregnancy were warned to sit up before turning over. As already indicated, frequent copulation between husband and wife in the early stage of pregnancy generated twins. A woman who persisted in an extramarital liaison during pregnancy might also come to deliver twins. Whatever their origin, twins symbolized good fortune. Male twins were destined to be good hunters. No case of triplets could be recalled.

The new parents did not resume sexual relations until about three months after delivery. Magically the avoidance protected a man from parturition danger with which his wife remained affected. During the length of the taboo the woman ate apart and used special utensils. Her stay in the birth camp, however, did not last beyond five days. No purification rites attached to the new father, who sought to occupy himself

[1] See below, pp. 137, 141, 142.

as fully as possible during the period immediately following birth. Lounging during the first ten days or so after delivery might canalize a man toward that kind of life.[2]

Wiped clean with moss the newborn baby was wrapped in a plaited rabbit skin robe. After 24 hours it first received the breast. Two considerations explained the delay in feeding. Immediate nursing of a newborn baby could be fatal because its stomach was still weak. Even when the child suckled for the first time, people took care that it received only enough milk "to wet his mouth." In the second place, the colostrum did not constitute suitable food in the minds of the Indians. Hence the substance was expressed on the ground by massage, a process in which the lactating woman was aided by a companion. In contrast to the colostrum breast milk must never be allowed to touch the ground, lest no milk would flow for a subsequent baby. When it became necessary to clear swollen breasts people collected the expressed milk in a gut container, which they cached in a tree. To "teach" a young infant to nurse, the mother brushed the nipple against its lips until the sucking started, whereupon she might offer further help by lightly squeezing her breast. The Kaska believed that mother's milk originated from ingested food and liquids. Meat stock and grease could increase the supply and nursing women had fat meat and grease urged upon them. If after three days of trying a woman lacked sufficient milk to content her child, she might solicit another woman to act as wet nurse. However, a nurse's milk was less beneficent than the mother's so that a baby fed through this means did not grow rapidly. Animal brain mixed with water was sometimes used as a substitute for milk, for example, in event of a mother's illness. Unless prevented by the mother's illness or pregnancy a child nursed for about three years. Weaning at that age was advisable because it would prevent the child from drawing blood from its mother's breast. An older sibling never shared the breast with a subsequent baby. Displacement of this kind not infrequently stirred up aggression toward a younger sibling, behavior that earned reproach but never corporal punishment. To assist weaning a mother sometimes forced the child's lip into its mouth with the nipple, repeating the act until all inclination to nurse disappeared. Beginning at about the age of two a child received fat to suck. After that feeding regularly included a little ground (pre-chewed?) meat.

A baby spent all of its time with the mother. Should the latter die, any woman might be asked to look after the child until it was grown. Then the child returned to its father who paid the foster mother for her care. It is likely that a woman's sisters provided foster motherhood and wet nursing when such needs arose and from these women a widower also secured a new spouse. Naming occurred when the child began to speak (earlier according to another informant). Either the father or mother assigned a suitable name and one that rarely reflected any special proclivity or trait of

[2] It is likely that a man's activity at this time served functions analogous to those realized by the couvade, namely, that the father "counter-balanced in this way his loss of participation in the birth." (Shimkin, *Childhood and Development among the Wind River Shoshone* [1947], 21.) The Chilkat Tlingit also secluded the parturient in a special birth hut. For four days the mother ate and drank little but remained in bed for twelve days. Hunting and work were avoided by her husband. Drucker, *Cultural Element Distribution: XXVI, Northwest Coast* (1950), 205–207.

the youngster. Instead the choice of a name depended on the whim of the parents. This name was retained until adolescence. Teknonymy was not admitted.[3]

For a year and a half or two years the moss bag served for carrying the baby. In this container he could also be hung from the lower branches of a tree and rocked. Following discontinuance of the baby pack children up to four continued to wear a knee-length dress or coat, a moose-hide diaper lined with moss. Trousers for a boy followed the achievement of cleanliness training. Before verbal instruction in the use of the bush came to be given, toileting habits were inculcated with the aid of a moss-lined bark vessel. In summer a child who had been released from the moss bag slept in a cradle swing. In winter for greater protection against cold he passed the night alongside his mother. Babies received encouragement to crawl but were not allowed to stand erect too early for fear of injuring the limbs. Nobody discouraged finger sucking and the "black dirt" collecting on the surface of the baby's palm was regarded as "baby food." A mother removed a loose milk tooth by pinching it between index finger and thumb. With the tooth she then described a circle on the crown of the child's head, repeating the formula, "Rabbit tooth, rabbit tooth." The rite promoted the rapid duplication of the lost organ. The extracted tooth ended up cached in the split of a dead tree. If it were discarded on the ground future teeth would grow in at wrong places. Young children amused themselves with bull-roarers, the blades of which were often decorated with charcoal or animal blood designs; buzz toys, twirled on rawhide lines, and simple swings. Dolls did not constitute playthings.

Kaska parents did not neglect disciplining in the event of a child failing to take over socially approved habits. Discipline ideally attached to the like-sexed parent, although manifestly the mother exerted more authority because she was in constant interaction with the young child. If toilet training did not occur in a reasonable time, a child's hands might be lightly whipped with a willow switch. Disgust for the body wastes was also inculcated. Children of the same sex could urinate and defecate together in the bush but children of opposite sex were early prohibited this degree of intimacy. Lying brought about whipping, while truthfulness won praise for its magical association with future hunting ability. A girl who stole might be hung by the feet and whipped on her legs. Only women witnessed this punishment. A father beat his son for theft. A child of either sex who stole might have an awl point pressed against the fingers or ears. A too aggressive boy received whippings with a length of braided babiche. People felt that a boy who showed early aggressive tendencies would become cowardly when he matured. Children were dissuaded from sex play by parents pointing out how it threatened a boy's hunting prowess and could cause a girl's death. Sexual curiosity met the warning, "Your eyes are going to be blind." A masturbator's hands were whipped with a willow switch.

Sex typing received serious attention in late childhood. A youth of 12 began to accompany his father hunting and so learned to track, ambush, and butcher game and became familiar with the habits of animals. A girl continued to spend much time with her mother, who encouraged feminine pursuits. Girls were dissuaded from playing with

---

[3] Teknonymy has been reported for the Tlingit. Jones, *Study of the Thlingets of Alaska* (1914), 37.

weapons like a bow. Persistence in such behavior, she learned, might affect a brother's heart. Upon approaching puberty a boy began to seek a power dream with the active encouragement of his father. From now on he began to sleep in his own camp or perhaps in the company of older unmarried brothers. The custom probably reinforced the brother-sister avoidance and is also said to have safeguarded youths in the event of a surprise enemy raid.

Dease River Kaska. To eat fowl, rabbit, and porcupine or other soft foods in pregnancy promised to facilitate delivery. Parturition took place in a birth camp, that consisted of a circular wall of willows surrounding a fireplace. Here older women brought food from the main camp and assisted in the process of delivery. An ordinary knife served for cutting the umbilicus. Later the stump of the cord was dried, wrapped in a piece of tanned skin and sewn to the baby's hat, where it remained until the child began to walk. An infant would cry for a long time if this amulet became lost. Eventually the cord would be cached in a tree, where the skin-wrapped afterbirth had already been deposited (although it was probably not necessary that the same tree be employed). Following delivery the woman remained isolated and avoided sex relations for about three months.

Twins represented good fortune and neither of such a pair was killed. The Indians preferred boy babies to girls because the former would become hunters. Apparently female infanticide was sometimes condoned.[4]

Breast feeding lasted until about the age of three. On journeys, when a child began to cry the whole group of women might halt while it nursed. In winter during outdoor feeding fire had to be made for the nursing woman's comfort. No principles of naming were specified and teknonymy was denied.

Either parent exercised discipline. Children beyond the age of five who misbehaved or refused to heed parents' warnings were struck with the hands alone. Crawling in a young child met no discouragement. Toys included the buzz toy, bull-roarer, rawhide rattle, hoop to be pushed by a pole, and hollow moose hooves hung on a pole, which a child delighted in shaking. Dolls were not played with but string figures, a pastime said to have been derived from the Taku Indians, furnished children with a pleasant occupation.

ADOLESCENCE

Upper Liard Kaska. Coinciding with the vision quest, which in a sense marked the completion of childhood, a boy received training in hardihood and endurance.[5] In autumn he stripped and plunged into icy water. When winter came, groups of naked boys rolled in soft snow, after which some older men whipped the youths with willows. A boy never cried out in pain during such a trial but he could protect his chest with crossed arms and might escape when he reached the limit of endurance. A mild com-

[4] Among the Tlingit, infant girls were sometimes strangled. Twins being regarded as an "evil omen" were also put to death. Jones, *Study of the Thlingets of Alaska* (1914), 121.

[5] Perhaps the exercises began earlier and finished at puberty, as among the Navaho. Leighton and Kluckhohn, *Children of the People* (1947), 56–57.

petitive element entered these exercises, as a boy who withstood whipping or remained in cold water longer than the others gained the reputation of toughness. It was predicted that he would be able to withstand considerable exposure to cold in later life.[6] It is reported that boys around the time of puberty showed fear of the bush. Overcoming their timidity no doubt constituted further training in hardihood.

With adolescence a child customarily received a new name, but the circumstances attending name changing could not be ascertained clearly. According to one informant (X), a girl retained her childhood name throughout life and the boy took over his father's at a memorial potlatch dedicated to that parent. Such a pattern hardly corresponds to a name change systematically associated with puberty. Only in anger did one ever call a grown person by his name. Normally people employed relationship terms even though no blood connection could be traced. Older men commonly received the designation "grandfather" while an age-mate responded to "brother-in-law." A child took special care not to utter his mother's name.

For the girl adolescence meant the beginning of reproductive life and ushered in menstrual avoidances that would continue until menopause except, of course, during periods of pregnancy. Although any connection between the menstrual flow and hymeneal bleeding was denied, people asserted that the initiation of sexual relations brought on menarche some five months later. As Ford points out, in conjunction with considerable premarital intercourse such a belief "would only rarely be challenged by contradictory facts."[7] Girls knew from warnings they had received that sexual experience led to bleeding, and not uncommonly a girl noticing the onset of menstruation seized her blanket and shamefully ran off. The mother followed, seeking her daughter where the latter hid under a tree. The girl was asked the name of the boy who had "started" her. The theory that accidents which caused internal injuries also brought on menstrual bleeding probably served as a rationalization for the appearance of the menses in girls whose chastity had been more than casually guarded. Nobody asso-

[6] Among the Tlingit, "in the winter time, in the extreme cold weather, men and boys would go down to the beach and, naked, jump into ice-cold water" or roll in the snow. "They would then switch their nude bodies, or have someone do it for them, until the blood would all but break through the skin. . . . Youngsters were treated in this way to teach them endurance and make them brave." (Jones, *Study of the Thlingets of Alaska* [1914], 120.) To the north of the upper Liard area in the country of the Pelly River, "after the winter set in it was the custom in the morning before they made a fire to cut a hole in the ice where the water would come about to the shoulders. All the men and youths that held any claim to being strong and being able to withstand hardship jumped in the water, each being armed with small bundles of willows. When they had stayed in the water as long as able, they climbed on the ice and beat each other with willows. The man who could stay in the water the longest and also the hardest whipping with the willows and ask for more was proclaimed the strongest man in the tribe." (Field, *Unpublished manuscript* [1913], 6–7.) Among the Tanaina, along with their value on early rising it was the maternal uncle who threw the boys into cold weather if they did not rise promptly. Osgood, *Ethnography of the Tanaina*, (1937), 135, 143. Compare with Honigmann, *Culture and Ethos of Kaska Society* (1949), 190; Honigmann, *Changes in Sarsi Social Culture* (manuscript).

[7] Similar beliefs in a relationship between coitus and menstruation occur among the Lepcha, Andamanese, and Murngin. (Ford, *A Comparative Study of Human Reproduction* [1945], 9.) In the Northern Athapaskan Area the middle Yukon River "Tena," too, held that menstruation was brought on by sexual intercourse. Jetté, *On the Superstitions of the Ten'a Indians* (1911), 700.

ciated lunation and the menstrual cycle. Amenorrhea was disturbing because it led to weakness, but occasionally to miss a period promised a long life—perhaps because of the association between the cessation of menstruation in advanced age. There existed no word to designate the menstrual flow. Men never mentioned the process and women spoke euphemistically about camping "way back" and then never in the company of the opposite sex.

With menarche the girl underwent her first menstrual sequestration in an open camp located about a quarter of a mile from the dwelling. At least during this initial period, the menstrual camp was sometimes encircled by a wall of brush that obstructed the occupant's view.[8] Although only a single adolescent usually occupied the camp, sometimes a younger girl went along to keep the menstruant company. During her first seclusion a girl wore a large hooded robe of smoked skin, lacking sleeves, and wide enough to envelop the whole body, while the hem was pegged to the ground.[9] For scratching her head she employed a bone rod about five or six inches long. A swan-quill drinking tube and a special awl also constituted part of her paraphernalia. All these objects were carried on a line that passed around the girl's neck. Across the hood a mother placed another line to which she fastened small pieces of dried meat. The meat would prevent the girl from being stingy with food in womanhood. Initial seclusion lasted one month, during which time specially prepared food was carried to the menstrual camp. The menstruant, however, ate lightly and took no more than four or five swallows of water daily through the drinking tube. Also she remained industriously occupied; when other tasks were completed the girl kept her fingers busy endlessly "counting" (picking?) the needles from spruce brush on the floor of her camp. Should the parents move camp during the sequestration period, the menstruant followed a distance behind the group and in the company of her mother. Young men dared not follow in her footsteps if they valued their dream power. At the end of the month a skin cape reaching to the elbows was substituted for the great hooded cloak. The second garment provided far greater freedom for the girl's working arms. Now, too, the pubescent returned to eat and sleep in the parent's camp, but she retained her menstrual camp for one more month. Then both garments were burned. A rich man sometimes provided a feast when his daughter completed her puberty seclusion.

Each month a menstruating woman re-entered sequestration, remaining in the menstrual camp for the duration of the period. At this time she avoided raw (fresh?) meat, moose head, and moose marrow but could drink any amount of water. Also she did not now cook for her husband or children. During seclusion the woman quit wearing

[8] Jones speaks of the Tlingit pubescent sequestrated from four to twelve months "in some cramped, cooplike place." (Jones, *Study of the Thlingets of Alaska* [1914], 133.) Swanton gives the period of seclusion as about two or three months. The girl "had to undergo many observances supposed to affect her future life, as also the existence of people around her. Her look might destroy the luck of hunter, fisher, or gambler, turn objects into stone, etc." Swanton, *Social Condition, Beliefs and Linguistic Relationship of the Tlingit Indians* (1908), 428.

[9] It is probably relatively fruitless to ask if historical connection exists between this robe, widespread in northwest America, and the cloak described by Mead for the Manus girl. Mead, *Growing Up in New Guinea* (1939).

her usual long dress and donned a knee-length garment specifically designed for such a time. She also padded her breech cloth with moss to absorb the blood. In the event that in following a traveling party she came across the scene of a moose kill, blue and red paint applied across her cheeks in horizontal lines was supposed to prevent her from seeing the animal's blood. Always the menstruant carefully avoided stepping across snowshoes, bows, or arrows. If her camp traveled by water she followed in her own canoe. A man avoided the camp where his wife stayed, fearing that close contact with the menstrual blood would cause his legs to become sore and thus render him incapable of hunting or performing other work. A menstruating wife who struck her husband's trail while he was on a war party imperiled him seriously. Hence such a woman did not move around when her husband was away fighting. Sexual intercourse with a menstruant caused a man to pass blood in his urine so that he would sicken and die. Despite this belief boys seized on the easy accessibility of girls in seclusion who, in turn, did not always resist their advances. When they became ill the youths might confess such an offense.[10]

Dease River Kaska. Even before a boy reached puberty he began to participate in exercises designed to toughen him and induce resistance to cold. Stripped to the skin, boys plunged into icy water. Upon emerging they were whipped on the upper arms by fathers or grandfathers using willow switches. A boy did not cry out or flinch under this treatment, which continued until he became adult. The informant lauded the effectiveness of these induration customs, explaining that because of them hunters could sleep outdoors in winter without a robe to protect them from the cold.[11]

Upon reaching menarche the Dease River girl retired to a camp located some distance from the family dwelling. Here she was surrounded by a circular enclosure made by planting willows in the ground and enclosing an area three feet in diameter. In winter a six-foot high spruce bark conical shelter provided the menstruant with a hut. Explaining sequestration, an informant said that it prevented the death of the girl's brother. During her seclusion the girl covered herself with a sleeveless robe of fully tanned caribou skin fashioned with a hood that extended nearly a foot in front of her

[10] Among the Pelly River people, "when a girl first comes to the age of puberty she was made to go away about a quarter of a mile from the main camp and camp alone in a skin tent. She was allowed to cook nothing. Food was sent by a female from her father's camp and no male was allowed to see her or pass close where she was stopping as if he did it was supposed to bring him bad luck either by sickness or hunting. She wore a mask over her face which she wore whenever she came out of her tent. If the Indians move camp she came last and camped behind them whenever she camped. If it was winter one or two of the other females travelled with her and they put green boughs across every track that crossed their trail when the track came on a trail no matter where it went or no matter what the track was they had to shut it off before the girl could pass. . . . After this, whenever she had her monthlies, whether she was married or not, she had to camp alone for at least four days, but did not have to wear a mask or put boughs across any track she might cross in travelling." Field, *Unpublished manuscript* (1913), 8.

[11] Among the Tahltan, adult men who wished to harden themselves reportedly whipped each other's backs with willow switches. Plunging nude into snowbanks and ice water was a common exercise. (Jenness, *The Indians of Canada* [1932], 372.) "Puberty ceremonials appear to be rather strongly developed," says Teit for the Tahltan, adding that "a whipping custom was prevalent. . . ." Teit, *On Tahltan (Athabaskan) Work* (1912), 485.

face. The hood obscured any view the sky, which was partly its intended function. Below the robe she wore ordinary garb. The pubescent used water sparingly during her seclusion, drinking through a quill or willow tube whose use prevented diarrhoea. To scratch the head with fingers threatened loss of her hair; hence the scratching stick of wood or bone. Initial seclusion is said to have lasted from three months to a year. If the parents moved camp in this period the girl was escorted by her mother. Upon crossing a frozen lake the girl occasionally planted a willow stick in the snow.[12] Menstruants did not have to break a fresh trail. Informants could not recall the bull boat or canoe used along the Fort Nelson and lower Liard rivers.[13] Subsequent to menarche the girl dispensed with the ceremonial paraphernalia but passed each period in a brush camp where she stayed for three or four days. A padding of dry moss inside the breech cloth served to absorb the menstrual blood.

Ideally it was dangerous to have sex relations with a menstruating woman, nevertheless boys eluding adult watchfulness, sometimes visited the camp of a sequestrated girl and engaged her in coitus. The following remarks transcribed from a 23-year old woman refer specifically to the post-contact period but probably reveal some of the sentiments and conditions formerly associated with menstrual ceremonialism.[14] Speaking of her initial seclusion, which she passed in the house, the girl said:

I stayed in the house one month and never see my brother. Mama had to cook two bannocks and I only eat dry meat. I had to pick needles off spruce brush so I could sew good. If I get fresh meat my uncle or my daddy have to chew it for me. Not allowed to laugh for one month! Not supposed to eat wild rhubarb. They say you get gray quick. Never eat fresh berries. My aunt had tent alone but me winter time and I stay in the house. When my grandpa come back I go with my aunt. When a man come into the house I must not look at him but I talk to him. My grandma always watch. Used to be that boy did same thing like girl.

I wanted to go to dance. I sneak out when grandma went but I hear grandma come and I come back. I tell grandma I want to go but she say no. Gee, I get mad. Mama and daddy they all go. Grandma always watch, just like policeman.

All the boys go in May's tent [the informant's aunt] when grandma sleep. In morning they all go. Grandma never know. That's why mama never lose one kid, we all live. My auntie [referring to another aunt, not May] lose lots of kids. My auntie never tell when she get sick. May she tell but she never do right. That's why we lose our auntie. They say that's May's fault.

When a woman sees moose or caribou she takes match box and turns it around and around [describes a circle with her hand]. First time you handle knife somebody hold your hand and make you cut. Woman does this. A man makes you chop things with ax. A woman makes you sew.

Attention may be called to the informant's statement, "Used to be that boy did same thing like girl." It is not clear if the informant intended to refer to the youth's vision quest or to his puberty ceremony. Such a ceremony is reported for other Athapaskan people.[15]

[12] This sounds reminiscent of the ritual followed by returning warriors among the Upper Liard Kaska. See above, p. 95.

[13] Honigmann, *Ethnography and Acculturation of the Fort Nelson Slave* (1946), 85, 91.

[14] The informant is Dorothy Plover. See Honigmann, *Culture and Ethos of Kaska Society* (1949), 24, 340–350.

[15] Osgood, *Ethnography of the Tanaina* (1937), 162–163.

Tselona. Because menstruation threatened a man's dream power thereby imperiling his success in hunting, women remained isolated during the period of the flow. Widow Matoit, at Fort Nelson, spoke of willow-bark enclosures surrounding the menstruant that prevented her from seeing out of the camp. A woman also stuffed feathers in her ears in order not to hear the hunters returning to camp. A Lower Post informant described all fresh meat and fish as being taboo to the menstruant. The avoidance referred to the dislike which the animals felt for the menstrual blood.

SEX

Upper Liard Kaska. Despite a certain ambivalence regarding sexual processes the Indians keenly appreciated the excitement of sexual situations. They also sought to explain the nature of sexual attraction by referring to the anecdote of an old man who could not understand why the sexes desired physical contact with each other and asked the people for their opinion. People felt that sexual desire ultimately stemmed from a desire for offspring. Informants localized sexual tension in the testes, the organs responsible for erection and sexual desire. The testes also influenced human thought processes, provoking imagery of "women" in the man. These ideas in turn helped to create physiological readiness for copulation. Internally women possessed the equivalent of testes. A certain measure of sexual intercourse was desirable because of the pleasure it aroused. Coitus was even beneficial if pursued in moderation. However, a boy might be weakened for life should he enter sexual relations before 18 or 19 years of age. Masturbation led to insanity or blindness and in a child was punished by whipping the hands with a willow switch. Coitus could also diminish a man's dream power; hence a shaman who wanted to maximate his strength abstained from sexual relations and dreamed of participating in heterosexual intercourse. The women in his dreams represented his animal sponsors. Men possessed stronger drives for coitus than women and some men were more highly sexed than others.

An informant believed that people engaged in sex acts more frequently in summer than in winter.[16] In summer unmarried couples copulated in daylight or at night, but always in the privacy of the bush. A husband and wife waited until after nightfall and the sex act between them always occurred in the dwelling. Sometimes a man reached orgasm two or three times in a night but that was uncommon and a mark of youth. When he was 18 the average man reached orgasm about seven times a week. An estimated six out of ten men 20 years old could copulate twice a night and three out of ten, three times a night but probably not every night. By the age of 30 marital relations were reduced to about once a week on the average and at 40 to about once every two weeks.

While sexual relations of a casual sort were common enough before marriage, the culture of the Kaska Indians included a notion of love and lifelong devotion. "If a man loved his wife very much he would not marry again when she dies. He'll remain single all his life." Similar sentiments motivated a man on journeys to carry mementoes of

[16] In 1944–45 we estimated a higher frequency of summer conception. Honigmann, *Culture and Ethos of Kaska Society* (1949), 37, 232.

his sweetheart, like a piece of her hair. Girls might extract a promise of faithfulness in return for a keepsake. No case of suicide for unrequited love could be recalled. The ideal girl was one who cared for her hair; possessed bright, good looking eyes; showed strong or "big" legs, and a wide chest. Physical beauty did not suffice to recommend a girl for marriage. As a matter of fact boys were advised to choose a plain girl, who would not attract other men and hence whose faithfulness could be depended on. An ideal bride was a girl thoroughly imbued with the virtue of generosity, who treated people well, offered food to guests no matter how numerous they might be, even if it meant using the last piece of meat in camp. Such a woman attracted visitors to a camp, always a gratifying experience for a host. This description of ideal womanly virtues suggests how strongly a woman dominated the food that a man brought home. Clearly her rights were final and by no means did such rights represent mere lip service on the part of the man.

Conventions pertaining to modesty were very important. It was indecent for a child beyond the age of three to expose the genitals. No woman revealed to a man any part of her body between the breasts and ankles but apparently the breasts were not as strongly concealed as other areas—at least not in a nursing woman. Few men ever saw their wives completely naked. Women also refrained from undressing before other women. A man took care not to expose his penis to a woman, but nudity before male companions produced little or no embarrassment. Modesty demanded that a woman sit with her legs folded under her, parallel to one another, the dress drawn over the knees. In a mixed group a man sat with his legs crossed. A youth was once severely reprimanded for facing parents-in-law with his legs spread apart. Blushing followed when people called immodesty to one's attention. This indicated shame. Strict rules governed the vocalization of sexual concepts. Boys were advised not to use the terms for the sexual organs until they were "half-old" and never to refer to sexual topics in the presence of siblings. The emphasis on modesty correlated with an interest in pornography and verbal obscenity. Pornography included pictorial and sculptural representations of the genitals. One man reportedly carved phalluses two or three feet long from wood and planted them on ridges at the heads of trails, where they would shock people who unexpectedly encountered them.[17] In anger a man who had lost his wife to a rival might caricature the latter in charcoal on a tree, showing him naked and holding his penis. Children were punished for making obscene drawings. Both sexes expressed verbal obscenity, common expressions including: "Somebody has had intercourse with you!" "You just know how to copulate!" "You have no father!" A woman angered another woman by crying, "You vagina!" Or she might tell her husband, "You copulate with me every night!" For the proper flavor vernacular terms must be substituted for the printed version of these expletives!

Patterned gestures served to communicate sexual interest between sexes. If a girl wanted to reciprocate such an advance she merely laughed. In verbally soliciting coitus

[17] One informant, who had been a member of boat crews freighting on Dease River, several times shaped sticks of driftwood into huge phalluses, leaving them to bob in the current to shock female passengers on other vessels.

a man employed euphemisms and circumlocutions. "I'm going to stay with you," made his intention quite clear as did, "I want you, sister-in-law." Only a girl who enjoyed no respect in her community solicited coitus. Lovers sometimes agreed to meet in specific places. As is so common in North America, a girl walking alone away from camp always provided a fair target for sexual advances provided she did not come under an incest rule. At night a boy might creep close to a camp containing an unmarried girl. He slipped his hand under the sleeping robes striving to reach her body and genitals. If she pressed his hand the boy slipped under the blanket. On the other hand, if she screamed out he might be caught and punished. Another way of winning a girl's favors was to sing love songs from a short distance beyond the camp. Girls often wept a little when they heard the rather mournful refrains of these tunes. An example of a love song in free translation follows:

asla patiaaa	My sweetheart is lovely
la patiiaaa naʔu̧ naʔu̧	Sweetheart, I am lonely today.

To which a girl might answer:

duʔela itcitla	How sad, little brother.

Most girls hung back shyly from physical intimacy; hence even a willing partner had first to be caught and "forced" into submission. When such a girl struggled in the arms of her lover the boy promised "I'm not going to leave you alone. I'm going to fight you." This was calculated to make her surrender, perhaps by stressing how little resistance would avail. The struggle in which a girl's ambivalence toward sex relations was overcome did not constitute rape in the eyes of the youths. Sometimes it happened that a girl truly resisted a boy's advances. "When a girl does not want a man she hits the man." To subdue such a girl the rapist punched her leg about half-way above the knee thereby relaxing the thighs sufficiently to force them apart. Rape occurred rarely and was the resort of men who could not obtain the favors of a girl in any way. Strong women also could throw down a man, undress him, and by sitting astride his thighs force intromission. Such behavior was described as rather pleasant for the victim.

Ideally a girl of 17 engaged in sexual relations with a boy of her choice as a prelude to marriage. Any tendency toward promiscuity was immediately stopped and promiscuous girls were beaten. Boys also received advice to limit their attentions to one girl. One gains the impression that corrective measures seldom applied to youths who manifested varietistic tendencies. A boy usually entered upon his sexual career without tutelage from any more experienced person. Sometimes a girl, knowing that an inexperienced boy desired coitus, kept after him until he submitted to her advances. The existence of the hymen remained unknown, the pain of first intercourse being associated with the girl's inexperience. Although most girls commenced sex relations at about 17, a girl rarely bore a child until about two years later. In the words of the informant, "Many people could get away with it for two years."

As already indicated males took the initiative in sex relations. Sometimes the couple preceded the sex act by lying together, the man talking to his partner, caressing her hair, and running his hand across her shoulders and body. Lovers did not kiss. Various terms of endearment were current, a youth saying, for example, "You're my grub," to indicate his affection. Sibling terms of opposite sex commonly expressed the idea of "sweetheart" or "lover" but lovers also addressed each other as "brother-in-law" and "sister-in-law." Tumescence might be aided through manual contacts undertaken by a boy but a girl never touched a man's sexual organs. Oral contacts with the female genitals rarely took place, people regarding the woman's sexual parts as poisonous. A man usually removed trousers but not breech cloth or moccasins in sexual situations. The woman assumed a supine position on her back while the man lay over her, supporting part of his weight on the forearms. For a woman to lay astride a man threatened his hunting ability. Women disliked and never permitted coitus á tergo. On the average five minutes elapsed between intromission and ejaculation. The contraceptive practice of a woman partially withdrawing at the moment of her partner's orgasm discomforted the man and interfered with the strength of his climax. Women frequently bit during copulation, particularly at the moment of orgasm. Should a man finish before a woman, she might seize him from behind to force him to remain in her until she reached detumescence. Men did not generally wait for the partner to finish first but proceeded with coition at a pace to suit themselves. No hygienic measures followed the sex act. In return for her favors a man gave gifts to a partner other than a wife, presents that were returned by a companion who desired to show her affection. When they were presented to a married man such gifts often caused great embarrassment as the wife questioned their origin.

Many women in refusing sex relations apparently rationalized their aversion saying that they wanted to hunt game successfully. Sometimes a married woman tried to reduce the frequency of coitus in order to avoid pregnancy and childbirth, one gathers without much cooperation from the husband. The incidence of impotence in the male could not be ascertained: "a man is ashamed to tell that."

One man denied wife exchange but ascribed the pattern to the Tahltan, among whom a woman was sometimes loaned to a brother or a friend. We are inclined to disbelieve our informant in view of the fact that the contemporary Kaska are not adverse to wife exchange.[18] The same informant did admit that sometimes an old man who required a young man's assistance in hunting might invite a real or classificatory brother to live with him, allowing the young man sexual access to his wife. The relationship, however, was generally phrased as marriage.[19] Under conditions of polygyny a husband slept with a different sexual partner about once every two nights. "The youngest wife always wants to get more and the man has to try to give her plenty." Nevertheless a polygynous husband remained careful not to neglect the older woman. When fraternal polyandry was practiced, the auxiliary husband enjoyed access to a wife only during the absence of the first husband. A woman reported her husband's brother's attentions to the senior husband when the latter returned.

In one reported case of homosexuality a man, disinclined to heterosexual relations,

18 Honigmann, *Culture and Ethos of Kaska Society* (1949), 163–164.
19 For additional information concerning fraternal polyandry, see below, pp. 133, 135.

sought young men as sexual partners, with whom he secured orgasm by apposing the glans of the penes. In the morning the homosexual rewarded his lovers with gifts, treating them "just as good as women." Although dressing as a man, the homosexual removed his clothing during sexual relations. Once he tried to secure anal intromission with a sleeping man who had been eating fat and who defecated against his would-be seducer. Female homosexuals simulated copulation by "getting on top of each other." Such women were often transvestites, but no male transvestites could be recalled. Sometimes if a couple had too many female children and desired a son to hunt for them in later years, they selected a daughter to be "like a man."[20] When she was about five year's old the parents tied the dried ovaries of a bear to her inner belt. She wore this amulet for the rest of her life in order to avoid conception. The girl was raised as a boy. She dressed in masculine attire and performed male allocated tasks, often developing great strength and usually becoming an outstanding hunter. She screamed and broke the bow and arrows of any boy who made sexual advances to her. "She knows that if he gets her then her luck with game will be broken." Apparently such a girl entered homosexual relationships.

Behavior corresponding to sexual sadism, masochism, and exhibitionism could not be recalled. Mentally ill women and old men sometimes publicly revealed their genitals. Voyeurs received a scolding but were not physically punished. Animal contacts occurred only rarely. Necrophilia appears to have been totally incompatible with the prevailing attitudes toward the dead, an interpretation concurred in by our informant.[21]

Dease River Kaska. Love songs constituted a means of winning girls' favors and also possessed magical properties designed to create favorable attitudes toward the wooer. In coitus the woman lay on her back. Cunnilinctus was denied but a rare woman performed fellatio as a preliminary to intercourse. Berdaches were unknown but the informant agreed that both male and female homosexuality sometimes occurred. Homosexual men engaged in sodomy, oral contacts being carefully avoided. Two women achieved orgasm through clitoral friction. An upper Liard River informant reported a case in which some Dease River youths who had killed a cow moose copulated with the animal, an act blamed for the subsequent depopulation of the Dease basin.

MARRIAGE

Upper Liard Kaska. Ideally marriages were for permanency and a man who tried to leave his wife would be urged by the community to reconsider his decision. Despite these ideal attitudes divorce was common.

A man sought a wife "to dry meat for him," sew clothing, cook his meals, and perform the many other services culturally allocated to women. Marriage brought a youth a certain increment in prestige, marking as it did the transition to adulthood. It promised

---

[20] In Montenegro and other Balkan countries it was not uncommon for a girl to swear virginity and occupy the role of a son in a family without boys. Durham, *Some Tribal Origins, Laws, and Customs of the Balkans* (1928), 211.

[21] See below, p. 137. Thus do cultures limit the scope of deviation. See Mead, *Male and Female* (1949), 147.

children, and when he realized this promise another reward accrued to the husband. Not only did marriage provide a dependable source of sexual gratification but a young man secured his reputation in the community when he no longer had to "bother" girls or other men's wives in order to obtain such satisfaction. On the other side, women welcomed marriage for its economic rewards, like an abundance of food and skins for clothing, as well as for sexual opportunities and the children that might follow.

Boys married around the age of 18; that is, when they were old enough to meet the primary qualification of a husband, namely, to be able to earn a living by hunting. Girls married when about 16 years old or shortly after menarche. An older brother ideally took a bride before his junior but an elder sibling's prerogatives were not so great that parents interfered with a younger brother's marriage plans. While great disparity between the ages of spouses sometimes occurred, it was never happily regarded. Public opinion maintained that because an old man could not make his living as easily as a younger man he could not expect to marry a young wife. The union of a mature woman and a young man received more tolerance but even then "much talk" might follow. Men incapable of making a living by hunting, or those who enjoyed the reputation for stinginess (they "try to hold on to meat and not share it; they hunt alone") sometimes never married. Also there were men who resembled the women previously described and showed little interest in women or sex. They too refrained from marrying.

Blood relatives as close as parallel cousins of the second and third generation came under the incest taboos as did members of the same matrilineal moiety. Marriage to a maternal cross cousin was preferred. Other unions were frequently concluded by sister exchange. Marriage outside of the tribe (macrocosmic group) was not too well regarded. People from abroad, it was felt, could rarely be trusted. Also intertribal marriage might lead to trouble in cases where the members of such a group learned about some mistreatment suffered by one of the outmarrying persons. Marriage to captive women certainly had a place, single men regarding the war party as an opportunity to secure a wife. If the defeated group happened to recognize moiety distinctions a warrior took only a woman of the opposite exogamous division. The initial treatment of captive wives was apt to be harsh but warmer relations usually followed the birth of children. Married men never secured additional spouses through war. Women objected strenuously to sharing a man with anyone but a closely related co-wife.[22] What appears to have been literal bride purchase obtained in unusual circumstances, as when a rich man negotiated for the daughter of a poor family. In return he paid clothing, other valuables, and presumably continued to supply food to his parents-in-law. Such a marriage was not highly esteemed.

Generally a period of bride service, lasting as long as two years, preceded marriage. During this interval a young man supplied meat, skins, and wood for the family of his intended bride, sometimes without directly announcing his intentions to the parents. His plans were probably well understood and he usually enjoyed sexual relations with the girl of his choice. Ideally the period of bride service allowed a youth to demonstrate

[22] But among the Sarsi a captive woman was said to have made an excellent co-wife. Honigmann, *Changes in Sarsi Social Culture* (manuscript).

his capacity as a provider and worker. With the consent of the girl assured, a boy communicated his plans to his parents. Following their approval his mother visited the girl's mother and the two families arranged a feast at which they exchanged gifts amidst much joking and expressions of good feeling.[23] The two fathers addressed each other "brother-in-law" while the mothers said "sister-in-law." Following the celebration the couple still refrained from openly sleeping together for another four or five days, perhaps out of shyness.

A variant pattern of marriage occurred when a young girl, who had begun to menstruate, named the boy who had "started" her. The mother then informed the youth's mother whereupon it was up to the latter to accept the girl as a daughter-in-law. Should the seducer have been a poor hunter, the girl's family might claim one of his more adept brothers for a son-in-law. Elopements when a girl's parents rejected a suitor took place with the young couple running off, sometimes to another country. With time the parents could usually be won over, perhaps after the advent of a grandchild. Two atypical forms of marriage widely distributed in the northern Athapaskan area remains to be mentioned, namely "wrestling for wives" and childhood betrothal. The first ensued when a strong, unmarried man visited a camp in which he was a stranger. Shaking hands he suggested to the husband that they wrestle for possession of the latter's wife. A man thus approached could decline the challenge. On the other hand his gambling impulse might be aroused. If defeated he saw his wife go with the opponent. Sometimes the angry loser directed sorcery against the successful challenger, aiming to destroy the latter's hunting power. Bystanders broke up a wrestling match that showed signs of developing into "bad trouble" like murder. Occasionally parents contracted engagements between children, exchanging gifts of children's clothing. A girl still in infancy might be betrothed to a boy two or three years old. If both children survived but later developed a distaste for each other, their fathers might press them to marry. In cases of extreme recalcitrance a sister or brother was substituted for one of the partners.

Matrilocal residence followed marriage. After two or three children had been born a husband usually asked his father-in-law for permission to camp by himself. A "good" father-in-law agreed, adding some such advice as, "Be careful; don't go up in the mountain in winter" (because of the many slippery and dangerous places where a hunter could meet injury). Monogamous families were most common. Few men could afford to support as many as two wives and the children they produced.[24] Polygyny

[23] "Among the Pellys and Little Salmons, the custom was that if a man wanted a wife he made her a present of some kind. If he was satisfactory as a son-in-law to the girl's parents the present was kept, if not, it was returned. If the present was kept he had to keep on giving game and skins to the girl and her parents. (Field, *Unpublished manuscript* [1913], 9.) Among the Tlingit, when an engagement between a boy and girl had been concluded, the boy's mother gave gifts to the girl's family which were distributed by the husband among his "daughter's people." Then he gave a dowry to the suitor's friends. Swanton, *Social Condition, Beliefs and Linguistic Relationship of the Tlingit Indians* (1908), 428.

[24] Informants reported that Taku men often had four or five wives. In the Pelly River area "there is no limit to the number of wives so long as you can support them, but of late years . . . there are very few with more than one wife." (Field, *Unpublished manuscript* [1913], 9.) Among the Tlingit polygyny was widely practiced. Jones, *Study of the Thlingets of Alaska* (1914), 120.

was sororal in type. Even a widower had trouble securing permission to marry a woman other than his deceased's wife's sister, parents-in-law showing particular possessiveness about a man renowned as a hunter. To bring an unrelated woman into the family constituted a signal for the first wife to quit her husband and go home. No bride service attended marriage to a subsequent wife. Polyandry appears to have been restricted to old men who were unable to hunt sufficiently to support their families.[25] As the informant expressed it, "Sometimes a man cannot feed all the children of his wife. He then asks a brother to stay with him and trap with him and help him feed his family." The plan required the consent of the woman, who generally approved. "When the husband goes away and comes back his wife will tell him that his brother stayed with her. Then the husband knows he has help." The younger man continued to look after the widow when his co-husband died. Children of a polyandrous household belonged to the biological father, but it is not clear how the assignment was determined. Polyandrous marriages were frequently fraught with jealousy, but physical violence between the brothers never took place. As already pointed out, a junior husband never copulated with the woman while the senior husband was home. Some women remained unamenable to entering a polyandrous relationship. The husband's brother then "bothered' her until she consented. Very rarely a man invited some man other than a sibling to become a co-husband.

While women worked hard in marriage they did not perform a role inferior to the man's. A wife had much to say about running her home. The husband faced the responsibility of supplying her with meat and skins. She controlled food and dispensed hospitality, from which her husband in turn gained prestige. In folk tales we encounter the motif of a wife hoarding food while the husband starves. Does this mean that a man felt insecure in the face of his wife's household dominance?[26] The following story illustrates such a plot and perhaps reveals something of the relationship between brother, married sister, and sister's husband.

There was an old woman and her husband. The husband was starving, when one day his wife's brother came along. This man knew that his sister had bear meat. He met his brother-in-law and said, "Brother-in-law, you have game. We saw the head back there." The old man said he knew nothing about it. The woman hearing them became afraid and didn't know what to do. She cooked some bear meat in a spruce-root kettle but her brother refused to eat it. At night the latter said, "I thought you treat my brother-in-law right. You don't. I can't eat that meat. I'm going home." This man later spoke to his younger brother and said, "I don't think our sister will live much longer. I feel it. If anything happens to our sister don't think anything about it till we see our brother-in-law." They went away for seven days and upon their return discovered that the old woman had been killed. Her husband

---

[25] Polyandry, levirate, and sororate are reported for the Tlingit and Chilkat. Drucker, *Culture Element Distributions: XXV, Northwest Coast* (1950), 215–216.

[26] See also the story titled "The Blind Old Man" in Honigmann, *Culture and Ethos of Kaska Society* (1949), 327–328. We hear that "the mountain women have very little to say in the management of affairs. The Pelly and Little Salmons are about even with the men in some cases the women being the boss entirely. In regards to camp work it depends entirely on what season of the year it is, if in fur season it keeps the men busy hunting and trapping and the women do practically all of the camp work. In the summer months they help each other. Field, *Unpublished manuscript* (1913), 16.

was gone. The children too had been killed. Her husband was gone. The older brother said, "Don't think anything about it till we see our brother-in-law and see how he treats us."

The widower found a beaver den and set a net. He got two beaver. From one he removed the fat and he ate the other. Then his brothers-in-law came along. The husband began to weep. He asked them, "Have you seen what I have done?" He added, "You can kill me if you want to." The older brother said, "I'll do nothing till you eat." The husband picked up a piece of fat and cooked it while holding it in his hand. This gesture demonstrated his courage. He knew he was in danger of being killed but was warding off danger with a show of fearlessness and resistance to pain. He offered some meat to the brothers. When they had eaten the elder said, "Ill let you go because your hand is half-cooked now. I'm not going to bother you. I still have a younger sister at home."

Two observations may be offered concerning this anecdote, first, the responsibility assumed by a brother for his sister's moral conduct in relation to her husband stands out. Second, the use of deliberately induced pain to demonstrate courage should be noted. Both of these patterns are strongly and formally developed in the Plains Culture Area. Not only is the husband in the tale forgiven for killing the stingy woman but he is promised one of her sisters as a new wife.

Divorce aroused neither sharp criticism or shame, although the deserted spouse might display more or less resentment. Sometimes a man used sorcery to kill the woman who had quit him or to cause her children by the subsequent husband to die. Reasons for divorce included the desire of one marriage partner for another man or woman (perhaps a man who could provide a richer living than the current husband), cruelty, and adultery. Women did not always permanently quit husbands who treated them badly. Sometimes a wife merely ran off to spend a night in the bush. In case of divorce older children remained with the husband while infants went with the mother. When he became grown-up, a son might return to his father. Both patterns suggest the recency and superficial imposition of matrilineal descent in the culture.

Economic benefits accrued to a widow and her children under the levirate. However, unless the real or classificatory brother were single or the husband of the widow's sister he could not live intimately with the woman but merely supported her and her children in his camp.[27] Under such circumstances a widow would remarry following a two year period of mourning and upon receiving the consent of her brother-in-law. To choose a new husband closely following a man's death, aroused the jealousy of the deceased husband's ghost. As already noted, when a wife died her father frequently invited the bereaved husband to choose a sister-in-law as his spouse and might even insist that the latter be taken.[28]

Dease River Kaska. Boys married when they could provide sufficient meat and skins for a family, a girl when she was capable of performing household duties and understood the responsibilities of married life, particularly its ideal of faithfulness. Incest rules extended to include one's moiety. Each sex normally secured the parents' consent

---

[27] Here lies a powerful incentive for two brothers to marry a pair of sisters. Such a marriage readily accomodates the levirate. It would be desirable to know if there is a significant correlation between these two traits when a large series of cultures are compared.

[28] Levirate and sororate have both been reported for the Tlingit. Among these coastal people a nephew sometimes inherited the widow or the niece of a deceased woman might marry the widower. Jones, *Study of the Thlingets of Alaska* (1914), 129.

to a proposed match. Where such permission was withheld, elopement might follow. The eloping couple then lived alone or, more often, joined another camp. Sometimes angry parents pursued the young people and beat the youth if they caught him. In the normal course of events a young man undertook bride service for a year in the home of his father-in-law. During this period he contrived to have secret sexual relations with his intended spouse. A wealthy father-in-law terminated bride service with a feast, after which the couple were regarded as man and wife. Occasionally fathers arranged engagements between children. Contracted without gift exchange, these agreements were not absolutely binding on the young people and could be abrogated for sufficient cause. Only single men utilized the war party to secure a wife. Residence after marriage was matrilocal.

Sororal polygyny remained limited to wealthy men. Never did a man live with more than two women, plural wives "always got along with each other." The idea of an unrelated woman as co-wife was strongly resented and the presence of such a woman in camp would provoke endless quarreling.[29] Fraternal polyandry existed and is illustrated in a tale reported by Teit, titled "The Deceitful Wife."[30] A woman, married to two brothers, happened to be raped by a war party that prepared to attack her people. The ordeal weakened the woman but the enemy offered her ptarmigan. In return she promised to conceal what had happened. The mother-in-law, however, became suspicious and spoke to her sons. As a result the two husbands sensed danger and proposed to the wife that they all three enjoy a last good meal together. They thereupon killed the woman and fled. An upper Liard River informant reported knowledge of a Dease River Indian who had shared his wife with nine brothers. The ten men alternated in cohabiting with the woman and no trouble ever occurred between them. However, the brothers became extremely jealous when they saw a stranger talk to their wife and reported the incident to the senior husband who warned off the intruder.

Divorce sometimes followed adultery and occasionally a man quit a barren wife. Upon her husband's death a widow became the responsibility of her brother-in-law.

Tselona. People favored marriage between cross cousins. "Its good for them," the informant explained. The levirate and sororate both obtained.

OLD AGE AND DEATH

Upper Liard Kaska. Many Indians did not live to see old age. Others found their declining years filled with waning prestige and dissatisfaction. With menopause cul-

---

[29] Allard says: "Polygamy existed among them when they were all pagans. One man would take as many wives as conditions would allow. For instance, if he were a good hunter he would take more than one wife. When I visited the Kaska for the first time in 1925, I found no polygamy among them ... they had never seen a Catholic priest in their country, but being in their native state more moral than the other races of Indians, the influence of their brethern, the Si kan ni, led them easily to abandon polygamy." (Allard, *Notes on the Kaska and Upper Liard Indians* [1928], 25.) We feel incined to ascribe the loss of polygyny much more to the influence of the white men who invaded the Dease River valley after 1872. Cf. Honigmann, *Culture and Ethos of Kaska Society* (1949), 44–45.

[30] Teit, *Kaska Tales* (1917), 461–462.

turally recognized as the end of the child-bearing period a woman knew that old age was at hand. The thought saddened her. Sometimes such a woman began to act youthful and sought to attract a young lover or husband. Very old people, when they became unable to walk, were sometimes abandoned alongside the fire with a large pile of wood. This usually happened in autumn. Then when the snow had crusted the people returned to bury the bodies that they found awaiting them. Often, however, the aged, like the blind and lame, were carried or drawn upon a toboggan.

The Kaska recognized several interrelated causes of death. People who exerted themselves, killed themselves, or suffered accidents like drowning, died of so-called natural causes. However, it was not improbable that sorcery had made them vulnerable to injuries or depression. Many deaths followed from malevolent magic as well as from the violation of avoidances like an incest rule. Finally, as we will see, the ghosts could take life. Illness, as already stated, represented the temporary alienation of the soul or wind (tajuc) from the body. Death on the other hand represented a permanent rupture between these entities. The wind, described as "just like" the photograph of a person, did not die but continued to exist in an afterworld from which it might return to be reincarnated. In addition death represented the loss of the shadow (mezi). This did not leave the earth but remained around the scene of death or at a burial place. At night the shadow sometimes manifested itself as a ghost (tsune).

There were several afterworlds about which informants remained vague. Up in the sky lay the realm reserved for the souls of the good where people spoke a language different from that employed on earth. Here the winds spent the time in play and eating but they did not hunt. To reach the sky the soul followed a trail leading across a clear country where its tears created a great river that presently blocked further progress. Only by restraining its weeping could the soul lower the waters and thus continue the journey until it came to a narrow passage guarded by two great swans. When they saw the deceased they cried out, "Person coming!" "Then God [Tenatiia] takes them in," the informant added.[31] The description of the afterworld reserved for the evil sounds very much as if it had been influenced by Christian teaching. No other explanation accounts as well for the presence of animals that are not indigenous to the Cassiar. In this realm the souls of the wicked suffered constantly. Snakes crawled around the individual; bad animals troubled, fought, and frightened him. "Elephants picked him up on their tusks and sharks with their teeth scraped the skin from his body. In all this torture the soul was never killed [i.e., the torture never terminated?]."

[31] The Tlingit realm of the dead is described as "an entirely happy region, elevated above the plane of this world." On the other hand we read that there were three such regions, one lower than the other. Below the world still another afterworld existed for the drowned. Bad people went to "Raven's home." (Swanton, *Social Condition, Beliefs and Linguistic Relationship of the Tlingit Indians* [1908], 466.) Jones says that the soul or "shadow" quit the body at death to go "if the person dies a natural death and was not a slave ... to the happy region of the spirits which is thought of as being in some remote part of the earth; if he die in war, then it goes to dwell in the sky; if drowned, then it descends to a region below the plane of the earth, provided the body is recovered, but if not recovered it is captured by Goosh-tă-kă' (Land-otter Man) and taken back into the woods." Jones, *Study of the Thlingets of Alaska* (1914), 234–235.

Indians who drowned entered neither of these afterworlds but turned into fish.[32] People who committed suicide also ended up in a distinctive realm but no informant could describe this beyond the fact that it was "a black place" and an abode of the "devil." Suicide, usually by hanging, might follow a period of extreme anger or a bitter quarrel.

The wind enjoyed only a single reincarnation. Informants did not agree as to whether the souls of the good or evil returned to life. One man said that by means of reincarnation the wind of a wicked person received "another chance."[33] Following rebirth, death became final so that the man who did evil during his second life not only went to the devil but remained there for eternity. Testimony of reincarnation came through a child saying, "I know this country. I been here before." According to one man, "My boy [aged ten] says this. 'First time I'm dead. Now I'm born again. I come back this country. I try again!'" (X).[34]

As already brought out, the shadow remained, for a time at least, around the death camp or the body's burial place. In apparitions the ghost's color seemed black. Apparently a ghost largely devoted itself to punishing relatives who had treated the deceased meanly during life. Sometimes ghosts sought "partners," particularly girls. They called prospective mates by name and to hear one's name called in ghostly fashion portended death. The younger siblings of a deceased child exhibited particular vulnerability to such solicitations. Sometimes ghosts threw stones, trying to hit a living person. When they succeeded the victim would die. Although regarded as an omen of impending death, it is not clear whether ghosts spoke through the cracking fire.[35]

All the "relatives" (i.e., members of the same moiety) in the vicinity visited the bedside of a dying man, wept with him, and shook his hand. They felt that in all liklihood they would never see him again. The company remained assembled until death occurred. Without receiving any change of raiment the body was then wrapped in a robe with the hands always open. For the fists to be clenched promised death to the next of kin. However, the eyes were closed; "otherwise he looks to see if another relative

---

[32] "It is believed that the spirit of the drowned is caught by the land-otter and dragged into his hole, and there it is turned into . . . the native hobgoblin, or ghost of the woods. On account of this superstition, drowning is considered the worst calamity that can befall one, especially if the body is not recovered." Jones, *Study of the Thlingets of Alaska* (1914), 165.

[33] That the evil dead should be reborn sounds reasonable and has been reported for the Kutchin. Osgood, *Contributions to the Ethnography of the Kutchin* (1936), 140.

[34] Kutchin children gave similar testimony. (Osgood, *Contributions to the Ethnography of the Kutchin* [1936], 140.) The Tlingit "believe that the soul transmigrates from relative to relative, but not from man to animals. For instance, if a nephew dies who has borne some peculiar mark (perhaps a birthmark) on his person and an aunt should afterwards give birth to a son who was similarly marked, it would be fully believed that the newly born was none other than the departed nephew and his name would be given to the child." Jones, *Study of the Thlingets of Alaska* (1914), 234; see also Swanton, *Social Condition, Beliefs and Linguistic Relationship of the Tlingit Indians* (1908), 463; Drucker, *Cultural Element Distributions: XXVI, Northwest Coast* (1950), 230.

[35] The Tlingit believed that spirits of the deceased communicated with the living through cracking in the fire. Swanton, *Social Condition, Beliefs and Linguistic Relationship of the Tlingit Indians* (1908), 461.

is following him."[36] People denied fear of a corpse, the informant having heard of such an attitude around Fort Simpson, where only old people could be persuaded to prepare a body for burial because the young men fled into the bush. The dead body was usually removed from the dwelling through the entry. Sometimes the corpse would be carried through the rear wall in order to conceal it from children. People thought that for a child to look at a dead body permitted the ghost to see and perhaps take a fancy to the youngster.[37] It would seem that ghost fear rather than fear of the corpse characterized the people of the Cassiar.

The dead were disposed of in four ways, through cremation, inhumation, abandonment, and caching in a tree. In "really cold" weather the corpse was burned. Members of the moiety opposite to that of the deceased built a coffin of lashed poles corresponding to the size of the body. Dry wood was included in the box along with the corpse. Then the workers struck a fire and departed. Nobody witnessed the actual cremation, as people disliked the odor of burning human flesh. When the blaze died down the men returned to see that the liver had been fully consumed. This organ always burned slowly and had to be destroyed or the "relatives" would become angry. Following complete destruction the skull and bones were raked together and deposited in a small hole dug on the site of the fire.[38] People planted a stick over the place of interment.[39]

In summer a pit three feet deep was dug with sharp poles to accomodate a corpse. Sometimes inhumation also occurred in winter when a fire had to be built to thaw the ground. The grave, usually located on a ridge, was lined with poles and a layer of spruce brush.[40] Grave workers took care not to bring extra poles to the site lest another per-

[36] Preparation of the corpse became somewhat more elaborate after contact, when the deceased was dressed in new clothes and his face covered with a handkerchief. For two or three days the body might be displayed to visitors who lifted the cloth for a last view.

[37] Tlingit bodies were never removed through the door but through an aperture in the roof or side of the house. The custom magically prevented the spirit from finding its way back to the death place. Jones, *Study of the Thlingets of Alaska* (1914), 151.

[38] The only other evidence of secondary disposal is contained in an anecdote about one man, Alec Chief, who in 1909 exhumed his wife's body at Lower Post. She was a Bear Lake (Sekani) Indian and her mother disliked the fact that she had been intered in a Kaska graveyard. Alec took the corpse to McDame Creek, where the people became alarmed at his act and felt that many of them would die because a corpse had been brought from so great a distance. "This is true," the informant assured us. "Many people have died there since then" (0). According to Jones, the Tlingit "will even exhume bodies and bones and bury them in some other spot in order to have an excuse for . . . feasting." Jones, *Study of the Thlingets of Alaska* (1914), 150.

[39] Jenness affirms that the Kaska had adopted cremation from the Tahltan and Tlingit but later superseded this form of disposal with ground burial. A Dease River informant said exactly this about his own people, as will be reported below. (Jenness, *The Indians of Canada* [1932], 399.) Jones reports that among the Tlingit "at one time cremation was the universal way of disposing of the dead, except of the bodies of slaves, which were embalmed and deposited in dead houses." The ashes collected after burning a corpse were placed in a box which was stored in a death house with clothing, food, and blankets. Disposal of the corpse was in the hands of another "totemic group" who were paid according to the rank of the deceased. Jones, *Study of the Thlingets of Alaska* (1914), 136–137. See also Swanton, *Social Condition, Beliefs and Linguistic Relationship of the Tlingit Indians* (1908), 430, who says that shamans' bodies were abandoned along the shore.

[40] McLean reports the Mackenzie River Athapaskans around 1844 were accustomed to "dispose of

son die. For the same reason they burned fragments of wood remaining from the construction of the burial cache. Preparations for interment rested with affinal relatives of the deceased who, of course, belonged to the opposite moiety. They also carried the body from the dwelling to the place of interment. The only grave goods were the clothes and ornaments worn at the time of death. A pointed stick thrust into the ground at the head of the grave served to remind survivors of its location. The Kaska did not practice flexed burial. Variant patterns of inhumation include use of a hollow-log coffin and the winter practice of burying the deceased within the dwelling. The family thereupon moved camp without demolishing the former residence.

After handling a corpse men participated in rituals to ward off the malevolent influences associated with death. Upon returning from the grave, instead of directly entering camp they first circled (danced around) the dwellings. Meanwhile those people who had not gone to attend the burial had prepared sharp sticks which they used to strike the grave workers as the latter made their circuit. "We kill game!" the people cried, whereupon the dancers fell to the ground. They rose immediately and entered the house, where each washed his hands and ate some meat that had been cooked by the opposite moiety. The meal constituted a "small" burial feast.. During the eating the hosts kept talking in loud voices saying, "You got moose meat; you kill it not long ago." Reference was being made to the corpse that had just been disposed of. The grave workers then thanked their hosts. If the workers belonged to the Crow moiety their gratitude was expressed in a circumlocution like, "You got wing and fly around and get game. We got no wing." Such an indirect expression of thanks appears to have been common in many social situations.[41]

---

their dead by placing them in tombs made of wood, and sufficiently strong to resist the attacks of wild beasts. The body is laid in the tomb at full length, without any particular direction being observed as to the head or feet. Neither they, nor any other Indians I am acquainted with, place their dead in a sitting posture." It is difficult to determine from the text whether surface or subsurface "tombs" are indicated. McLean, *Notes of a Twenty-Five Years' Service in the Hudson's Bay Territory* (1932), 343.

[41] Among the post-contact Pelly River people a gun and blanket went into the grave with the corpse. "The men were supposed to follow him to the grave. On the way their chief or head man was supposed to walk ahead and call their God that one of his children was coming to him, occasionally firing the gun belonging to the dead man. When they arrived at the grave and had lowered the body into it, they fired two more shots, then loaded the gun again and left it at full cock and placed it on top of the coffin pointing west. Then the head man spoke to the dead person, calling him by name two or three times, then telling him, 'You are leaving us now to go to our great Father according to the life you have led here below whether good or bad is the reception he will give you. You see the trail ahead of you leading from here to his camp in the star that we on earth are not permitted to see, you must follow this trail, neither turning to the right or to the left on small hunting trails, but keep to the well beaten one. We will put food in the fire every time we cook for you to eat on the way. . . .' They then fill in the grave and return to camp where the relatives make a feast for the opposite moiety from the deceased, whether Wolf or Raven in honor of the dead, and throw food into the fire for him to eat.

"When the dead person arrives at the star, if he is a good Indian he is met by God, who gives him a hearty welcome and leads him to where the other Indians are stopping that have died before him, who also give him a hearty welcome and make a big feast for him. When they are through eating they dance and sing and gamble and have a general good time. If the Indian dead should not have been a good Indian on earth, the God is liable to turn him into a bear or a moose or any kind of animal and

The bodies of men who had died in warfare remained where they had fallen. Abandonment of a corpse also occurred when starvation killed many people and left the survivors too weak (and too few?) to undertake disposal of the corpse.

One informant (X), who had been born in the Fort Simpson area, spoke of tree burial. His reference may have been to customs prevailing there. The same man denied cremation for the "Kaska," saying that the practice had been confined to the Tahltan.[42] For tree burial an ordinary platform cache was constructed between three or four trees. The unflexed corpse, wrapped in a skin, was lifted to the stage and left there. The disposal of bodies on elevated caches was unusual according to our principal upper Liard River informant (O). He knew of one case where a man had specifically asked for such treatment and people granted his request. For an orphaned baby people sometimes constructed a diminutive spruce-bark canoe in which they placed the live child wrapped in blankets. Then they launched the vessel. This pattern of canoe "burial" occurred only when nobody could rear the small orphan. Tradition says that once a child survived its voyage to be reared by a beaver, from whose teats it nursed.

Following disposal of the corpse the close relatives of the deceased, including siblings, sons, daughters, and spouses, cut their hair to about the length customary in American society. A person of the opposite group did the cutting. Sometimes a parent detached a finger at the death of a child or an old woman might pound her chest with a stone following a grandchild's departure. Mutilation tended to be rare, however. Relatives also covered themselves with ashes or blackened their faces with charcoal to advertise their anguish. "For about a year" after the loss of her husband a widow refrained from washing.[43] Women led the wailing at death and continued the practice periodically for several months or a year. Sunrise and sunset constituted favorite times for wailing. Widows and widowers passed the year abstaining from porcupine and beaver meat. They might die if they broke this avoidance. To prevent the loss of additional children a bereaved mother lost little time before she resumed sewing and cutting with knife or ax. As already explained, a widow remained in control of her brother-in-law, who had to consent before she could take a new spouse. Generally a widow avoided remarriage or cohabitation for one or two years lest the husband's ghost claim her out of pique.

---

send him back to earth, and leave him there until such time as he thinks he has punished him enough when he will be taken back and he will be received with the same honor as a good Indian." Field, *Unpublished manuscript* (1913), 11–12.

Among the Tlingit articles of clothing and bedding were interred with the deceased along with a vessel of water. A death feast was celebrated in honor of the dead and to feed his spirit as it travels "and to pay off all who have any claim on the family of the deceased for any services rendered in their bereavement." Jones, *Study of the Thlingets of Alaska* (1914), 149. Swanton refers to feasts following cremation in his *Social Condition, Beliefs and Linguistic Relationship of the Tlingit Indians* (1908), 431.

[42] Tahltan warriors who had died in a foreign country might be cremated where they had fallen and the bones then transported back home.

[43] "Widows paint their faces black as a sign of mourning . . . sometimes the living shaved their heads as a sign of mourning, and widows cut their hair." Jones, *Study of the Thlingets of Alaska* (1914), 152. Cf. Swanton, *Social Condition, Beliefs and Linguistic Relationship of the Tlingit Indians* (1908), 429–430.

A widower also had to remain single for a time. No visits took place to the burial ground. People avoided that area because of their fear of ghosts.

Beigaben remained conspicuously absent, objects being neither burned nor buried with a corpse. After the body had been disposed of the deceased's clothing, to which the ghost might be attached sentimentally, together with the dwelling in which death had occurred, were burned. Informants said that the destruction of the house helped to get rid of the illness lurking there. We are not certain in our mind if this statement represents an awareness of contagion, nor if the explanation has been derived from European sources. Certain objects of the deceased like knives, unworn clothing, arrows, snowshoes, and tanning tools were distributed as mementoes by a surviving brother. Close relatives shared in these goods. Food left by the deceased went to the opposite moiety, probably in the death feast.[44] It is by no means clear whether a dead person's name was regularly inherited at a memorial potlatch. Sometimes, at any rate such names did come to be assumed by the oldest surviving, like-sexed sibling (real or classificatory) or by a deceased's brother's son or sister's daughter. These heirs directed the potlatch which, coming about a year after death, terminated the period of mourning.

Dease River Kaska. Old men possessed enhanced supernatural power, their longevity being a result of "good living." Such a belief perhaps compensated them for the disabilities brought about by age. An informant claimed that the aged were never abandoned but provided with walking sticks that helped them keep up with travelers. When incapable of walking the old were carried on the backs of strong, young relatives and drawn on toboggans. Sometimes people delegated a young relative to fish and otherwise care for an oldster until the group returned with some meat.

The origin of death is given in a tale recorded by Teit as constituting Bear's revenge for the theft of fire. Had it not been for Bear's interference constant renewal of life would have been the rule.[45] Death denoted the complete separation of wind (tuntaj?uc) and body. The wind continued to exist in one of two afterworlds. The souls of good people went to "heaven" and "God" while the evil found punishment in the company of the devil. The informant volunteered little concerning life after death. Prompting elicited admission of a path leading to a large body of water that had to be crossed in a boat. Crow might have operated the ferry. Only good people enjoyed reincarnation, the wind returning to life in an infant of opposite sex.[46] The appearance of a ghost (tsunetsina) provided a frightening experience.

[44] Among the Pelly River people "the dead person's goods, if he has any, is packed up by the head of the family. That . . . of any value are cached, the rest is either thrown into the river or burned after a year or two. The valuable stuff is then divided amongst the relatives of the dead person . . . it would be given to the ravens if the dead person happened to be a wolf or vice versa." (Field, *Unpublished manuscript* [1913], 13.) The Tlingit destroyed food and property with the aim of sending it on to the deceased "who then actually received its spiritual counterpart." Swanton, *Social Condition, Beliefs and Linguistic Relationship of the Tlingit Indians* (1908), 431; see also 429–430.

[45] Teit, *Kaska Tales* (1917), 443–444.

[46] Among the Tahltan "there is a strong belief in the rebirth of souls. A deceased relative is often born again by a mother, aunt, sister, or other relative. . . . The dead go to three different places: a

Everyone in camp assembled when death seemed inevitable. Long ago bodies were disposed of by cremation and the Tahltan continued the custom a long time after the Dease River people began to inter their dead in the ground. Coffins as well as any form of tree burial were denied. Members of the opposite moiety handled the corpse. Mourning rites included hair cutting but not mutilation. The dwelling in which death had taken place as well as most of the possessions left by the deceased came to an end by destruction, a practice designed to avoid illness.

Tselona. Death followed when the wind deserted the body and journeyed to an afterworld about which the informant knew little. The corpse was cremated and the bones intered in a small pit about one foot deep. Anyone who had handled the corpse avoided food and drink for two days but no particular relatives were charged with this responsibility. Elevated cache and canoe burials could not be recalled. In mourning a widow cut short her hair, fasted for several days, and wore ragged clothing. At night she slept little, deliberately keeping herself awake by means of sharp sticks planted under her head. Her plans for remarriage demanded the approval of her brother-in-law or he might wed her himself. Scarification, face blackening, and hair singeing were denied. A widower observed food and drink taboos but did not cut his hair.

Property destruction following death was denied.

Frances Lake Kaska. A person's wind or soul, located in the stomach, resembled the breath or the air that one inhaled. Just as breathing sustained life the loss of the wind (breath) produced death. The informant denied that there could be a temporary alienation of body and wind. The soul continued to survive after quitting the body and if it had belonged to a good man became reincarnated. Following death the ghost (tsune), which was always dangerous, remained in the neighborhood for a period ranging from ten days to a year. During this time it hunted, copulated with women, visited its birthplace, and completed any tasks that the deceased throughout his life had left uncompleted. In appearance the ghost resembled a living Indian but could only be seen and not sensed tactually. Ghosts also avenged themselves for injuries that had been sustained in life. To announce themselves they sometimes whistled. Knocking did not constitute a ghostly signature.

---

rather cool, dingy place underground to the west; a light agreeable place on the same level as the earth to the east; and a place above in the sky. Only people killed in battle go to the last. Sometimes they come out, and dance as the aurora. When the latter consist of red clouds, people say there is a war somewhere. When the streamers of the aurora descend, forming a kind of chute, it is said that the spirits are receiving a brave warrior whose soul ascends through this chute, and is borne away as the streamers ascend. The sky heaven is said to be the best abode. That to the east is somewhat like this earth, but better in so far as food is always abundant. Most people go to it. They have to descend a slippery hill, and cross a river. Some are afraid, and turn back to be reborn again, or wander about until they reach the place of shades in the west where conditions are not as good as in the other places, and food is often scarce. Teit, *On Tahltan (Athabaskan) Work* (1912), 486. Cf. Speck, *Naskapi* (1935), 51, who also speaks of the dead appearing in the northern lights.

APPENDIX A: THE POSITION OF THE KASKA IN THE NORTHERN ATHAPASKAN CULTURE AREA

IF we follow Osgood's classification, the Kaska Indians belong in the Arctic Drainage division of the Northern Athapaskan Culture Area.[1] To make such a classification is tantamount to describing Kaska culture as comprising "essentially simple patterns of behavior." Nevertheless, comparison of the Kaska to peoples living in the east, like the Slave, Beaver, and other Indians, reveals quite clearly that the former possess certain features relating their culture to the cultures of the more complex Pacific Drainage division. The Kaska are, of course, one of the westernmost of the Arctic Drainage Athapaskans and hence peripheral to the Pacific Drainage cultures. Therefore simply on grounds of geographical position a transitional character might be expected for the culture.[2] Indeed it is surprising that the transitional features are not more numerous or stronger. We are quite certain that the absence of salmon in the Cassiar is quite firmly related to the predominantly inland character of intermontane living. That region simply lacked the environmental base which, in conjunction with an appropriate exploitative technology, could support an expanding population, relatively sedentary habitations, and complex ceremonial life.

Among the traits of Kaska culture which clearly link that system to the Pacific Drainage division (and also with the Northwest Coast cultures) first mention may be given to the potlatch, with such associated elements as grease drinking contests, messenger stick, songs, dances, animal masks, and others. However the potlatch in the Cassiar appears to have been a much attentuated form of that ceremony as it occurred further westward. In the first place, although the give-away brought honor to a donor, it does not seem basically to have been a social climbing feast.[3] Furthermore, the amount of wealth distributed was limited. These two interrelated conditions follow from the fact that in comparison to the Pacific Coast people wealth remained more limited among the Arctic Drainage Indians with their severer struggle for existence. The attentuation of the potlatch is a quality shared by other features of social organization that make Kaska transitional, like unilinear (matrilineal) descent; economic-prestige classes, which appear scarcely formalized; and transitory villages, which are limited to periods spent at some productive fish place. Servants may be another linking trait[4] but as long as they remain occasional the pattern is not clearly diagnostic. Even the eastern Arctic Eskimo sometimes use an orphan or ne'er-do-well as a handyman.[5] A list of further Pacific Drainage and Northwest Coast traces in Kaska culture may

[1] Osgood, *Distribution of the Northern Athapaskan Indians* (1936), 20–21.

[2] Osgood, *Distribution of the Northern Athapaskan Indians* (1936), 4.

[3] We adopt this term to designate ceremonies whose end is focussed on prestige enhancement and status mobility. Of course, any ceremony may *contribute* to those ends. Cf. Chapple and Coon, *Principles of Anthropology* (1942), 334.

[4] Osgood reports commoners working for aristocrats among the Tanaina. Osgood, *Ethnography of the Tanaina* (1937), 134.

[5] Honigmann, Great Whale River Field Notes (1949, 1950).

include: line dancing, fire drill, labrets, nasal plugs, dugout canoes, horn spoons, horn adz, enemy dummies for war magic, ceremonial cannibalism, shield, armor, scalping, tattooed war records, thunder bird concept, cremation. Perhaps also to be included are the shaman's ceremonial doll, special respect for the otter, crutch-like paddle handle, and weregild. The number of such traits is not great and fails to give Kaska culture the overall Pacific Drainage complexion that would follow from the presence of patterns like salmon fishing and marine hunting, surplus production, sedentary life, hereditary nobility, and intense ceremonialism. In form, the Kaska community resembles overwhelmingly the small, mobile, hunting and fishing band characteristic of the northern forest, producing no surplus that would allow time for leisure activities, egalitarian, lacking chieftainship, and possessed of few forms of wealth.

We have also sought to isolate unanalyzable terms from vocabularies collected from several Kaska informants with the object of ascertaining the material traits in the local culture that are fundamental to Athapaskan material culture as a whole. Such terms are presented below. A single asterisk before any trait indicates that the Fort Nelson Slave also identify the item with an unanalyzable term. A double asterisk shows that the trait occurs with an unanalyzable term in Osgood's analysis of Ingalik material culture.[6] A triple asterisk is used to show that the trait occurs in similar fashion in Slave, Ingalik, and Kaska cultures.

***Arrow[7]	***Man's awl[7]
***Bark canoe	*Moccasin[7]
*Bow	***Outer belt
Breech cloth	**Parka
***Broiling stick	Robe
Buzz toy	Shirt
***Canoe paddle	*Snare
Clothing bag	***Semi-tanned skin line
*Club	Sinew line
Digging stick	***Snowshoe[7]
Drinking cup	Snowshoe staff
Drinking tube	***Square raft
Dwelling	***Stone ax[7, 8]
*Fish weir	*Stone knife[7]
***Hat[8]	***Tambourine drum
Inner belt	***Trigger deadfall
Kettle	***Trousers[7]
	**Wood bowl

A brief analysis of these 35 items from Kaska culture reveals that 14 are similarly designated with unanalyzable terms by Slave and Ingalik speakers. Of these, 5 can be shown to occur similarly among the Sarsi Indians. These traits may be basic in Northern Athapaskan culture in the sense of enjoying great age. They certainly enjoy a wide distribution.

[6] Osgood, *Ingalik Material Culture* (1940), 431.
[7] Also given in unanalyzable form by the Sarsi Indians of Alberta.
[8] Added to Ingalik list by Osgood but without linguistic evidence.

APPENDIX B: TABULATION OF ABORIGINAL KASKA CULTURE TRAITS

THE following list represents the occurrence of aboriginal culture traits among the Kaska groups for which information was available. The list summarizes traits referred to in the preceding text. So few data were obtained for the Espatotena that they have not been included in the tabulation.

Symbols employed have the following meanings:

X	Present	I	Incipient
O	Absent	T	Taboo
R	Rare	?	Applicability of data doubtful
F	Occurs in folktale		

The symbol for the absence of a trait indicates that informants did not know of the trait within their areas. It must be noted that items in the following tabulation do not follow the order by which they are presented in the text. Rather, in order to facilitate comparisons we have conformed fairly closely to the trait lists already published in the Athapaskan ethnographies of Cornelius Osgood.

	Upper Liard Kaska	Dease River	Kaska Tselona	Frances Lake Kaska
FOOD				
Fish:				
Salmon	R			O
Whitefish	X	X		X
Trout	X	X		X
Grayling	X			X
Jackfish	X	X		
Loche (ling)	X			X
Sucker	X	X		X
Pickerel	X			
Fish eggs		X		
Land animals:				
Caribou	X	X		X
Moose	X	X		X
Elk				O
Bison (wood buffalo)				O
Black bear	X	X		X
Brown bear	X	X		
Grizzly bear	O	R		
Beaver	X	X		X
Muskrat	X	O?		X
Lynx	X	R		X
Rabbit	X	X		X
Porcupine	X	X		X
Ground hog	X	X		X
Tree squirrel	X	X		
Mountain sheep	X	X		
Mountain goat	R	X		X

145

	Upper Liard Kaska	Dease River Kaska	Tselona	Frances Lake Kaska
Fox	O	O	O	
Otter	O, T	O, T	O, T	O, T
Mink	O, T	O, T	O, T	
Marten	X	X	X	
Ermine (weasel)			O	
Wolverine	O	O		
Wolf	O	O		
Dog	O	O		
Frog	O, T	O, T	O, T	
Fisher			O	
Gopher (marmot)	X	X		
Birds:				
Owl	X	R	X	
Goose	X	X	X	
Eagle	X	O	O	
Hawk		O	O	
Raven	O			
Ducks	X	X	X	
Grouse	X	X	X	
Ptarmigan	X	X	X	
Spruce	X	X	X	
Swan	X	X	X	
Loon	X	X		
Crane	X		X	
Whiskey jack		R		
Woodpecker		O		
Crow	O	O	O	
Birds' eggs		X		
Vegetable foods:				
Berry eating	X	X	X	X
Blueberry	R	X	X	
Cranberry, high bush	X			
Cranberry, low bush	X	X	X	
Strawberry	R	X	X	
Red raspberry	X	X	X	
Salmon berry	X	X		
Currant	R	X	X	
Soap berry	X	X	X	
Spruce fiber	X	X	X	
Birch fiber	O	X	X	
Jackpine fiber	X		X	
Willow bud	O		O	
Wild rice	O	O		
Wild peas	O			
Wild onion	X	X	X	
Wild rhubarb	X		X	
Wild carrot		X		
Wild roses	X	X		
Muskeg "tea"			X	
Muskeg "apples"	X			
Fern roots	X			

	Upper Liard Kaska	Dease River Kaska	Tselona	Frances Lake Kaska
Lily bulb	X	O	X	
Mushrooms	X	O		
Birch sap	X	X	X	
Poplar sap	O		X	
Chewing spruce gum	X	X	X	
Mud eaten	O	O	O	
Agriculture	O	O	O	
Fish primary food	X	X		
Starvation	X	X	X	
Gormandizing	O?	O?	X	
Starvation cannibalism	X	X	X	
Taboo on cannibals	X	X		
Fish spearing	X	X	X	
Torch fishing	O?		O	
Hunting:				
Cohabitation taboo	X	X	O	
Hunting songs	X	X		
Bear spearing	X			
Bear "tipi" ambush	X			
Hunting with dogs	X	X	X	
Caribou skin decoy	X		X	
Caribou surrounds	X	X	X	
Sheep surround		X		
Carved hunting charms	X	O		X
Semicircular moose tracking	X	X	X	
Moose called by rubbing scapula	X	X	X	
Moose called with bark horns	X	X		
Footwear removed in hunting	X	X	O	
Human moose surrounds	X	X	X	
Scapulimancy	X	X		O
Giving away kill	X	X	X	
Smoke (sun) drying	X	X	X	
Pemmican	X	X	X	
Eating raw meat	R	R	R	
Stuffed viscera	X	X	O	
Foetal animals eaten	X	X	X	
Fish intestines eaten	X	X		
Blood soup	X	X	X	
Milk drinking	R	X	X	
Antler "velvet" eaten	X			
Skin-lined boiling pit	X	O	O	
Grass-lined boiling pit	R	O	O	
Hot-stone boiling	X	X	X	
Boiling in stomach	X	X	O	
Broiling stock	X	X		
Food served in dishes	X	X		
Food served in bark	X	X		
Men-women-children eating order	O	O	O	
Youth's water taboo	X	X	X	
Youth's grease taboo	X	O	O	
Youth's marrow taboo	X			

	Upper Liard Kaska	Dease River Kaska	Tselona	Frances Lake Kaska
Bear taboo for women	O	O	O	
Taboo on eating leg tendons	X		X	
Taboo on dog's eating	X	O	X	
Taboo on eating hind quarters	X			
Pets	O			
Special respect for bear	X			
Special respect for otter	X	X	X	X
Special respect for wolverine			X	
Special respect for wolf	X		X	
Special respect for mink	X	X	X	
Special respect for caribou	X		O	
Special respect for flying squirrel	X			
Special respect for toad	X?	X	X	
Fire drill	O	X?	O	
Strike-a-light	X	X	X	
Fungus for tinder	X			
Dry grass for tinder	X			
Fire carriers	X		X	
DRESS				
Tailored clothing	X	X		
Caribou skin most important	X	X		
Gut clothing	O	O	O	
Fish skin clothing		O	O	
Bird skin clothing	X	X		
Woven skin clothing	X	X	X	
Rabbit skin weaving	X	X	X	
Open coat	X	X	X	
Parka	X	X	X	
Parka stretching frame	X			
Shirt	X	X		
Combination trousers and footwear	X	X	O	
Combination trousers and coat	X	O	O	
Trousers	X	X	X	
Moccasins	X	X		X
Breech cloth	X	X	X	
Leggings	X	X	X	
Fur duffel	X	X	X	
Grass duffel	X	X	O	
Feather duffel	X	X		
Moose-hair duffel	X			
Goat's-hair duffel			X	
Robe	X			
Mittens	X	X	X	
Non-detachable mittens on parka	X			
Gloves		X?	O	
Inner belt	X	X	X	
Ornamented (outer) belt	X	X	X	
Head band	X	X	X	
Skin hat	X	X	X	
Woven spruce-root hat	X	X	O	
Birch-bark hat	X	X		

	Upper Liard Kaska	Dease River Kaska	Tselona	Frances Lake Kaska
Birdskin hat	X		X	
Sewn-wood hat		X	X	
Pillow	O	X	X	
Moss-bag baby carrier	X	X	X	
Bark-chair baby carrier	O	O	O	
Woven spruce-root cradle		X		
Cradle swing (hammock)	X	X	X	
Clothing decoration:				
Skin fringe	X	X	X	
Feather	R	O		
Fur	X	X	X	
Hair		O		
Paint	X	X	X	
Porcupine quills	X	X	X	
Bone	X	X	X	
Personal adornment:				
Tattooing (needle and sinew)	X?	O?	X	
Tattooing (puncture)	O	O		
Painting	X	X	X	
Greasing	X	X	X	
Urine used for washing body		O		
Face lightening	X	X?		
Labret	X	X	O	
Earings (lobes)	X	X	X	
Earings (helix)	O		O	
Nasal-septum plug	X	X	X	
Nose rings	X	O	O	X
Necklaces	X		O	
Wristlets	X	X	O	
Combs	X	X	X	
Cut hair	O	O	O	
Depilation	X	X	X	
Garters	X	X	X	
Urine for washing clothes		X		
SHELTER				
Surface rectangular house	O			
Semisubterranean house	O	O		
Rectangular birch-bark house	O	O		
Rectangular grass-mat house	O	O		
Skin tipi	R			
Conical pole shelter	X	X	X	
Simple lean-to	X	X	X	
Inverted V-shaped house	X	X	X	
Snow house	X	X?		
Cave shelters	X			
Roofing:				
Moss	X		X	
Sod	X		X	
Skin	R	R	R	
Bark	X	X		
Spruce bough	X	X	X	

	Upper Liard Kaska	Dease River Kaska	Tselona	Frances Lake Kaska
Grass thatch	O		O	
Snow		X		
Mat floors	O			
Brush floors	X	X	X	
Sleeping platform	O	O		
Pits for protection	X			
Dugout fireplaces	O	O		
Raised fireplaces	O	O		
Fire screen	X			
Dance house	O	O		
Menstrual house	O	O		
Smoke house	O			
Sweat house	X	X	O?	
Sweat bathing	X	X		
Open camp	X	X		
Caches:				
4-pole platform cache	O	X		
4-pole shelter cache	O	X		
Ground shelter cache		X		
Single-pole cache	X	X		
Tree platforms	X			
Stone cairn	X			
Snow cache	X			
Special ceremonial ground	O	O		
Two-family shelters	X			
Women erect shelters		X		
TRAVEL AND TRANSPORTATION				
Birch-bark canoe	R	O		
Spruce-bark canoe	X	X·		
Canoes fastened in pairs	R	O		
Hunting canoe	X	X		
Transport canoe	X	X		
Decked canoe	O	O		
Dugout canoe	X	X		
Moose-skin boat	X	X		
Single paddle	X	X		
Double paddle		X?		
Square raft	X	X		
v-shaped raft	X	X		
Sails	O	X		
Simple-log bridge	X	X		
Multiple-log bridge	X	X		
Trail blazing:				
Notched tree trunks		X		
Moss or grass hung on trees	X	X		
Bent brush	X	X		
Stone cairns	X	X		
Snowshoes	X	X		
Loucheux-type snowshoe	X	X		
Hunting and trail shoes distinguished	X	X		

	Upper Liard Kaska	Dease River Kaska	Tselona	Frances Lake Kaska
Willow snowshoe	X	X		
Men lace snowshoes	R	R		
Women lace snowshoes	X	X		
Snowshoe staff	X	X		
Snowshoe pins	X	O		
Sleds	O	O		
Toboggans	X	X		
Skin toboggan	X	X		
Men pull toboggans	X	X		
Women pull toboggans	X	X		
Human packing	X	X		
Men do packing	X			
Women do packing	X			
Tump line	X	X		
Shoulder strap	X	O		
Chest pack stick	O	O		
Dog packing	X	X		
Dogs hitched in tandem	X			
Dog shoes	X	X		
Ability to swim	X	X		
Trade	R	R		
MANUFACTURES AND IMPLEMENTS				
Techniques:				
Tanning	X	X		
Woven basketry		X		
Matting	O	O		
Pottery	O	X		
Skin weaving	X	X		
Wool-fiber weaving	X?			X?
Metal working	O	O		
Porcupine-quill weaving	X	X		
Lines:				
Babiche	X	X		
Rawhide	X	X		
Sinew	X	X		
Willow bark	X	X		
Willow bast	O			
Whole willow	X	X		
Spruce root	X	X		
Willow root	X	X		
Spruce wood	O	O		
Fish skin	O	O		
Special bear skin	X	X		
Tanned skin	X	X		
Grass line	X	X		
Braided	X			
Twisted	X	X		
Feather line		X		
Cold-weather babiche drying	X			
Dyed babiche	X			
Babiche stretching frames	R			

	Upper Liard Kaska	Dease River Kaska	Tselona	Frances Lake Kaska
Nets:				
Gill	X	X		
Seine	O	O		
Dip net	O	O		
Willow bark	X	O?		
Netting of beaver	X	X		X
Fish weir	X	X	X	
Fish drags	O			
Fish spear	X	X	X	
Fish hooks		X	X	
Beaver gaff hook	X	X		X
Club (for fish)	X			
Lance (spear)	X	X	X	
Ice chisel	X	X		
Ice scoop	X			
Snares:				
Caribou	X	X	X	X
Moose	X	X	X	
Mountain sheep	X	X		X
Mountain goats			X	
Bear	X	X		
Beaver	X	X		
Ground hog	X			
Lynx	X			
Rabbit	X			
Bird	X			
Fish	X		O	
Bear spear	X	X	X	
Deadfalls	X	X		X
Bear	X	X		
Beaver	X	X		
Fisher	X			
Ground hog	X	X?		
Marten	X	X		
Snowshoe trap for birds	X			
Pitfalls for animals	F	O		
Bows and arrows:				
Sinew-backed bow		X		
Tanned-skin-backed bow	X			
Bow with guard	X			
Blunt arrows	X			
Detachable point arrows	X			
Multi-tipped arrows	X			
2 rows of feathers	X	X		
3 rows of feathers	X	X		
Mediterranean release	O			
Under-arm quiver	X	X		
Shoulder quiver	O			
Sling	X			
"Stick gun"	F	X		

	Upper Liard Kaska	Dease River Kaska	Tselona	Frances Lake Kaska
Knives:				
Bone	X	X		
Stone	X	X		
Copper	O			
Drawknife	O?	X		
Ulu	O			
Horn hafts for knives	X	X		
Wood hafts for knives	R	X		
Scabbards		X		
Scrapers:				
Bone	X	X		
Stone	X	X		
Tooth		X		
Horn	X	X		
End scraper	X	X		
Tooth awl	X	X		
Wood awl	X			
Stone adz	O	O		
Horn adz	X	X		
Stone ax	X	O		
Stone hammer	X			
Stone pestle	X			
Wood wedge	X	X		
Wood maul	O			
Stone maul	X			
Containers:				
One-piece wood dishes	X	X		
Sewn-wood dishes	O			
Horn spoons	X	X		X
Wood spoons	X			
Birch-bark baskets	X	X	X	
Birch-bark dishes	X	X		
Spruce-bark baskets	X	X		
Willow baskets	X			
Woven-grass baskets		X		
Skin bags	X			
Fish-skin bags	X			
Babiche game bags	X			
Intestine bags	X			
Clay pots	O?	X?		
Clay-lined bark vessels	X			
Snow shovel	R			
Netting needle (shuttle)	X			
Net measure	X			
Bark remover	X	X		
Rabbit-skin weaving frame	O			
Skin snow glasses	X			
Bark snow glasses	X			
Willow broom	X			
Form-board skin stretchers	X			

	Upper Liard Kaska	Dease River Kaska	Tselona	Frances Lake Kaska
Willow-pole beaver skin stretchers	X			
Woman's work board	X			
Bow loom	X	X		
Bone needle	X	R	X	
Bone thimble	X			
Skin thimble		X		
WAR				
Causes:				
To protect territory		X		
To gain women	X	X		
To gain property		X		
To gain prestige	O			
Revenge	X	X		
Weapons:				
Bow	X	X		
Knife	X			
Club		X		
Lance	X			
Bear-skin armor	X			
Bark and skin helmets	X			
Shields	X			
Scouts	X			
Sentries or look-outs	X			
War chiefs	X			
Face painting	X			
Cohabitation taboo	X			
Ritual with human dummies	X			
Hiding of children	X			
Canoe warfare	O			
Exchange of prisoners	O			
Scalping	X			
Decapitation	O			
Mutilation of enemy	X			
Torture	X			
Ceremonial cannibalism	X	O		
Dancing with scalp	X			
Tattooing as war record	X			
Hunting taboo	X			
ARTS AND AMUSEMENTS				
Measures and directions:				
Monthly time units	X	X		
Body-part measures	X			
River-valley directions	X			
Cures:				
Bleeding for snowblindness	O			
Gum for snowblindness	O	X		
Sweat bathing	X			
Bathing in hot springs	O			
Urine fumes for colds	X?	X		
Fireweed brew for muscle aches	X			
Broken limbs set		X		

	Upper Liard Kaska	Dease River Kaska	Tselona	Frances Lake Kaska
Rock painting	X			
Blue-green color confusion	X			
Paints:				
Red	X	X	X	
Blue-green	X	X		
Yellow	O			
Black	X	X		
White		X		
Dyeing	O	X		
Wood carving	X			
Carved wood masks	X			
Animal-skin masks	X	X		
Bark masks		X		
Grotesque attire	X	X		
Incising by burning	O			
Porcupine-quill work	X	X	X	
Weather omens	X			
Drawing on snow	X			
Smoke signals	X	X		
Circle dances	O?	X		
Line dances	X			
War dances	O			
Musical instruments:				
Tambourine drum	X	X		
Plank drum	O	O		
Rattle	X	X		
Willow whistle	X	X		
Songs:				
Luck	X	X		
Mourning	X			
Shaman's	X	X		
Love	X	X		
Potlatch	X	X		
War		O		
Victory	X			
Amusement	X			
Canoeing	O			
Gambling	X	X		
Stone working		X		
Individual ownership	O			
Toys and dolls:				
Dolls	O	O		
Miniature weapons	X	X		
Skin sling toy	X			
Buzz toy	X			
Bull-roarer	X			
Games:				
Wrestling	X	X		
Relative avoidance in wrestling	X			
Running races	X	X		
Boat races	X	X		

	Upper Liard Kaska	Dease River Kaska	Tselona	Frances Lake Kaska
Rope tug-of-war	O	X		
Pull pole tug-of-war	O	X		
Push pole tug-of-war		X		
Tossing in moose skin	O	O		
Stick games	X	X		
Blind man's bluff	X	X		
Drag-skin	X	O		
Swings	X			
Bow and arrow	X	X		
Hide and seek	X	X		
Breaking beaver bone	X			
String figures	X	X		
Story telling important	X			
Ownership of stories	O			
Riddles	X			
Gambling	X	X		
SOCIAL ORGANIZATION				
Matrilineal sibs	O	O		
Exogamous moieties	X	X	O	X?
Moiety face painting	X			
Band organization	X	X		
Social classes	I	I		
Slaves	X			
Strong chieftainship	O	O		
Weak chieftainship	X	X		
Inherited chieftainship (patrilineal)	X	X		
Wealth a prestige factor	X	X		
Councils	X			
2-family social unit	X		X	
Ritual friendship	O	X		
Individual ownership	X			
Fishing sites	O	O		
Hunting sites	O	O		
Beaver creeks	X			
Ownership marks	O			
Patrilineal inheritance	X			
Family-owned beaver creeks	X			
Hospitality	X			
Hot-food hospitality test	O			
Cool food served visitors	X			
Adoption	X			
Berdache female	X	O		
Berdache male	O	O		
Position of women:				
Women do packing	X			
Shelter wife's domain	X			
Control of children	X			
Control of food	X			
Blood revenge	X	X		
Weregild	X	X		
Murder and manslaughter distinguished	X			

	Upper Liard Kaska	Dease River Kaska	Tselona	Frances Lake Kaska
Adoption of murderer	X			
Joking relationship	X	X		
Uncle-nephew relationship	X			
Brother-sister avoidance	X	X		
Crow-type cousin terminology	X	X	O	X
Iroquois-type cousin terminology	O	O	X	O
Mother called by same term as MoSi	X	X	O	X
Reciprocal term between MoBr-SiSo	X	X	X	X
Joking relationship with FaSis	X			
Feasts:				
Birth	X			
First game	X	X		
Girl's puberty	X	X		
Marriage	X	X		
Death	X			
Vision quest		X		
Anniversary of death	X	X		
Rich man's feast	X			
Mock feast (wolverine feast)	X			
War		X		
Potlatch:				
Between moieties	X	X		
Loaning to accumulate wealth	O	O		
Messenger staff	X			
Competitive games	X			
Grease drinking	X			
Special songs	X	X		
Ceremonial wigs		O		
To avoid intermoiety conflict	X			
Social customs:				
Skin band worn for fertility	X			
Skin band worn during pregnancy	O			
Repeated copulation for conception	X			
Nausea during pregnancy	X			
Food preferences during pregnancy	X			
Contraceptive magic	X			
Birth:				
Woman isolated	X	X		
Stooping (supported by women)	X			
Hanging to pole	X			
Secreting placenta	X	X		
Cohabitation taboo	X	X		
Infanticide		X		
Killing one twin	O	O		
Purification of father	O			
Unwed motherhood punished	X	X		
Circumcision	O			
Speaker's name taboo	X			
Teknonymy	O	O		
Girl's puberty:				
Puberty sequestration	X	X		
Menstrual sequestration	X	X	X	

	Upper Liard Kaska	Dease River Kaska	Tselona	Frances Lake Kaska
Menstrual hood	X	X		
Drinking tube	X	X		
Scratching stick	X	X		
Special dishes	X?			
Food or drink taboos	X		X	
Trail taboos	X	O		
Idleness taboo	X			
Menstrual pads	X	X		
Boy's puberty ceremony		X?		
Marriage:				
Engagement of children	X	R		
Monogamy prevalent	X	X		
Polygyny	X	X		
Polyandry	R	X		
Wife exchange	O?			
Wife capture	X	X		
Wrestling for wives	X			
Wife purchase	X			
Levirate	X	X?	X	
Sororate	X	X	X	
Matrilocal residence	X	X		
Mother controls marriage	X			
Boy works for bride's parents	X	X		
Divorce simple	X	X		
Mother-in-law avoidance	X	X		
Cross-cousin marriage	X	X	X	
Chastity belt	F			
Death:				
Due to evil spirits or ghosts	X			
Due to sorcery	X			
Due to natural causes	X			
Due to broken taboos	X			
Suicide	X			
Abandonment of living	X	O		
Disposal of corpse:				
Abandonment	X			
Elevated cache	X	O	O	
Cremation	X	X	X	
Second disposal	X		X	
Canoe burial	X	O	O	
Log burial	R	O		
Interment in ground	X	X		
Burial in house	R			
Body ceremonially displayed	X			
Body removed through rear wall	X			
Burial by another group	X	X	O	
Flexed burial	O			
Grave-worker's taboo	X		X	
Grave objects	O			
Mourning:				
Widow cuts hair	X			

	Upper Liard Kaska	Dease River Kaska	Tselona	Frances Lake Kaska
Survivors cut hair	X	X	X	
Widow scarification	R	O	O	
Widow blackens face	X		O	
Survivors blacken face	X		O	
Food taboos	X		X	
Widow controlled by brother-in-law	X	X	X	
Taboo on cohabitation	X			
Taboo on remarriage	X			
Severe demeanment	X		X	
Periodic wailing	X			
Distribution of deceased's property	X	X		
Destruction of deceased's property	X		O	
Mourning songs	X	X		
RELIGION				
Animism	X			
Belief in afterworld	X	X	X	X
Special afterworld for drowned	X			
Special afterworld for suicides	X			
Reincarnation	X	X		X
Belief in superior being	O?	O?	O	
Monsters	X			
Giants	X	X		
Dwarfs	X	X		
Special regard for otter	X	X	X	X
Nakani belief	X	X		
Animals with human attributes	X			
Cold being	O			
Moon being	X			
Water being		O		
Wind being	X			
North-wind being	X			
Fire being		X		
Feeding the fire	X	X		
Offerings to rocks	O			
Magic formulas	X	X		
Amulets	X			
Earth-diver tale	X	X		
Ceremonial number 4	X			
Shamanism:				
Public performances	X	X	O	
Power from animals	X	X	X	
Vision quest	X	X	X	
Power through dreams	X	X	X?	
Cures by sucking	X			
Plank drum	O		O	
Tambourine drum	O		O	
Rattle		X	O	
Clappers (snapping sticks)	X			
Ceremonial doll	X			

	Upper Liard Kasha	Dease River Kaska	Tselona	Frances Lake Kaska
Bear-skin dress		X		
Payment	X	X		
Divination	X			
Confession	X	X		X?
Illness by soul loss	X	X		
Illness by intrusion	X	X		X
Fear of sorcery	X	X		X

BIBLIOGRAPHY

ALLARD, E. *Notes on the Kaska and Upper Liard Indians* (Primitive Man, vol. 1, pp. 24–26, Washington, 1928.)

ALLEN, F. A. *The American Bisons, Living and Extinct* (Memoirs of the Museum of Comparative Zoology, vol. 4, no. 10, Cambridge, 1876).

BARBEAU, M. *Mountain Cloud* (Caldwell, Idaho, 1944).

CAMPBELL, R. *The Discovery and Exploration of the Pelly (Yukon) River* (in The Royal Reader, Fifth Book of Reading Lessons, Toronto, 1883).

CANADA. *Annual Report of the Department of Indian Affairs for the Year ended March 31* (Ottawa, 1915). *Annual Report of the Royal Canadian Mounted Police for the Year ended September 30* (Ottawa, 1926).

CHAPPLE, E. D., AND C. S. COON. *Principles of Anthropology* (New York, 1942).

DALL, W. H. *Travels on the Yukon and in the Yukon Territory in 1866–1868* (in Trimmer, F. M., ed., The Yukon Territory, London, 1898).

DAWSON, G. M., *Report of an Exploration in the Yukon District, N. W. T., and Adjacent Northern Portion of British Columbia, 1887* (Annual Report of the Canadian Geological Survey, n.s., vol. 3, Ottawa, 1887–88).

DRUCKER, P. *Culture Element Distributions: XXVI, Northwest Coast* (Anthropological Records, vol. 9, no. 3, Berkeley, 1950).

DURHAM, M. E. *Some Tribal Origins, Laws, and Customs of the Balkans* (London, 1928).

FIELD, P. *Unpublished manuscript* (in Department of Anthropology, Yale Peabody Museum, New Haven, dated Ross River, Feb. 8, 1913).

FISHER, M. W. *The Mythology of the Northern and Northeastern Algonkians in Reference to Algonkian Mythology as a Whole* (in Johnson, F., ed., *Man in Northeastern North America*, Andover, 1946).

FORD, C. S. *A Comparative Study of Human Reproduction* (Yale University Publications in Anthropology, no. 32, New Haven, 1945).

GODSELL, P. H. *Romance of the Alaska Highway* (Toronto, 1945).

GROUARD, E. J. B. *Souvenirs de mes soixante ans d'apostolat dans l'Athabaska-Mackenzie* (Winnipeg and Lyon, n.d.).

HALLOWELL, A. I. *The Size of Algonkian Hunting Territories: a Function of Ecological Adjustment* (American Anthropologist, n.s., vol. 51, pp. 35–45, Menasha, 1949).

HANSON, C., AND D. A. McNAUGHTON. *Eagle-McDame Area, Cassiar District, British Columbia* (Memoirs of the Canadian Department of Mines, Geological Survey, no. 194, Ottawa, 1936).

HARRINGTON, LYN. *The Alaska Highway* (Canadian Geographical Journal, vol. 42, pp. 238–259, Ottawa, 1951).

HODGE, F. W., ed. *Handbook of American Indians North of Mexico* (Bulletin of the Bureau of American Ethnology, vol. 30, Washington, 1907–10, 2 vols.).

HOIJER, H. *Linguistic History* (in Human Origins: an Introductory General Course in Anthropology, Selected Readings, Series II, second edition, Chicago, 1946, mimeographed).

HONIGMANN, J. J. *Attawapiskat Cree field notes* (1947–48).
Changes in Sarsi Social Culture (manuscript).
Cultural Dynamics of Sex (Psychiatry, vol. 10, pp. 37–47, Baltimore, 1947).
Culture and Ethos of Kaska Society (Yale University Publications in Anthropology, no. 40, New Haven, 1949).
Ethnography and Acculturation of the Fort Nelson Slave (Yale University Publications in Anthropology, no. 33, New Haven, 1946).
Great Whale River field notes (1949–50).
Intercultural Relations at Great Whale River, P. Q. (American Anthropologist, n.s., vol. 54, pp. 510–522, Menasha, 1952).

Witch-Fear in Post-Contact Kaska Society (American Anthropologist, n.s., vol. 49, pp. 222–243, Menasha, 1947).

HONIGMANN, J. J., AND IRMA. *A Kaska String Oracle* (Man, vol. 47, article 159, London, 1947).

HORNELL, J. *Water Transport* (Cambridge, 1946).

HUNTER, F. *Frances Lake, Yukon* (Flushing, N. Y., 1924).

JENNESS, D. *The Indians of Canada* (Bulletin of the Canadian Department of Mines, National Museum of Canada, no. 65, Ottawa, 1932).

The Sekani Indians of British Columbia (Bulletin of the Canadian Department of Mines, National Museum of Canada, no. 84, Anthropological Series, no. 20, Ottawa, 1937).

JETTÉ, J. *On the Superstitions of the Ten'a Indians* (Anthropos, vol. 6, pp. 95–108, 241–259, 602–615, 699–723, Vienna, 1911).

JOHNSON, F. *An Archaeological Survey Along the Alaska Highway, 1944* (American Antiquity, vol. 11, pp. 183–186, Menasha, 1946).

JOHNSTON, W. A. *Gold Placers of Dease Lake Area, Cassiar District, B. C.* (1925 Summary Report of the Canadian Department of Mines, Geological Survey, pt. A, Ottawa, 1926).

JONES, L. F. *A Study of the Thlingets of Alaska* (New York, 1914).

KEITH, G. *Letters to Mr. Roderic McKenzie* (in Masson, L. R., ed., Les bourgeois de la compagnie du nord-ouest, vol. 2, Quebec, 1890).

KERR, F. A. *Dease Lake Area, Cassiar District, B. C.* (1925 Summary Report of the Canadian Department of Mines, Geological Survey, pt. A, Ottawa, 1926).

KING, W. C., AND M. WEEKES. *Founding Fort Nelson* (The Beaver, December, pp. 42–43, Winnipeg, 1943).

KLUCKHOHN, C. *Patterning as Exemplified in Navaho Culture* (in Spier, L., A. I. Hallowell, and S. S. Newman, eds., Language, Culture and Personality, Menasha, 1941).

KRAUSE, A. *Die Tlinkit-Indianer* (Jena, 1885).

KROEBER, A. L. *Cultural and Natural Areas of Native North America* (University of California Publications in American Archaeology and Ethnology, vol. 38, pp. 1–242, Berkeley, 1939).

LANTIS, M. *Alaskan Eskimo Ceremonialism* (Monographs of the American Ethnological Society, No. 9, New York, 1947).

The Social Culture of the Nunivak Eskimo (Transactions of the American Philosophical Society, n.s., vol. 35, pt. 3, pp. 156–323, Philadelphia, 1946).

LEECHMAN, D. *Caribou for Chipewyans* (The Beaver, March, pp. 12–13, Winnipeg, 1948).

The Pointed Skins (The Beaver, March, pp. 14–18, Winnipeg, 1948).

Prehistoric Migration Routes Through the Yukon (Canadian Historical Review, vol. 27, pp. 383–390, Toronto, 1946).

LEES, E. J. *Geology of the Teslin-Quiet Lake Area, Yukon* (Memoirs of the Canadian Department of Mines, Geological Survey, no. 203, Ottawa, 1936).

LEIGHTON, D., AND C. KLUCKHOHN. *Children of the People* (Cambridge, 1947).

LE JEUNE, P. L. *Dictionnaire général du Canada* (2 vols., Ottawa, 1931).

McCONNELL, R. G. *Report on an Exploration in the Yukon and Mackenzie Basins* (Annual Report of the Geological and Natural History Survey of Canada, n.s., vol. 4, pt. D, Montreal, 1890).

McLEAN, J. *Notes of a Twenty-Five Years' Service in the Hudson's Bay Territory* (Wallace, W. S., ed., Toronto, 1932).

MEAD, M. *Growing Up in New Guinea* (in Mead, M., From the South Seas, New York, 1939).

Male and Female (New York, 1949).

MORICE, A. G. *The Carrier Language* (St. Gabriel-Moedling, 1932).

The Fur Trader in Anthropology and a Few Related Questions (American Anthropologist, n.s., vol. 30, pp. 60–84, Menasha, 1928).

The Great Déné Race (Anthropos, vol. 1, pp. 229–277; vol. 2, pp. 1–34, 181–196; vol. 4, pp. 582–606; vol. 5, pp. 113–142, 419–443, 643–653, 969–990; St. Gabriel-Moedling, 1906–10).

The Nah·ane and Their Language (Transactions of the Canadian Institute, vol. 7, pp. 517–534, Ottawa, 1900–03).

MURDOCK, G. P. *Social Structure* (New York, 1949).

ONRAET, T. *Sixty Below* (New York, 1949).

OSGOOD, C. *Contributions to the Ethnography of the Kutchin* (Yale University Publications in Anthropology, no. 14, New Haven, 1937).

　　The Distribution of the Northern Athapaskan Indians (Yale University Publications in Anthropology, no. 7, New Haven, 1936).

　　The Ethnography of the Tanaina (Yale University Publications in Anthropology, no. 16, New Haven, 1937).

　　Ingalik Material Culture (Yale University Publications in Anthropology, no. 22, New Haven, 1940).

PARNELL, G. *Campbell of the Yukon* (The Beaver, June, pp. 4–6; Sept., pp. 16–18; Dec., pp. 23–27; Winnipeg, 1942).

PETITOT, E. F. S. *Autour du grand lac des Esclaves* (Paris, 1891).

PIKE, W. *Through the Subarctic Forest* (London, 1896).

RAY, V. F. *Culture Element Distributions: XXII, Plateau* (Anthropological Records, vol. 8, no. 2, Berkeley, 1942).

RICHARDSON, J. *Arctic Searching Expedition* (New York, 1852).

SCHWATKA, F. *Report on a Military Reconnaissance made in Alaska in 1883* (Washington, 1900).

SCIDMORE, E. R. *The Stikine River in 1898* (National Geographic Magazine, vol. 10, pp. 1–15, Washington, 1899).

SHELDON, C. *The Wilderness of the Upper Yukon* (New York, 1919).

SHIMKIN, D. B. *Childhood and Development among the Wind River Shoshone* (Anthropological Records, vol. 5, no. 5, Berkeley, 1947).

SKINNER, A. *Notes on the Eastern Cree and Northern Saulteaux* (Anthropological Papers of the American Museum of Natural History, vol. 9, pt. 1, pp. 1–117, New York, 1911).

SPAULDING, A. C. *Northeastern Archaeology and General Trends in the Northern Forest Zone* (in Johnson, F., ed., Man in Northeastern North America, Andover, 1946).

SPECK, F. G., *Naskapi* (Norman, 1935).

STANWELL-FLETCHER, J. F. AND T. C. *Naturalists in the Wilds of British Columbia* (Scientific Monthly, vol. 50, pp. 17–32, 125–137, 211–224, New York, 1940).

STEEDMAN, E. V. *The Ethnobotany of the Thompson Indians of British Columbia* (Forty-fifth Annual Report of the Bureau of American Ethnology, pp. 441–522, Washington, 1930).

STERNBERG, C. M. *Canadian Dinosaurs* (Canadian Geographical Journal, vol. 30, pp. 186–199, Ottawa, 1945).

STEVENSON, J. J. *Some Notes on Southeastern Alaska and Its People* (Scottish Geographical Magazine, vol. 9, pp. 66–83, Edinburgh, 1893).

SWANTON, J. R. *Social Condition, Beliefs and Linguistic Relationship of the Tlingit Indians* (Twenty-sixth Annual Report of the Bureau of American Ethnology, pp. 391–486, Washington, 1908).

TEIT, J. *Kaska Tales* (Journal of American Folklore, vol. 30, pp. 427–473, Boston and New York, 1917).

　　Notes on the Tahltan Indians of British Columbia (in Boas Anniversary Volume, New York, 1906).

　　On Tahltan (Athabaskan) Work (Summary Reports of the Canadian Geological Survey, pp. 484–487, Ottawa, 1912).

　　Unpublished manuscript (in the National Museum of Canada, Ottawa, 1915?).

THOMPSON, S. *The Folktale* (New York, 1946).

TURTON, M. C. *Cassiar* (Toronto, 1934).

VADEBONEOEUR, E. R. *Flower of the Blitz* (New York Times Magazine, August 25, p. 28, New York, 1946).

WILLIAMS, A. B. *Game Trails in British Columbia* (London, 1925).

WILLIAMS, M. Y. *Geological Reconnaissance along the Alaska Highway from Fort Nelson, British Columbia, to Watson Lake, Yukon* (Canadian Department of Mines and Resources, Mines and Geology Branch, Geological Survey Paper 44–28, Ottawa, 1944, mimeographed).

WILSON, G. AND M. *The Analysis of Social Change* (Cambridge, 1945).

The Medicis
A Ruling Dynasty

Heather Lehr Wagner

CHELSEA HOUSE
PUBLISHERS

A Haights Cross Communications Company ®

Philadelphia

COVER: Lorenzo de' Medici "The Magnificent," among the artists, Palazzo Pitti, Florence, Italy.

CHELSEA HOUSE PUBLISHERS
VP, NEW PRODUCT DEVELOPMENT Sally Cheney
DIRECTOR OF PRODUCTION Kim Shinners
CREATIVE MANAGER Takeshi Takahashi
MANUFACTURING MANAGER Diann Grasse

Staff for The Medicis
EXECUTIVE EDITOR Lee Marcott
EDITORIAL ASSISTANT Carla Greenberg
PRODUCTION EDITOR Noelle Nardone
COVER AND INTERIOR DESIGNER Keith Trego
LAYOUT 21st Century Publishing and Communications, Inc.

First Printing

9 8 7 6 5 4 3 2 1

Library of Congress Cataloging-in-Publication Data

Wagner, Heather Lehr.
  The Medicis: a ruling dynasty/Heather Lehr Wagner.
    p. cm.–(Makers of the Middle Ages and Renaissance)
  Includes bibliographical references and index.
  ISBN 0-7910-8630-5 (hard cover)
  1. Medici, House of–Juvenile literature. 2. Florence (Italy)–History–
1421–1737–Juvenile literature. 3. Florence (Italy)–Kings and rulers–
Biography–Juvenile literature. I. Title. II. Series.
  DG737.42.W34 2005
  945'.5'0099–dc22
                                                    2005007488

CONTENTS

Murder in
the Cathedral

A large crowd had gathered for the celebration of Easter Mass on Sunday, April 26, 1478, at Florence's magnificent cathedral, the Duomo. Many distinguished and important men were inside. The nephew of Pope Sixtus IV, Cardinal Rafaello Riario, was there, as well as Francesco de' Pazzi, son of the wealthy Pazzi family.

1

Perhaps the most distinguished attendee, however, was young Lorenzo de' Medici, "Lorenzo the Magnificent," as he was known.

Lorenzo de' Medici was the head of the city-state of Florence, having inherited the role at the age of 21, upon the death of his father. For nine years, he had provided Florence with glory and prosperity. An astute politician and statesman, and an extraordinarily generous patron of the arts, Lorenzo de' Medici had overseen a period in which Florence became the intellectual and artistic capital of Europe, while ensuring itself a place of prominence among the most powerful city-states in Italy. By spending his own wealth for the public benefit, Lorenzo de' Medici's dominance of Florentine politics had provided its citizens with a time of great prosperity.

In addition to being a generous and wise statesman, Lorenzo de' Medici also knew how to have fun. He organized splendid tournaments and festivals, breathtaking fireworks displays, and grand pageants. The people of Florence loved him. As he stood in the cathedral, however, Lorenzo de' Medici did not realize that among the

Lorenzo de' Medici became head of the city-state of Florence at age 21, upon the death of his father. Lorenzo de' Medici was an astute politician and an extraordinary patron of the arts.

crowd were four men who were preparing to kill him before Mass ended.

THE PAZZI CONSPIRACY

The plot to assassinate Lorenzo de' Medici was organized by Pope Sixtus IV and his nephews in Rome. Joining them in the plot were members of Florence's noble Pazzi family, whose name would be used to describe what became known as the Pazzi Conspiracy. Pope Sixtus IV was, by all accounts, a cruel and ruthless representative of the Catholic Church, intent on using his office to obtain land and power for his family—principally his nephews. He was determined to add Florence to his conquests, and he decided that this goal would best be accomplished by eliminating Lorenzo de' Medici and his younger brother, Giuliano. Once both of the Medici brothers were out of the way, Pope Sixtus IV planned to make his nephew, Girolamo Riario, the new head of state of Florence. Riario could be counted on to be completely loyal to the pope.

Pope Sixtus IV was assisted in his plan by the Pazzi family, wealthy and proud Florentines who held an intense grudge against all members of the Medici family—their rivals for power and influence in Florence—and Lorenzo de' Medici in particular. The Pazzi family supported the idea of assassinating the two Medici brothers, but intended to seize power for themselves once the Medicis had been eliminated.

Banks in Rome operated at the invitation of the pope. First the pope cancelled the Medici bank concession in Rome and transferred that right to the Pazzi family's bank. Next he appointed as archbishop of Pisa a member of the Salviati family, another family unfriendly to the Medicis. Lorenzo de' Medici was unhappy with the appointment, but he still seemed unaware of the diabolical plot that was unfolding against him.

By early 1478, the plans for Lorenzo de' Medici's assassination were in place. Among the conspirators were Girolamo Riario (who, in the pope's plan, would become Florence's head of state), the young cardinal Rafaello Riario (another of the pope's nephews who would travel to Florence to oversee the plan while Girolamo remained in Rome), Francesco Salviati (the archbishop-designate of Pisa, who had been promised by the pope that he would become archbishop of Florence if the plan was a success), several members of the Pazzi family, and a mercenary soldier named Montesecco, who had been hired by the pope as the chief assassin.

In the first phase of the plot, troops led by men loyal to Pope Sixtus IV were sent to occupy various points along Florence's border. It was thought that once Lorenzo de' Medici and his brother had been assassinated, chaos would break out in Florence, allowing the troops to march in and seize control.

The other conspirators arrived in and around Florence, with many of them staying just outside the city at the home of Jacopo de' Pazzi, the head of the Pazzi family, whose villa bordered that of the Medicis. The Medicis, learning of the presence of the distinguished guest Rafaello Riario at the Pazzi villa, cordially invited the cardinal and his friends to a banquet at their home on Saturday, April 25. The conspirators were thrilled with the invitation, and quickly decided to poison Lorenzo de' Medici and his brother Giuliano during the party. Unfortunately for the plotters, Giuliano was not well and did not attend the banquet, so the plan had to be reworked.

Hoping to create a new opportunity, the Pazzi family informed Lorenzo de' Medici that Cardinal Riario had heard much about the famous art treasures of the Medicis, and the gracious host quickly invited the cardinal and his friends to be his guests at the palace.

They all traveled to the palace in Florence, where the conspirators had determined that, after Mass, they would murder the two Medici brothers at their dinner table. To the plotters' dismay, it quickly became clear, however, that Giuliano de' Medici was still too ill to attend the celebratory dinner. He would attend the Easter Mass, but would then return to his room to rest and recover.

A new plot had to be formed, and quickly. By nightfall, the troops would be outside the gates of Florence and the element of surprise would be lost if their presence was discovered. The only solution was to seize the one moment when the two brothers would be in the same place at the same time—the Easter service at the Duomo. The cathedral would be crowded, allowing the murderers to act quickly and then disappear in the confusion. They would strike during the sacred ceremony, when the host was raised and all heads were bowed.

The plot proved to be too much for Montesecco, the hired assassin, who had traveled to Florence with Archbishop Salviati. Montesecco vowed that he would commit murder but not sacrilege, and backed out of the plan. Two priests were willing to step in for Montesecco, and the details of the plot were finalized, at last. The two Medici brothers would be separated in the cathedral. The two priests would place themselves near Lorenzo de' Medici while Francesco de' Pazzi and his accomplice, Bernardo Bandini, would occupy Giuliano de' Medici.

MURDER IN THE CATHEDRAL

Near midday on Easter Sunday, Lorenzo de' Medici left his palace, accompanied by his guest Rafaello Riario, and began the walk toward the cathedral. Giuliano de' Medici was still not feeling well, but an anxious Francesco de' Pazzi and Bernardo Bandini persuaded him to join them for the Easter Mass, urging him out of bed. Francesco, pretending to help Giuliano as he limped along, put an arm around him, secretly feeling around his waist to determine whether or not he was armed or wearing a mail shirt, a type of protective armor, under his clothes. He had neither a weapon nor protective clothing.

As planned, the two brothers were led to separate sections of the cathedral. Giuliano was taken to the northern side of the choir, near a door, while Lorenzo was placed at the south side of the choir. The host was raised and thousands of worshippers bowed their heads.

As Giuliano de' Medici bowed, Francesco de' Pazzi and Bernardo Bandini began stabbing him. Francesco de' Pazzi stabbed Giuliano a total of 18 times, with such fury that in the confusion he accidentally stabbed himself in the leg. Giuliano de' Medici immediately fell dead.

Had the expert soldier Montesecco remained with the plot, Lorenzo de' Medici might have met the same fate, but the priests who were the last-minute substitute assassins lacked Montesecco's expertise in handling weapons. Less quick to act than Bandini and de' Pazzi, they succeeded only in slashing Lorenzo de' Medici in the neck before he quickly pulled off his cloak and wrapped it around

Lorenzo's brother, Giuliano de' Medici (above), was stabbed multiple times and killed as a result of the Pazzi Conspiracy.

himself as a kind of makeshift shield. They had also failed to check Lorenzo for weapons. He was carrying a sword, which he quickly drew and used to fight off his attackers.

Lorenzo de' Medici jumped over the low rail surrounding the choir, ran across the front of the high altar, and quickly barricaded himself in the sacristy, the room in the church where the clergy dressed and sacred vessels were kept. He was joined by a few friends who bolted the heavy bronze doors and stood at guard. With the cathedral in chaos, worshippers screamed and attempted to determine who was responsible for striking at the Medicis. In the confusion, the assassins were able to escape and Cardinal Riario hid in the high altar.

As the cathedral emptied, one of Lorenzo de' Medici's aides climbed to the top of the organ gallery, over the sacristy door. From there, he could see the whole empty cathedral, and it was then that he spotted the dead body of Giuliano de' Medici, lying in a puddle of blood. Soon a knock was heard at the sacristy door. A group of Lorenzo's friends had arrived to carry him home to safety.

THE ATTACK ON THE SIGNORIA

In addition to the assassination attempt on the Medicis, another key element of the plot had revolved around seizing control of Florence in the chaos. Archbishop Salviati, the would-be arch-bishop of Florence, had been given the job of seizing control of the government, helping to para-lyze Florence just before the troops marched into the city. As the attackers were striking the Medicis in the cathedral, Archbishop Salviati arrived at the Palazzo della Signoria, the palace where Florence's chief legislators were meeting. Salviati and his followers planned to make a ceremonial entrance into the council chamber and then, using the element of surprise, seize the government and kill all members of the legislature—known as the *Signoria*—who resisted.

Something about the arrival of Salviati and his entourage aroused the suspicion of the *gonfaloniere*, one of the chief officials of the Signoria, who cor-dially invited the archbishop and his entourage into his own private rooms and then sent out a messenger to determine whether anything unusual was going on in the city. The messenger quickly

In addition to plotting the murders of Lorenzo and Giuliano de' Medici, another key element of the Pazzi Conspiracy revolved around seizing control of Florence in the chaos following the assassinations. A view of the city is shown here.

returned to relate the reports of chaos in the cathedral. Accompanying him was the noise of an angry mob forming in the streets.

In the midst of the crowd, elderly Jacopo de' Pazzi and other members of his family, accompanied by 100 armed men, rode on horseback, urging the crowds with cries of "Liberty!" and "Down with the

Palle!" *Palle*, or balls, were the symbol on the crest of the Medici family. Instead, the crowd responded with angry cries of "Long Live the Palle!" [1]

Quickly determining what had happened—and what was about to happen—the gonfaloniere seized Archbishop Salviati and hanged him, leaving his body dangling from the corner window of the council hall. Five of his conspirators were also hanged from other windows. The remaining 26 members of Salviati's group were struck down in the stairway as they attempted to flee.

These actions were not sufficient for the angry mob, however, which quickly hunted down the other conspirators. Francesco de' Pazzi, weak from his own wounds, had escaped to his home. He was dragged from his bed and hanged next to the body of the archbishop. Few stopped to ask questions or determine guilt or innocence. Anyone suspected of being part of the plot was seized and killed. Seventy people were killed in the first four days. Some 200 more people would be killed before the chaos had ended. Old Jacopo de' Pazzi, who had attempted to inspire the crowds with his shouts of "Liberty!," was also killed. After his burial, his body was pulled out of its grave and dragged through the streets, before his naked remains were finally dumped into the Arno River.

Bernardo Bandini, one of Giuliano de' Medici's assassins, escaped to Constantinople, but the sultan of the Ottoman Empire ordered that he be returned to Florence in chains, where he was immediately executed. The Pazzi family name, by public decree, was forever erased. Any places in Florence that bore the Pazzi name, including their own palaces, were renamed. Anyone married to a Pazzi was barred from public office. Lorenzo de' Medici showed mercy to a few members of the plot, however. Having escaped the cathedral, upon reaching his own home, he ordered a guard to protect Cardinal Riario, one of the chief conspirators who had been hiding in the high altar. The cardinal was taken to the Medici Palace, where he was kept hidden for several days before being secretly conveyed back to Rome.

A PAPAL WAR

The pope was furious at the plot's failure, and angry that his part in the conspiracy had been uncovered. He immediately denounced the Florentine government for what he called the criminal and sacrilegious hanging of his representative, the archbishop, and demanded that Lorenzo de' Medici surrender himself to religious authorities. Medici refused, protesting that his only crime had been not allowing himself to be murdered.[2] The Florentine legislature joined Lorenzo de' Medici in his protest, offering as proof the signed confession of one of the conspirators who linked the pope to the plot, and calling upon other European rulers for support.

Events quickly spiraled out of control. The pope announced that the entire state of Florence was excommunicated, expelled from the Catholic Church. Clergy in Florence responded by outlawing the pope. Pope Sixtus IV then declared war on Florence. He announced that all Catholics were forbidden from trading with Florence, and enforced treaties he had formed with Siena and the king of Naples, whose troops invaded Tuscany.

The war and the barriers to trade placed a heavy burden on the Florentine people, and Lorenzo de' Medici soon determined that he must surrender, if only to protect his people. The legislature refused to allow him to do so, however, and Lorenzo was

TEMPLA DOMVM EXPOSITIS VICOS FORA MOENIA PONTES
VIRGINEAM TRIVII QVOD REPARARIS AQVAM
PRISCA LICET NAVTIS STATVAS DARE COMMODA PORTVS
ET VATICANVM CINGERE SIXTE IVGVM
PLVS TAMEN VRBS DEBET NAM QVAE SQVALORE LATEBAT
CERNITVR IN CELEBRI BIBLIOTHECA LOCO

Pope Sixtus IV (seated at right) was furious at the Pazzi
plot's failure, and angry that his part in the conspiracy
had been uncovered. He immediately denounced the
Florentine government for what he called the criminal
and sacrilegious hanging of his representative, the
archbishop. He also demanded that Lorenzo de' Medici
surrender himself to religious authorities.

forced to slip away secretly. He traveled first to Pisa and then to Naples to meet with King Ferrante, an ally of the pope's.

King Ferrante was impressed, both by Lorenzo de' Medici's courage in slipping through the war zone to travel to Naples, and with his argument that, should the pope become too powerful, a weakened Florence under the pope's domination would not prove to be in Naples's best interest. For three months, Lorenzo de' Medici stayed in Naples, where he was treated as an honored guest, rather than a political prisoner. In the end, Lorenzo de' Medici had achieved a treaty with Naples that promised some land and financial support for Naples in exchange for an end to the fighting. The pope was furious at this turn of events, but an attack on Italian soil by Turkish troops forced him to agree to peace with Florence so that a unified Italy might fight off the Turkish invasion.

Lorenzo de' Medici returned to Florence having achieved an honorable peace. His people cheered him as their hero. Throughout Italy, he was hailed as a brilliant diplomat, a skillful financier, and the man who brought greatness back to Florence.

The Pazzi Conspiracy ultimately ended in failure. Its consequences, however—the death of Lorenzo de' Medici's beloved younger brother, the war that followed, and the threats to Lorenzo and his family— would forever mark the reign of Lorenzo de' Medici. The carefree young man who loved poetry and pageants was gone. In his place was a more serious ruler, determined to consolidate all power under his control and eliminate any potential rivals.

The story of the Medici Dynasty might have ended in the Duomo on that Easter Sunday. Instead it marked another interesting event in the saga of a single family that dominated the politics of Florence for three centuries—a family whose rise to power would signal the beginning of the Renaissance in Italy.

Test Your Knowledge

1 What is the name of Florence's cathedral?

   a. The Vatican

   b. The Duomo

   c. The Medici Palace

   d. The Pazzi

2 What was the name of the plot to kill to Medici brothers?

   a. The Florence Conspiracy

   b. The Pope Sixtus Conspiracy

   c. The Pazzi Conspiracy

   d. The Medici Conspiracy

3 How many times was Giuliano de' Medici stabbed?

   a. 50

   b. 18

   c. 10

   d. 32

4 In addition to the assassination attempt on the Medicis, another key element of the plot involved what?

   a. Seizing control of Florence in the chaos

   b. Taking control of the Vatican

   c. Installing the pope in power

   d. Seizing control of the legislature

5 For how long did the Medici family dominate Florentine politics?

a. 50 years

b. 10 centuries

c. 200 years

d. 3 centuries

ANSWERS: 1. b; 2. c; 3. b; 4. a; 5. d

Bankers to the Republic

By the late fourteenth century, Florence had witnessed triumph and tragedy. Rival groups had battled for control over the city whose territory and power were much greater than the Florence we know today. Florence had conquered Pisa, Prato, Volterra, and Pistoia—among other Italian cities—and comprised a region with autonomy and independence more similar to a state than a city. The following four city-states controlled most of the power in Italy: Venice, Naples, Milan, and Florence. Their rulers were constantly challenging each other for prestige, territory, and alliances with foreign powers.

Authority within Florence rested, in large part, within a system of guilds—groups of merchants or craftsmen—which had been organized in the city. There were 21 guilds in total, among them wool merchants, silk merchants, judges, lawyers, doctors, and bankers. Young Giovanni de' Medici belonged to the guild of bankers.

Giovanni de' Medici was born into a middle-class Florentine family in 1360. Florence was, at the time of his birth and during his early years, quite powerful. Small wars with neighboring states had added to its territory and power. The region then known as Florence would today more accurately be identified as Tuscany. Florence was a European leader in trade and commerce, and through its banking industry, Florentines were beginning to make their influence felt around the world.

Members of the Medici family were well known as bankers, and for their political activism in Florence. Giovanni de' Medici's father, Averardo, was a banker, and his great-grandfather, also named Averardo, had operated a successful trading business. His grandfather Salvestro had been sent, in 1336, as a diplomat to finalize the treaty between Florence and Venice, while a distant cousin, also named Salvestro, had contributed to the riot of the *ciompi*, the cloth guild workers, which helped to bring about the fall of the noble class in Florence.

The Medici family tradition included examples of hard work, and of success both in finance and politics. This was Giovanni's heritage, but it was his life and accomplishments that would mark the rise of the Medici ruling dynasty.

WEALTH AND POWER

By the time Giovanni de' Medici had reached middle age, he was a millionaire. Of the 80 banking families in Florence, the Medicis had risen to the top, with branches of their bank in 16 European capitals. The most important men in the Florentine guilds were expected to become involved in politics, and Giovanni de' Medici could have become a very influential political figure. Instead he chose to spend his money and energy on public works. He contributed toward building churches and he donated to charity, funding the construction of the Foundling Hospital of Florence. He also employed as the hospital's architect Filippo Brunelleschi, who would go on to become one of Florence's leading architects of the time, overseeing the construction of the impressive grand dome over Florence's largest cathedral. Giovanni de' Medici supported young artists, commissioning a group of them to decorate his home with frescoes. He also incurred much criticism and gossip in the process, as that type of decoration—most often used in churches—was considered excessive for a private home.

Giovanni de' Medici had married Piccarda Bueri in 1386. Their oldest son, Cosimo, was born on September 27, 1389. Six years later, a second son, Lorenzo, would be born. The family lived a fairly simple life, not merely because Giovanni had gained a reputation for being a prudent man. Homes, even of the wealthiest Florentines, were not built or furnished for beauty or comfort. Floors were bare stone; the walls were whitewashed and seldom covered with any hangings or tapestries; chairs were made of wood, straight-backed, covered only with leather; beds were wide and hard. Even

The Duomo

The Duomo (Italian for "cathedral") of Florence was finally completed in 1436, while Cosimo de' Medici was in power. Its soaring dome has become a symbolic part of the Florence skyline. The cathedral itself was built over the course of six centuries, its construction ebbing and flowing in reflection of the turmoil in Florence at the time. It was built on the site of an earlier cathedral, Santa Reparata, which had been a place of worship for Florentines for nine centuries. In 1293, the Florentine Republic decided to finance a larger and grander cathedral, and the people of Florence were expected to contribute to this project. In fact, a law was passed stating that the wills of all Florentine citizens must include a tax to help finance the cathedral's construction.

The first architect, Arnolfo di Cambio, designed a soaring place of worship and oversaw the beginning of its construction, in 1296. Work continued until

the wealthiest of homes contained only these pieces, plus, perhaps, a large credenza holding the family's best vases, glass, and silver for formal dinners, and a chest for linen and clothes.[3]

his death in 1302. A succession of architects contributed to other parts of the design, including the bell tower, the center nave, and the south doors, as well as the plan for external marble and the decorative side entrances. One problem remained: how to construct and support a cupola large enough to soar over the massive cathedral. The architect Brunelleschi was eventually chosen to manage this most challenging part of the cathedral's plan, and the brilliant system of supports he designed made the Duomo a masterpiece of Renaissance architecture.

Pope Eugene IV dedicated the Duomo on March 25, 1436, some 140 years after construction began. Forty-two years later, Lorenzo de' Medici would narrowly escape assassination while celebrating Easter Mass at the cathedral. Final design elements, including the addition of white, green, and red marble to the exterior, were made to the facade in 1886.

The same simple, plain style was used for clothing, as well. There were actually laws in Florence
to govern what was and was not considered appropriate dress for the people. Women were strictly
instructed on what material dresses might be made
of, and they took care to avoid any of a long list of
forbidden decorations. These same rules specified
acceptable length—and width—for women's dresses.

Men also were restricted in what they could wear.
For most men, the required clothing was a simple,
plain, long garment, with buttons down the front,
resembling the long black cloak or cassock a priest
might wear. This plainness and simple style would
gradually slip away, however, as the artists that
Giovanni de' Medici was employing, and other
artists that future generations of Medicis would
support, began to carve out a new style that would
become known as Renaissance style.

A JUST TAX

In the early 1400s, as a sign of his prominence
within the banking guild, Giovanni de' Medici was
chosen to serve as one of the seven priors, or representatives, comprising the legislature of Florence,

known as the Signoria. In 1421, he was elected gonfaloniere of Florence, literally meaning "standard bearer," but actually an important ceremonial office.

Giovanni de' Medici's most significant political action came in 1426, when he fought fierce opposition from the noble class to oversee the passage of a new and fairer tax, known as the *catasto*. Up until that time, taxes had been enacted arbitrarily, when a war or government shortfall meant that Florence needed additional cash. For years, the wealthy families of Florence had benefited from a system of indirect taxes, which imposed heavy, random taxes—sometimes several in a single year—and an additional random poll tax on all Florentines. Giovanni de' Medici's proposal was a new, 1.5 percent tax on all capital, with the wealthier citizens paying more than the poorest. All citizens were required to declare their possessions—gold and silver, jewels, property, income, and investments. In the event of an emergency, such as a war, however, the tax would be collected with the heaviest burden falling on the wealthiest families. The tax was regarded as a significant step toward social progress, and it made Giovanni de' Medici a hero to the poorest citizens of Florence.

When Giovanni de' Medici was killed on February 28, 1429, his family was one of the wealthiest in all of Florence. His vast fortune was passed on to his two sons, Cosimo and Lorenzo.

IN HIS FATHER'S FOOTSTEPS

As the oldest son, it was Cosimo de' Medici's responsibility to run the family business. At the time of his father's death, Cosimo de' Medici was 40 years old, and had already formed an important alliance with the current pope, John XXIII. Having helped to save the pope's life, Cosimo de' Medici had earned for the Medici family the pope's loyalty, plus—perhaps more important—the lucrative and prestigious responsibility of serving as official banker for the vast wealth of the Catholic Church.

As Cosimo de' Medici assumed control of the family's business, he seemed likely to follow closely in his father's footsteps. He was similar to his father in personality, modest and tactful in his business dealings, and generous with artists and others in need.

Two years after his father's death, Cosimo de' Medici decided to build a new home—a palace—for his family, near the Church of San Lorenzo. He

When Giovanni de' Medici was killed on February 28, 1429, his family was one of the wealthiest in all of Florence. His vast fortune was passed on to his two sons, Cosimo and Lorenzo. Cosimo, shown here, was the oldest son. As such, he assumed responsibility for the family business.

determined that his palace would be something extraordinary, something that would reflect the new styles in architecture and design that were beginning to flourish in Florence. He hired talented artists and sculptors to create masterpieces to adorn his new home. The result was the Medici Palace, a building that still stands as a landmark of architectural achievement from the early years of the Renaissance.

Cosimo de' Medici was passionately interested in art, and he became a great patron of Florentine artists. He would eventually build three villas for his family and a convent for the Dominicans at San Marco. He supported the sculptor Donatello, as well as painters Fra Filippo Lippi, Fra Angelico, and Benozzo Gozzoli. He also supported learning and philosophy, paying for the construction of several libraries and schools.

Unfortunately, Cosimo de' Medici's wealth, success, and popularity, and the grand family palace he was constructing sparked jealousy among the other wealthy families in Florence. In 1433, one of the Medici family's rivals, the Albizzi family, accused Cosimo and his family of posing a danger to the state because of their wealth and ambition.[4]

Two years after his father's death, Cosimo de' Medici decided to build a new home—a palace—for his family. Medici Palace, shown here, still stands today.

The proof, the Albizzis claimed, could be found in Cosimo de' Medici's elaborate new palace, far more luxurious and extravagant than that of an ordinary Florentine citizen.

The charges were successful. On September 7, 1433, Cosimo de' Medici was arrested, charged with treason, and imprisoned in a cell in the tower of the Palazzo della Signoria. The Albizzis, and others intent on eliminating the Medicis, sought the death penalty for Cosimo de' Medici's crimes. Cosimo de' Medici, meanwhile, possibly fearing that his enemies might attempt to poison him while in prison, refused to eat anything for four days, until one of his jailers shared his own food, eating at the same time, so that Cosimi de' Medici might be assured that the food was safe.

With the help of his jailer, Cosimo de' Medici was able to smuggle a bribe to members of the Signoria who were deciding his fate, and instead of execution, he, his brother, and other members of the Medici family were banished from Florence. A few days after the sentence was passed down, Cosimo de' Medici was taken by an armed guard to the frontier of Florence and was ordered never to return.

LIFE IN EXILE

With Cosimo, Lorenzo, and other members of the Medici family scattered throughout Italy, the Albizzis and others, no doubt, felt confident that they had successfully eliminated the Medici family's power and influence from Florence. The nobles quickly set out to undo many of the laws that the Medicis had supported, attempting to once more assure the dominance of the noble class in Florence.

All friends of the Medicis were punished for their association with the family, either by being similarly forced into exile or imprisoned. Many of the artists the Medicis had supported quickly left Florence. The architect Brunelleschi was imprisoned; his work on the construction of the cathedral's soaring dome abruptly halted.

The Albizzis soon launched Florence into a war against the small city-state of Lucca. The war proved expensive, massively unpopular, and ultimately unsuccessful. Lucca had an alliance with Milan, however, so the war against Lucca also led Florence into war with Milan. This conflict would drag on for several years.

Within one year, however, a new Signoria had been chosen, and many of the members were hostile to the Albizzis. They quickly passed a law canceling the banishment of the Medicis and on October 5, Cosimo de' Medici returned to Florence, welcomed

Cosimo de' Medici (on horseback at right) returns to Florence from exile. The people welcome him with great joy.

with great joy by the people. Machiavelli, the famous political tactician and author who spent many years studying and attempting to win the favor of the Medicis, noted, "Seldom has a citizen returning from a great victory been greeted by such a concourse of people and with such demonstrations of affection as Cosimo on his return from exile."[5]

Shortly after his return, as proof of his popularity, Cosimo de' Medici was elected gonfaloniere. His term in that office would last only three months. He had in mind a different, more powerful role to help avoid another exile from Florence. His enemies, upon his return, were forced out of office; many of them fled Florence. Those in the Signoria, acknowledging Cosimo's status, were now quick to show their support for the Medicis. Cosimo de' Medici took advantage of their support to have himself appointed as banker to the republic and advisor to the government.

BANKER TO THE REPUBLIC

Cosimo de' Medici placed much of his own money at the disposal of the republic. He was generous with loans, and generous with expenses he personally undertook on behalf of all of Florence. He entertained important dignitaries and foreign leaders at his own expense, housing them in his palace. Emperors, princes, diplomats, and the pope were all his guests at one time or another. Through his hosting and entertaining, Florence gradually became a center for political and religious deliberations, glittering cultural events, and thriving commerce.

Through these activities, Cosimo de' Medici also became recognized as Florence's head of state, even when he held no official title and was not considered a part of the government. Florentines and foreigners knew that Cosimo de' Medici had the diplomatic connections, financial resources, and status to get things done.

His investments and loans in foreign countries made it possible for Cosimo de' Medici to influence foreign relations. When the leaders of Venice and Naples threatened Florence, Cosimo de' Medici was able to use his bank's investments and loans in those two city-states to stabilize the conflict. Rather than having the Medici banks call in their loans, which would have brought the economies of those two regions to collapse, their leaders reluctantly negotiated peaceful settlements.

Cosimo de' Medici also continued to invest generously in the arts. Some of the greatest artists of the day worked on his commissions at the Church of San Lorenzo, the Medici Palace, and the monastery of San Marco. He collected many different kinds of art, and opened his collections to all artists. In 1436, Brunelleschi completed his work on the grand dome soaring above Florence's cathedral and as Brunelleschi's patron—and a generous donor to the

In 1436, Filippo Brunelleschi completed his work on the grand dome soaring above Florence's cathedral. As Brunelleschi's patron—and a generous donor to the dome's construction—Cosimo de' Medici took credit for the completion of the cathedral.

dome's construction—Cosimo de' Medici took credit for the completion of the cathedral, after 138 years of construction.

PATER PATRIAE

Cosimo de' Medici's control of Florence marked a period of prosperity and artistic achievement. In 1440, his grand palace on the Via Larga was finally ready, after some ten years of construction. Joining Cosimo de' Medici and his wife were their two sons, Piero and Giovanni, who were then 24 and 19 years old respectively. Only a few years after the move into the palace, both sons married. Still later, grandchildren (sons and daughters of Piero) would join the family.

Cosimo de' Medici appreciated having his family by his side, but his sons were not healthy, and in 1463, his younger son, Giovanni, died. His son's death was a great tragedy for Cosimo de' Medici, who was carried through the rooms of the palace muttering, "Too large a house for so small a family." [6]

After some 30 years of dominance, Cosimo de' Medici died on August 1, 1464, at the age of 75. The people of Florence, who had retained their love and respect for him until the end, wanted to honor him with a grand funeral, but the Medici family declined. Instead the Signoria issued a public decree, conferring on Cosimo de' Medici the title *Pater Patriae* ("Father of his Country"), noting that the title should be inscribed on his tomb. He was buried in the Church of San Lorenzo, a church for whose construction he had paid.

Machiavelli wrote of Cosimo de' Medici:

> He was one of the most prudent of men; grave and courteous and of venerable appearance. His early years were full of trouble, exile, and personal danger, but by the unwearied generosity of his disposition he triumphed over all his enemies and made himself most popular with the people. Though so rich, yet in his mode of living he was always very simple and without ostentation. None of his time had such an intimate knowledge of government and of State affairs. Hence even in a city so given to change, he retained the Government for thirty years.[7]

The day after Cosimo de' Medici's death, his son Piero told his sons, Lorenzo and Giuliano, of their grandfather's legacy:

Piero de' Medici, Cosimo de' Medici's son, is shown here. It was not Piero de' Medici, but rather his sons, who would eventually rule Florence and continue the Medici legacy.

He counselled me that, as you had good abilities, I ought to bring you up well, and you would then relieve me of many cares. . . . He said that he did not wish any pomp or demonstration at his funeral. . . . He reminded me, as he had told me before, of where he wished to be buried in San Lorenzo, and said all in such an orderly manner, and with so much prudence and spirit, that it was wonderful. He added that his life had been long, therefore he was well content to leave it when God willed. [8]

Cosimo de' Medici's final words would prove prophetic. For it was not in Piero's hands, but in the hands of his sons, that the Medici family would again dominate Florence.

Test Your Knowledge

1 Authority within Florence rested principally in what?

    a. A system of guilds

    b. An organized legal system

    c. The authority of the Catholic Church

    d. Local governments

2 To what guild did Giovanni de' Medici belong?

    a. The guild of silk merchants

    b. The guild of doctors

    c. The guild of bankers

    d. The guild of lawyers

3 At the time of Giovanni de' Medici's birth, the region then known as Florence would today more accurately be identified as

    a. Tuscany.

    b. Rome.

    c. Pisa.

    d. Venice.

4 How long did Cosimo de' Medici rule Florence?

    a. 100 years

    b. 30 years

    c. 35 years

    d. 50 years

5   Where was Cosimo de' Medici buried?

a. The Duomo

b. The Vatican

c. The Medici Palace

d. The Church of San Lorenzo

ANSWERS: 1. a; 2. c; 3. a; 4. b; 5. d

Lorenzo the Magnificent

Cosimo de' Medici knew his son Piero well enough to have feared the fate of the Medici dynasty when it lay in his son's hands. Forty-eight-year-old Piero suffered from gout, a disease whose symptoms include painful inflammation of the joints, and lacked the energy and focus of his father and grandfather.

In Cosimo de' Medici's final years, loans to Edward IV of England and Charles the Bold of Burgundy had placed the Medici bank's finances at risk. When Piero de' Medici assumed control of the family's banks, he was confused by what seemed to be the precarious state of the Medici financial holdings. One of his father's advisors was called in to assist, and he suggested that Piero stabilize things by demanding repayment of the Medici loans. Chaos quickly followed. Those businesses that were unable to promptly repay their loans failed and Florence itself was put at risk, as the state struggled to repay its debt. Critics labeled Piero de' Medici a miser who was willing to destroy Florence in order to protect his own fortune.

During one of Piero de' Medici's frequent illnesses, a plot was hatched by the Poggios, enemies of the Medicis and of Florence—including the Duke of Ferrara and leaders of rival Venice—first to destroy the Medici bank, and then to murder Piero and assume control of Florence. Piero de' Medici was warned of the plot by a letter from the ruler of Bologna, stating that troops belonging to the Duke of Ferrara were massing on the Florentine border.

Despite his illness, Piero de' Medici ordered his attendants to put him on a stretcher and carry him to the Signoria to warn of the impending attack.

On August 27, 1466, Piero de' Medici made his dramatic appearance, and the sudden revelation of the plot was enough to bring it to a halt. The Signoria quickly approached Ferrara and Venice with offers to negotiate, while ordering troops— and their allies, the Milanese army—to assume defensive positions on the border. When the plot ended, the Signoria passed death sentences against all conspirators, but Piero de' Medici refused to have the men executed. With his actions, he was able to avoid the division of Florence into pro- and anti-Medici factions, and the rebellion against him ended peacefully.

A GRAND WEDDING

Piero de' Medici had two sons, Lorenzo and Giuliano, and two daughters, Bianca and Nannina. Weddings in the Medici family were an opportunity to form strategic alliances. Bianca and Nannina de' Medici were both married at a young age to sons of distinguished Florentine families, and it was expected that

Lorenzo de' Medici, the oldest son, would also be married to a member of a wealthy family in Florence.

Piero de' Medici and his wife, Lucrezia, however, had greater ambitions for their oldest son. One of the most powerful families in Italy was the Orsinis of Rome. Members of the Orsini family had played a leading role in many of Italy's wars, and in much of its politics. They had close connections to the Catholic Church, and many members of the family were noblemen and women.

It was decided that Lorenzo de' Medici would marry Clarice Orsini, the beautiful, red-headed daughter of a baron, and the niece of a cardinal. A grand jousting tournament was held to celebrate the engagement, and all of Florence's most important citizens were invited to attend. Handsome young men, dressed as knights, were accompanied by heralds, trumpeters, and pages, all displaying their knight's colors. Crowds watched the tournament from balconies and roofs. First the knights paraded around the square, before changing into their armor for the combat.

Lorenzo de' Medici was perhaps the most dazzling of all, with a shield studded with diamonds, a cap dotted with rubies and more diamonds, and a velvet coat fringed with gold. His helmet bore three blue feathers, and his horse was draped with red and white velvet, embroidered with pearls.[9] Lorenzo de' Medici won first prize in the tournament, earning a silver helmet with a statue of Mars, the Roman god of war, on top.

One year later, on June 4, 1469, in another grand celebration, Lorenzo de' Medici and Clarice Orsini were married. A gala party given by the groom's parents followed, to which all of Florence was invited. The party, which lasted three days, was marked by feasting, dancing, and music. Simultaneously, the wealthier members of Florentine society were entertained at five separate banquets held at the Medici family palace.

Six months after Lorenzo de' Medici's wedding, the young man became head of the Medici family when his father, Piero, died on December 2, 1469, and was buried next to the tomb of his brother Giovanni. When he was older, Lorenzo wrote:

Two days after the death of my father, although I, Lorenzo, was very young, being only in my twenty-first year, the principal men of the city and the state came to our house to condole on our loss and encourage me to take on myself the care of the city and the state, as my father and grandfather had done. This proposal being contrary to the instincts of my youthful age and considering that the burden and danger were great, I consented unwillingly, but I did so to protect our friends and our property, for it fares ill in Florence with anyone who possesses great wealth without any control in the government.[10]

YOUNG AND CAPABLE RULER

Lorenzo de' Medici's early years as head of the family and ruler of Florence were a time of great prosperity for all. He was a poet, a patron of the arts, and a young man who loved beauty. He invited the great thinkers and artists of the day to his home, hosting parties where the men who were shaping the Renaissance in Florence came together to inspire and be inspired.

During the first nine years of his reign, Lorenzo de' Medici and his younger brother, Giuliano, organized tremendous costumed themed spectacles, parades, and midnight tournaments with fireworks.

Lorenzo de' Medici was a brilliant statesman, considered by many to be the greatest of all the Medicis. The people of Florence paid homage to him.

The artist Botticelli was inspired by these events to create some of his most famous masterpieces, including *Birth of Venus*, *Mars and Venus*, and *Return of Spring*. During these years of splendor and spectacle, Lorenzo de' Medici provided lavish entertainment for himself and his people, noting in one of the many poems he wrote as a young man:

> *How passing fair is youth,*
> *Forever fleeting away;*
> *Who happy would be, let him be;*
> *Of tomorrow who can say?* [11]

Lorenzo de Medici's words proved prophetic, for his happy, carefree years as unofficial ruler of Florence did not last long. As early as 1474, he came into conflict with the new pope, Sixtus IV, arguing over land. Florence had on its southern, eastern, and northern borders, states under the control of the pope, and these so-called papal states came into question when Pope Sixtus IV decided to seize the small city of Imola for his nephew.

Imola had been loosely under Florentine control, and with its loss, Lorenzo de' Medici was determined to take a more forceful position against any other papal conquests, to ensure that towns near Imola did not slip away. Lorenzo de' Medici formed an alliance with Venice and Milan, aiming to "safeguard the peninsula's [Italy's] peace."[12] In reality, the alliance only angered the pope and prompted him to form his own alliance with the king of Naples. The pope's anger against Lorenzo de' Medici grew, and as we learned earlier, led to an assassination attempt against Lorenzo, the murder of his brother, an attempted revolt in Florence, and a war.

THE MAGNIFICENT

When Lorenzo de' Medici returned to Florence, having successfully negotiated peace with Naples, he was greeted as a hero, and labeled "Lorenzo the Magnificent." Lacking an official title, he was, nonetheless, determined to ensure Florence's safety, consolidate his power in Italy, and protect himself from future threats. The Florentine people were willing to support him in whatever way he deemed necessary.

Lorenzo de' Medici chose not to seize an official title. He chose not to have himself named a prince or crowned king of Florence. Instead he chose to ensure his power by establishing a kind of dominance over all aspects of Florentine life—its politics, its diplomacy, and the establishment of schools, libraries, and churches—while still maintaining the appearance of a democracy in the continuation of the elected legislature, the Signoria. In reality, however, it was with Lorenzo de' Medici that foreign rulers and dignitaries met, and it was also to Lorenzo de' Medici that people went with their requests for a public building, a favor, or an appointment to an important position.

Lorenzo de' Medici was able to retain his power in part because, like his father, grandfather, and great-grandfather, he was extraordinarily generous. He donated his own money to build libraries and churches. He supported artists and then opened his extensive collections to the public.

He was also a brilliant statesman, considered by many to be the greatest of all the Medicis. He understood that the true threat to the Italian city-states came not from within but from outside. It was not the small wars for territory between individual Italian city-states that were to be feared, but the threat of invasion from foreign powers, like France and Spain.

Lorenzo de' Medici also proved to be a great judge of art. Many young artists came to the Medici gardens to learn, copying the styles of great artists of the past. Lorenzo de' Medici enjoyed walking among the young art students, spotting talent. One young man who particularly impressed him was invited to live in the palace, joining the family for meals as he pursued his art. This young man, unofficially "adopted" by Lorenzo de' Medici, was the great artist Michelangelo. Lorenzo de' Medici also sponsored Leonardo da Vinci, another young artist who would become closely identified with the Renaissance.

LORENZO DE' MEDICI'S CHILDREN

Lorenzo de' Medici had four daughters and three sons. Lorenzo married two of his daughters to relatives of those who had participated in the Pazzi Conspiracy, to help heal any ongoing wounds in Florence. He followed the example of his own parents by selecting a member of the Orsini family of Rome, Alfonsina Orsini, to be his son Piero's wife.

Michelangelo

Michelangelo Buonarroti was born on March 6, 1475, in Caprese, Italy. His mother died when he was only six, and at a young age he was sent away to school, where he learned Latin and studied art. His father was horrified at Michelangelo's decision to become an apprentice to a painter at the age of 13, wanting his son to become a businessman instead. Michelangelo studied painting and sculpture in the Medici gardens, where he came to the attention of Lorenzo the Magnificent, and soon was living in the Medici Palace. While there, he spent time with the two Medicis who would become Popes Leo X and Clement VII.

During the regime of Girolamo Savonarola, Michelangelo went to Rome, to study its classical statues and ruins. Michelangelo produced his famous sculpture *Pietà* during this time, finishing it before he was 25.

He returned to Florence in 1501, sculpting the giant marble statue *David* to symbolize his desire that Florentines mimic the biblical leader in courage and a sense of duty. Seven years later, Pope Julius II called him back to Rome, to paint 12 figures of apostles on the ceiling of the Sistine Chapel in the

Vatican. Michelangelo had thought of himself as a sculptor, but by the time the project was completed (in 1512), he had painted more than 400 figures in a masterpiece of artwork containing numerous scenes from the Bible. Michelangelo was also commissioned to create a fitting tomb for Pope Julius II in St. Peter's, and the Medici tombs for Lorenzo de' Medici (the Duke of Urbino) and Giuliano de' Medici (the Duke of Nemours).

Michelangelo left Florence forever in 1534, disgusted by the brutality of Alessandro de' Medici. He returned to Rome, where Pope Clement VII commissioned him to paint a fresco of the Last Judgment in the Sistine Chapel. It would become the largest fresco created during the Renaissance, and a target of criticism for its depiction of nudity. Completed in 1541, the fresco was later "edited" by an artist who added drapes to cover the nude figures.

In 1546, Michelangelo was made chief architect of St. Peter's Basilica. He considered it a sacred duty, and would accept no payment for his labors. Michelangelo died on February 18, 1564. He is remembered today as one of the greatest artists of the Renaissance.

As a patron of the arts, Lorenzo de' Medici sponsored artists Michelangelo and Leonardo da Vinci. Michelangelo's *Man's Face* is shown here.

Lorenzo de' Medici was also anxious to mend ties with the Catholic Church. Through lobbying, Medici's second son, Giovanni, was admitted into a training program for high office in the Catholic Church when he was only seven years old. King Louis XI of France, a friend of Lorenzo's, appointed

Giovanni archbishop of Aix-en-Provence when
he was only 12 years old. With the death of Pope
Sixtus IV, Lorenzo's former enemy, the election
of a new pope, Innocent VIII, made Lorenzo de'
Medici's efforts complete. In 1492, 17-year-old
Giovanni de' Medici was named a cardinal.

As Giovanni de' Medici left for Rome to take his
position as the youngest cardinal, Lorenzo de'
Medici wrote his son a letter. He urged his son to
lead a simple, virtuous life, by avoiding temptation
and keeping his temper. Lorenzo de' Medici told his
son to first use his ears rather than his tongue, to rise
early, eat simple food, and get plenty of exercise.
Finally he urged his son to be a good priest, to place
the honor and advantage of the church first, but to
note that he would have many opportunities to
serve his city and his house, for the alliance of the
church was essential to Florence, and Giovanni was
to be the link between them.[13]

By 1489, facing the decline of his health, Lorenzo
de' Medici focused more of his energy on his children.
The late 1400s, though marked by great achievements in the arts, was not a time of greatness in
medicine, and Lorenzo feared for the future. His

oldest son, Piero, he described as headstrong (*pazzo*); Giovanni was discreet (*savio*); the youngest, Giuliano, was virtuous (*buono*).[14]

Lorenzo de' Medici knew how difficult it was to hold a state together. He also knew that the Medici fortunes were not endless. He worried that his son Piero might not be strong enough. He worried, too, about the annoying problem of Father Girolamo Savonarola, a new, outspoken priest in Florence.

PREACHING DOOM

The focus of Father Savonarola's preaching was that the lavish excesses of the Medicis were leading Florence into destruction. Father Savonarola loudly criticized Lorenzo de' Medici's lifestyle, urging the people of Florence to turn away from sin, and to choose a more sober, religious life before God punished them.

The fundamentalist preaching drew many to Father Savonarola's side, and Lorenzo de' Medici, who understood the threat, attempted, unsuccessfully, to appease Father Savonarola. Soon Father Savonarola was loudly denouncing the Medicis from his pulpit at the Duomo, warning of a terrible

Father Girolamo Savonarola, shown here, was an outspoken priest in Florence. He openly criticized Lorenzo de' Medici's lifestyle, urging the people of Florence to turn away from sin and choose a more sober, religious life before God punished them.

fate that was coming, and divine punishment for the Medicis and their supporters.

"Tell Lorenzo to do penance for his sins," Father Savonarola warned, "for God will punish him and his." [15] Father Savonarola predicted that, within a year, Lorenzo de' Medici would die, and his prediction proved correct. On his deathbed, Lorenzo de' Medici sent for Father Savonarola to hear his confession. The priest appeared, but before he agreed to hear Lorenzo de Medici's confession and offer repentance, he demanded three things. First he asked that Lorenzo de' Medici admit his faith in God's mercy. Medici quickly agreed. Second, Father Savonarola demanded that Lorenzo de' Medici agree to repay any public funds he had used for his own expenses. Again Medici agreed. Finally Father Savonarola demanded that Lorenzo de' Medici restore full liberty to Florence, removing it from Medici control. To this demand, the proud Medici was not willing to concede, and he turned his face to the wall. He died only a short while later, on April 8, 1492, bringing the rule of Lorenzo the Magnificent to an end. Machiavelli offered the following tribute to Lorenzo de' Medici: "Of

Fortune and of God he was supremely loved, wherefore all his enterprises ended well and those of his enemies ill . . . . All the citizens mourned his death and all the princes of Italy." [16]

THE BRIEF RULE OF PIERO DE' MEDICI

Lorenzo de' Medici's fears had proved true, for his son Piero lacked the courage and wisdom of his father, and was little match for Father Savonarola, the enemies of the Medicis, and the scheming of foreign rulers. In 1492, the year of Lorenzo de' Medici's death, Europe was going through a period of tremendous change. Pope Innocent VIII had also died, and was replaced by Pope Alexander VI, who proved not to be a friend to the Medicis. At the same time, the rulers of England, France, and Spain were building mighty empires.

Twenty-two-year-old Piero de' Medici was unable to recognize this shift in the balance of power, nor to understand that Florence and the other Italian city-states were rapidly becoming insignificant players in global politics. His father had warned of the threat posed by foreign nations, but his handsome, arrogant son did not take heed.

Piero de' Medici ignored the cautious foreign policies his father had advocated in his final years, preferring something bolder. He chose sides in a dispute between Milan and Naples, siding with Naples, and prompting the ruler of Milan to call upon the French king, Charles VIII, for aid.

France was quick to respond. In the late summer of 1494, a French army began its march across the Alps into Italy, where it was joined by forces from Milan. The French army was a terrifying force as it marched southward across Italy. The Italian city-states were accustomed to quick battles with each other, fought by small forces of hired soldiers. They were unprepared for the well-trained, heavily armed French army of some 60,000 men marching across their land. The French were a force with a highly skilled infantry and the best artillery in all of Europe, equipped with light, mobile cannons that fired iron rather than stone balls.[17]

Within a few weeks, French forces were marching into the Florentine territory of Tuscany. Rather than rallying his forces and urging unity among the Italian city-states, Piero de' Medici left Florence and traveled to the place where the French king had camped. He quickly offered the French certain key fortresses in Florence as the terms of surrender.

The people of Florence were outraged at Piero de' Medici's cowardly actions. When he returned from the French camp to report on the peace treaty, the Signoria refused to allow him to enter the building. Instead, members rang the great bell outside that was used to summon the people of Florence in times of crisis. Unable to fight his way through the growing crowd, and fearing for his life, Piero de' Medici was forced to flee with his brother Giuliano. The crowd, when they learned of the surrender, rummaged through the palace, stealing its treasures. Cardinal Giovanni attempted to appease the crowd, but his efforts were in vain. Fearing for his life, the cardinal disguised himself and escaped, joining his brothers in exile.

For 60 years, the Medici family had ruled over Florence. Their name had symbolized power, and they had become a dominant force in Italy. Now, only two years after Lorenzo's death, the Medicis were forced out of Florence. They would spend the next 18 years in exile.

Test Your Knowledge

1 How was the engagement of Lorenzo de'
   Medici and Clarice Orsini celebrated?
   a. A jousting match was held.
   b. A boxing match was held.
   c. A fox hunt was conducted.
   d. A singing contest was conducted.

2 Which famous artist was inspired by Medici
   spectacles to create *Birth of Venus*?
   a. Botticelli
   b. Michelangelo
   c. da Vinci
   d. Machiavelli

3 Lorenzo de' Medici established dominance
   over which aspect(s) of Florentine life?
   a. Politics
   b. Diplomacy
   c. Establishment of schools and libraries
   d. All of the above

4 Lorenzo de' Medici understood the true
   threat to Italian city-states to come from
   a. the pope.
   b. foreign nations.
   c. within.
   d. the king.

5 Which famous artist was unofficially "adopted" by Lorenzo de' Medici?

a. Botticelli

b. Machiavelli

c. Michelangelo

d. Van Gogh

ANSWERS: 1. a; 2. a; 3. d; 4. b; 5. c

A Medici Pope

For 18 years, the sons of Lorenzo de' Medici were banished from Florence. With them was Giulio, the illegitimate son of Lorenzo's murdered brother Giuliano, who had been adopted by Lorenzo after Giuliano's death. When the Medicis were forced to flee for their lives, they had taken young Giulio de' Medici with them, fearing for their cousin's safety. Eventually they separated. Cardinal Giovanni took Giulio and traveled throughout Europe. The youngest of the Medici brothers, Giuliano, spent time as a guest in various palaces in Italy and throughout Europe. The unlucky Piero de' Medici, still hoping to reclaim his family's name and power, allied himself with various political leaders, fighting with them and nearly always choosing the wrong side. He died in a battle in Naples, drowned in a river, and left behind two children—a son named Lorenzo and a daughter named Clarice.

In 1503, Pope Alexander VI died, and with this Medici enemy gone, Cardinal Giovanni felt safe to return to Rome with his cousin Giulio. He was again able to serve as cardinal under the new pope, Julius II.

Pope Julius II supported the Medicis and was willing to help them in their effort to reclaim their role in Florence. During their 18 years in exile, Florence had suffered through poor governments, corruption, the presence of the French, and a religious government set up by Father Savonarola that banned excess, luxury, and finery. Citizens of

Florence were called upon to discard their jewels, their fine clothes, and even their wigs by throwing them into large bonfires. Once Father Savonarola had purged Florence of its excesses, however, it was difficult for him to ignore the excesses of the Roman Catholic Church. The Catholic Church, under Alexander VI, had been highly corrupt, and Florence joined with much of Europe in calling for a reformation of church policies.

Meanwhile, Pope Alexander VI was able to put pressure on a weak Signoria to call for Father Savonarola's trial on charges of heresy. He endured days of torture without renouncing his views before finally being executed in a public square.

Without a strong leader, Florence sank into chaos. Power changed hands many times. New constitutions were drafted and then overthrown. Those in power were increasingly corrupt. Florence was mismanaged, weak, and no longer a significant political player.

The new pope, Julius II, was determined to place Florence in the hands of his allies, the Medicis. Pope Julius II was disturbed that Italy had become a kind of battlefield for France, Spain, and Germany to

Father Girolamo Savonarola was found guilty on charges of heresy, a crime punishable by death. He was hanged on May 23, 1498, in a public square in Florence, shown here.

attempt to win land and power, and he understood that his own power depended on a stable Italy. He also was a skilled warrior with his own army of troops to command.

By 1512, the pope's troops were marching near Prato, about ten miles north of Florence. The

Florentine leadership dispatched a force, woefully unprepared for the challenge, which was quickly defeated, and the army turned toward Florence. Learning that Prato had collapsed, a number of Florentines formed a revolution in the city, blaming the shameful defeat on poor leadership and forcing the head of the government to resign. The rest of the government quickly sent a message to the pope's forces, expressing its willingness to allow the Medicis to return.

On September 1, 1512, Lorenzo de' Medici's sons Giovanni and Giuliano and their cousin Giulio—accompanied by their nephew, Pietro's son Lorenzo—rode back into Florence. They were welcomed by enthusiastic crowds of cheering Florentines who were tired of the years of chaos and corruption, and remembered the glory days that Florence had experienced under Medici rule. The Medicis had fled Florence as young men of 18, 16, and 15 respectively. They were now mature adults of 36, 34, and 33.

These Medici men conducted themselves with honor. Although they had been forced into exile, fearing for their lives, they made no effort to execute or force into exile those who had been their enemies. When they returned to a family palace that was bare of its priceless collections of art and antiques, they demonstrated the same spirit of forgiveness that Lorenzo de' Medici had shown after the assassination attempt.

It was soon decided that the youngest of Lorenzo de' Medici's sons, Giuliano, would assume control of Florence. Cardinal Giovanni was anxious to return to Rome, and Giulio went with him. Shortly after the return of the Medicis, Pope Julius II died. Cardinal Giovanni wanted to be in Rome when the new pope was elected.

GIULIANO DE MEDICI'S RULE

During his years in exile, Cardinal Giuliano—who was known for his cheerful and intelligent personality—had been a welcome guest of many of the noble houses of Italy. He was talented, and had also proved his military skill. The decision to make him the Medici ruler in Florence—rather than Pietro's 20-year-old son, Lorenzo—was a wise one. Many still remembered Pietro de' Medici's cowardly surrender to France, and Lorenzo had the same stubborn, inflexible personality as his father. Giuliano de' Medici, on the other hand, was generous, peaceful, diplomatic, and a great student of the arts—a man very similar, in fact, to his father.

Giuliano de' Medici demonstrated respect for his people by adopting the plain and simple style of dress then in fashion in Florence. He avoided any outward appearance of luxury, and even shaved off his beard, as facial hair was a foreign style in that part of Italy.

The hope of many Florentines was that, under Giuliano de' Medici, the city-state would once more recapture the glory it had known under Lorenzo, but Giuliano de' Medici's reign would unfortunately be cut short when, in March 1513, Giuliano's older brother, Giovanni, was elected pope.

POPE LEO X

The choice of 36-year-old Giovanni de' Medici as the new pope meant a time of great rejoicing in Florence. Giovanni de' Medici was the first Florentine to become pope, and most Florentines expected that Giovanni, or Pope Leo X as he was now known, would be quick to bring favors and

Once Giovanni de' Medici became Pope Leo X, he outlined a more ambitious plan to expand papal authority in Italy. Pope Leo is shown here with cardinals Giulio de' Medici and Luigi de' Rossi.

benefits to his homeland. His speech on becoming pope certainly seemed to support this: "Since God has given us the Papacy, let us enjoy it." [18]

Scholars of the Medicis have surprisingly different views of the family at the time that Leo X began his service as pope. Some view the new pope as an ambitious man, eager to instill his policies on Florence and exert his influence on other members of his family. Some view Giuliano de' Medici as the villain of the history—a man too weak to confront his brother, and too pleasure-loving to exercise any real authority in Florence. Still others point to Giulio de' Medici as the "power behind the pope"—a man who schemed to have his cousin named pope so that he could manipulate him and gain the rights to the kingdom.

There is, without a doubt, a bit of truth in each of these views of the three Medici men who shaped the family's history in the early 1500s. Once Giovanni de' Medici became Pope Leo X, he outlined a more ambitious plan to expand papal authority in Italy. The most logical place to begin to exercise this new authority was in the city where he was most beloved, Florence. The Medici then ruling over Florence, Giuliano, instead was named "gonfaloniere of the papal forces," a position requiring him to stay close to the pope and, consequently, to move to Rome.

Pope Leo X did not intend to directly rule Florence himself, however. Instead, his nephew

Choosing a Pope

The process of selecting a pope has changed little over the last 500 years, and the systems that were in place when members of the Medici family became heads of the Roman Catholic Church remain largely intact. When a pope dies, all of the cardinals (the most important priests in the Catholic Church) go to Rome to attend the funeral and choose from among themselves the man who will be the next pope.

The pope is chosen in one of three ways: by a unanimous voice vote of the cardinals; by a unanimous selection by the cardinals of anywhere from a 9-member to a 15-member committee, which then chooses a pope; or, most commonly, by ballot. In ballot voting, a morning meeting is scheduled within ten days of the pope's death. The approximately 120 active cardinals (those under the age of 80) all write the name of one man on their ballot. After the votes

Lorenzo—the son of Pietro—became the unofficial leader of Florence. Pope Leo X remained in almost daily contact with Lorenzo, offering guidance and assisting him in choosing his advisors. Pope Leo X next turned to one of the territories of Italy that was rebelling against his authority,

are counted, the ballots are burned. If there is no winner, a chemical is added to the ballots to produce black smoke when they are burned. Another vote is taken, until a winner is produced. Then the ballots are burned without the chemical, producing white smoke. Observers watch the color of the smoke coming from the roof of the Vatican in St. Peter's Square in Rome to determine whether or not a pope has been chosen.

The man chosen is then asked if he accepts his election. If so, he then chooses the name he will use as pope. Finally, the oldest cardinal walks out onto the balcony overlooking St. Peter's Square and announces to those gathered below, *"Habemus papam."* ("We have a pope.") The new pope is introduced, and he begins his service by offering a blessing.

the province of Urbino. The pope used both the papal and Florentine armies to attack Urbino, removing its duke from his throne, and instead naming young Lorenzo de' Medici as the new Duke of Urbino.

The previous generations of Medicis had furthered their ambitions through marriage, selecting members of noble families as spouses for their children. Pope Leo X set his ambitions even higher, arranging for the marriage of his brother Giuliano to the young aunt of the king of France, 17-year-old Philiberte of Savoy. The French king named him Duke of Nemours to honor the marriage. Giuliano de' Medici died, however, only a year later, at the age of 37, and was buried in San Lorenzo, where a statue by Michelangelo was placed over his tomb.

The Medici family had risen far from its early days as wealthy bankers. Now its members included dukes, and even a pope. Still the family's ambitions continued to grow. The new pope was determined to increase both his own influence and the influence of the Medici family. Unfortunately these two ambitions would not peacefully coexist.

LORENZO, DUKE OF URBINO

Lorenzo de' Medici, the new leader of Florence and Duke of Urbino, had experienced great tragedy during his early life. He had been only two years old when his family was forced into exile, and his childhood had been marked by his father's desperate efforts to reclaim his good name and power. When Lorenzo was only 11, his father had died, and when he was 21, his uncle had made him ruler of Florence.

Lorenzo de Medici's uncle, remembering the tragic events that had led to Medici exile, warned his young nephew to adopt a simple lifestyle in Florence, to remain respectful of the ways of the Florentines, and above all to avoid the arrogance that had led to his father's downfall. Apparently these instructions were difficult for a young man who had suddenly been given power over an entire city-state and granted a noble title. He was, after all, a young man who had been brought up on stories of the injustices bestowed upon his family by the Florentines.

The naming of Lorenzo de' Medici as Duke of Urbino also carried a hefty price tag. Francesco della Rovere, the man who had been Duke of

Urbino before the papal and Florentine armies overthrew him, had no intention of letting his land go without a fight.

Soon Lorenzo de' Medici would be elevated even higher. Pope Leo X determined that his nephew should be married to French royalty as a way to cement an alliance with France. The French king, Francois I, agreed to the marriage of Lorenzo de' Medici and Madeleine de la Tour d'Auverne, and the ceremony was a time of extraordinary extravagance in the court of France. The celebration lasted an entire month, after which the young couple returned to Florence. The Florentines welcomed the lovely young French princess, but Lorenzo de' Medici quickly offended Florentines by following the French tradition and growing a beard, as well as mimicking the more extravagant customs and clothing that had been the fashion in France. It was with mixed feelings that Florentine citizens celebrated the birth of Lorenzo and Madeleine's daughter Catherine.

An extraordinary future awaited the young baby who would be known as Catherine de' Medici. She would become queen of France, and the mother of three kings, but the celebration of her birth quickly turned to mourning when her mother died as a result of complications following the birth, and her father died less than a month later. Pope Leo X would not allow Florence to slip out of Medici control. So he sent his cousin Giulio, now a cardinal, to manage Florence until a legitimate ruler could be found.

CARDINAL GIULIO

Giulio de' Medici had remained behind the scenes during the early years of the Medicis' return to power. He had served as an advisor to Pope Leo X, supported the efforts to install Lorenzo de' Medici as ruler of Florence, and had been an invaluable aide in the complicated politics of the Catholic Church. It was as administrator of Florence, however, that the illegitimate son of Giuliano de' Medici was finally able to allow his talents and skills to shine.

Giulio de' Medici quickly began changing many of Lorenzo de Medici's policies that had caused ill will and trouble in Florence. He ensured that Florence's finances were put into good order, he lowered the taxes on Florentines, and quickly took steps to eliminate some of the corrupt influences that had begun to rise under Lorenzo de' Medici's rule.

At the same time, he remained a modest and simple man in public, doing his best to adapt to the ways of the Florentines and in all things to avoid giving offense. He frequently sought the advice of leading citizens in Florence. Within five months, Giulio de' Medici had skillfully mended ties, and had once more assured the support of Florence for Medici rule.

Meanwhile, both Giulio de' Medici and Pope Leo X worried about exactly who would continue the Medici rule after they were gone. Baby Catherine was the only legitimate heir to the family throne. The question was whether she could prove worthy and able to sustain Medici power.

Test Your Knowledge

1 Which of the sons of Lorenzo de' Medici was the youngest?

a. Lorenzo

b. Giuliano

c. Piero

d. Giovanni

2 How long did the Medici brothers spend in exile?

a. 25 years

b. 18 years

c. 40 years

d. 12 years

3 How did Guiliano de' Medici demonstrate respect for his people?

a. By growing his hair long

b. By sponsoring great artists

c. By organizing lavish festivals

d. By adopting a plain and simple style of dress

4 What was Lorenzo de' Medici's other title?

a. Pope Leo X

b. Gonfaloniere of Florence

c. Duke of Urbino

d. Cardinal Lorenzo

5 What title would Catherine de' Medici have?

    a. Queen of England

    b. Queen of France

    c. Princess of Florence

    d. Duchess of Rome

ANSWERS: 1. a; 2. b; 3. d; 4. c; 5. b

Catherine de' Medici

Upon first meeting his infant great-niece, Pope Leo X said with a sigh, "She brings with her all the misfortunes of Greece!"[19] Obviously someone had to be in charge of caring for young Catherine, but an even larger problem remained—the fortunes of the Medici family were now being entrusted to a baby girl.

87

Pope Leo X soon discovered that there were two other people who might have a claim on the Medici fortune, a young boy named Ippolito, thought to be the illegitimate son of Giuliano, and Alessandro, who was claimed to be the illegitimate son of Lorenzo, but was probably the illegitimate son of Cardinal Giulio, instead. While the pope debated how and what to do with these complicated family ties, all three children were sent to live with Cardinal Giulio in the Medici Palace in Florence.

Meanwhile, France and Spain began vying for power in Italy. The king of Spain, Charles V, met with Pope Leo X and signed an alliance with him, promising Milan—then under French control—to the pope, in exchange for his support in a war between France and Spain. When the conflict ended, the French had evacuated Milan and retreated toward the Alps. Pope Leo X was so excited by this news that he ordered a grand celebration. When the party ended, however, Leo X came down with a severe fever and he had the chills. On December 1, 1521, only three days after his joyful celebration, Pope Leo X was dead at the age of 45.

His successor was not an Italian, and his support came from the king of Spain. The new pope, Hadrian VI, had high hopes for reforming the Catholic Church, but within a year, he too died, as a result of a fever.

POPE CLEMENT VII

For seven weeks after the death of Pope Hadrian VI, the cardinals argued over who would be his successor. Finally on November 19, 1523, the new pope was named; it was Giulio de' Medici, who would now take the name Clement VII.

Pope Clement VII's first crisis was the question of who would rule over Florence. Catherine de' Medici was only four years old, and the two supposed sons of Lorenzo and Giuliano de' Medici—Alessandro and Ippolito—were, at 13 and 15 years old respectively, still too young for such a responsibility. At first, Pope Clement VII appointed Cardinal Passerini as his representative in Florence, and, for three years, Cardinal Passerini administered the city-state under Pope Clement VII's direction.

At the same time, Pope Clement VII openly announced the existence of the two illegitimate heirs to the Medici name, noting that Cardinal Passerini would govern for the boys only until they became old enough to assume the responsibility. Up until this point, the people of Florence had only heard rumors of the boys' existence. Confronted with the facts, the people were angered, both at the sudden revelation of two young Medicis who would be trained to rule them, and at the arrival of Cardinal Passerini, who proved to be a greedy and foolish administrator.

Meanwhile, a question of war would pose the next crisis for the Medicis. In 1527, France and Spain were, once more, at war over Italy. Pope Clement VII tried to play one side against the other, and found himself without allies when a Spanish-German army began its slow march down through Italy, toward Rome. The soldiers had not been paid for many months, nor had they been given adequate supplies. Their response was to seize everything they could, and each Italian town and village in turn was ransacked, its citizens attacked and killed.

By May 5, 1527, the Spanish-German army was camped outside Rome, and the next day the attack began. Pope Clement VII hid in his castle, as

In May 1527, German soldiers of fortune attacked the city of Rome as Pope Clement VII hid in his castle, and eventually escaped the city. Rome was destroyed and finally abandoned by the army after nine months, when the plague swept through the streets.

churches, palaces, and houses were all ransacked. The soldiers attacked anyone and everyone in their path. The pope's army was quickly defeated, and, for seven months, Pope Clement VII remained in hiding as his city was occupied. Finally, on

December 8, 1527, the pope was able to escape, disguised as a peddler. Rome was destroyed and finally abandoned by the army after nine months, when the bubonic plague swept through the streets.

Hearing the news of the capture of Rome, the Florentines determined that the time had come for them to overthrow the Medici government. They were not interested in being ruled by one of two boys who had emerged seemingly out of nowhere; nor were they willing to listen to the representative of a pope who was no longer in power. On March 19, 1527, the Medici family was once more banished from Florence.

A POPE IN EXILE

Pope Clement VII remained focused on recapturing power and ensuring the continuation of Medici rule. By October 1528, he was able to return to Rome, where he discovered a city in ruins. Half of the population had died, most as victims of disease and war. Most of the major buildings had been burned. Pope Clement VII realized that there was little left in Rome for him, but the Medici family fortune could still be revived in Florence.

Accordingly, he arranged a secret meeting with the Spanish emperor, Charles V, in Spain. The pope signed a treaty agreeing to assist the emperor in cementing his control over all of Italy, in exchange for one small piece of land—Florence. With Emperor Charles's army under his direction, Pope Clement VII was able to order an attack on Florence, in September 1529, with the aim of reinstating Medici power in the city-state. The conflict lasted for nearly 12 months, before Florence was finally forced to surrender in August 1530.

Florence would now be governed by a duke— none other than 20-year-old Alessandro de' Medici, the illegitimate son of Pope Clement VII. On May 1, 1532, Alessandro de' Medici summoned the members of Florence's Signoria to the Medici Palace and announced that, under the orders of Emperor Charles V, the Signoria was being abolished. Alessandro de' Medici would be the only ruler of Florence. The presence of the Spanish army ensured order, and the Florentines could do little to protest or question this change.

Pope Clement VII had achieved his aim—to reinstate Medici power in Florence—but Emperor

Charles V and his army ensured control. To gain Florence, Alessandro de' Medici had essentially made himself subservient to Emperor Charles V, throughout all of Italy.

Meanwhile, Pope Clement VII continued his schemes. King Henry VIII of England wished to divorce his first wife, Catherine of Aragon, to marry Anne Boleyn. Henry VIII, a Catholic, needed the pope to agree to annul his first marriage. Queen Catherine, however, was the aunt of Emperor Charles V, and Pope Clement was not in a position to alienate Charles V by granting King Henry VIII's plea. Finally, in January 1533, Henry VIII married Anne Boleyn without the pope's blessing.

Pope Clement could not ignore this public act of defiance. Through Henry VIII's example, all of England was being encouraged to ignore the direction of the Catholic Church. In March 1534, the Church of England and the English parliament separately declared that the pope did not have supreme authority over England. From then on, the Church of England would be the sole religious authority in England. Pope Clement responded with a threat of excommunication against King Henry VIII, unless he agreed to immediately return to Catherine of Aragon. Henry VIII refused, and Pope Clement VII was forced to excommunicate him. Under Pope Clement VII, the Church of England and the Church of Rome were formally and finally separated.

Less than two months later, on September 25, 1534, at the age of 56, Pope Clement VII died. Pope Clement's ambition had left the Catholic Church divided, Florence in turmoil, and the Medici name hated and feared, rather than honored. Any hope of restoring family honor, rested squarely on the shoulders of young Catherine de' Medici. The pope, in one of his final acts, had married her off to the youngest son of the king of France.

A YOUNG GIRL ALONE

Catherine de' Medici has become one of the best known of the Medicis. It is important to remember, however, that the powerful woman who became the queen of France spent most of her childhood alone and unwanted, a pawn in a power struggle between the people of Florence and the pope.

Only weeks after Catherine de' Medici's birth, both of her parents were dead. At the time, she was believed to be the sole heir to the Medici fortune. At six months old, she was taken to Rome, where her great-uncle, Pope Leo X, oversaw her care while she lived with an aunt. She lived there until she was six years old, when her uncle had replaced her great-uncle as pope, becoming Clement VII. As noted earlier, Rome soon became a very dangerous place and, in 1525, the young girl was sent back to Florence, to live under the supervision of Cardinal Passerini in the family palace with Ippolito and Alessandro.

When Catherine de' Medici was eight years old, Rome was attacked and Pope Clement VII was forced into hiding. Very quickly, Florence turned against the Medicis, and, as her relatives fled, Catherine de' Medici was seized by representatives of the government and imprisoned. Government officials hoped to use the eight-year-old girl to negotiate with the pope, once he fled Rome.

The young girl was sent to a convent, and there, behind the walls of the religious community of nuns, Catherine lived for three years, prevented from communicating with any friends or relatives. The nuns focused on educating the young girl, as well as teaching her proper behavior and manners. Despite her status as a political prisoner, this was a happy and peaceful time for Catherine de' Medici. She was kept ignorant of the political squabbling in Florence, and the wars raging through Italy. The nuns grew so fond of her, that, by 1530, the government began to worry that support for the Medici family might be growing within the convent walls.

On July 20, 1530, in the middle of the night, three representatives of the government knocked on the convent door and demanded that Catherine de' Medici be turned over to them. She was convinced that they wanted to kill her. After much discussion with the nuns, it was agreed that Catherine de' Medici would be allowed to stay in the convent until morning. Quickly she put on the traditional dress of the nuns and cut off her long hair. When her escort reappeared in the morning, she refused to go with him. She claimed that she had decided to become a nun and dared them to carry off a nun by force from the convent walls. Finally they took her away, and the nuns cried bitterly. She was not murdered, but instead taken to another convent where, it was thought, she was less likely to stir up support for her family.

Catherine de' Medici's exile did not last long. By August 1530, Florence had surrendered to the troops of Pope Clement VII. Alessandro de' Medici was installed as Florence's ruler, and Catherine de' Medici was summoned to Rome to be with her cousin Ippolito, now 22 years old, and her uncle, who quickly busied himself with finding an appropriate husband for his 12-year-old niece.

Pope Clement VII finally chose the second son of King Francis I of France, a rather unimpressive young man named Henry, to be Catherine's husband. By the time she was 14, Catherine de' Medici's marriage arrangements had been finalized, and, in September 1533, she set out for France in a grand procession accompanied by her uncle.

On October 28, 1533, Catherine de' Medici and Henry of Orleans were married in Marseilles, France. The pope performed the marriage. The bride wore a cloak of dark blue velvet lined with ermine fur, and a crown on her head.

Despite the grandeur, however, the marriage did not mark a time of rejoicing. The people of France were furious at the choice of someone who was not a member of a royal family—and was a foreigner—

Catherine de' Medici (shown here) married Henry of Orleans, son of the king of France, on October 28, 1533. She was not well liked, however, by the people of France.

as a wife for the son of their king. Catherine de' Medici, in French eyes, was merely the daughter of some wealthy bankers whose uncle happened to be the pope. They described her sarcastically as "that

Italian woman," and, while her father-in-law admired her intelligence, her passion for hunting, and her witty conversation, her new husband ignored her.

A STRANGER IN A STRANGE COUNTRY

Within a year of her marriage, Pope Clement VII was dead, and Catherine de' Medici was deprived of her most politically important relative. Married to a man who did his best to avoid her, in a country where she was hated, she maintained her self-control and poise.

The emotions of the French people grew even more intense, however, when in August 1536, nearly three years after Catherine de' Medici's marriage to Henry of Orleans, his older brother, the crown prince, died suddenly. Rumors quickly spread that Catherine de' Medici, "the Italian woman," had poisoned her brother-in-law so that her husband would inherit the throne. King Francis I quickly made it clear, however, that these rumors would not be tolerated.

Catherine de' Medici's pain increased when her husband began a very public love affair with Diane de Poitiers, an older woman. Soon it was Diane de Poitiers who was being honored at court, traveling at Henry's side, and hosting parties with him at one of the palaces he bought for her, while Catherine was left alone and humiliated.

By the time she was 23 years old, Catherine de' Medici had been married for nine years, and during that time she had remained childless. Many began to suggest that Henry should divorce her and marry someone else—someone who would be capable of bearing children to continue the royal family. She quickly went to the king, and according to one report, told him:

she had heard that it was his intention to give another woman as wife to her husband, and since it had not, up to the present time, pleased God to grant her the grace to have sons, it seemed to her quite proper that he did not think it best to wait any longer to provide properly for the succession of heirs for so great a kingdom.[20]

The king replied:

My daughter, have no fear. Since God has willed that you should be my daughter-in-law and wife of the Dauphin, I do not wish to make any change and perhaps it will please Almighty God in this matter to grant to you and to me the gift we so much long for.[21]

Within a year, King Francis's prediction proved true. Catherine de' Medici gave birth to a son named Francis, after his grandfather. Over the next 12 years, she gave birth to nine more children. She had, in all, four sons—three of whom would become kings of France—and three daughters; three other children died as infants.

QUEEN OF FRANCE

In March 1545, when King Francis I died, Henry became King Henry II, and, at the age of 28, Catherine de' Medici was now queen of France. The new king had grown wiser and more mature as he aged, and now, at 29, he was a serious and popular ruler. Catherine de' Medici was deeply in love with her husband, and in letters later written to her sons and daughters, her pain during this period is revealed, as she dealt with the constant knowledge that her husband did not care for her in the same way.

Henry of Orleans became King Henry II in March 1545, when King Francis I died, and thus Catherine de' Medici became queen of France.

Catherine de' Medici focused on the education of her children. Her sons were given tutors as they grew older, and she also continued to educate her daughters, who would become noteworthy for their extraordinary intelligence. For many years, Catherine de' Medici remained quietly in the background, appearing

A Mother's Advice

Catherine de' Medici wrote many letters during her years as a young bride, a queen, and still later, as Queen Mother. This correspondence was often written for political or diplomatic reasons, to explain a position, request aid, or urge a particular response. The most honest and revealing of her letters, however, were those she wrote to her daughter Elizabeth. Shortly after the death of her husband and her oldest son, she wrote to Elizabeth, reminding her of the sacrifices she had made for the sake of her marriage and kingdom, and the importance of faith:

> For this reason, my dear daughter, recommend yourself well to God, because you have seen me as contented as you are, without a thought of ever having any other trouble than not to be loved as much as I wanted to be by the King

in public only for formal state occasions, such as the wedding, in April 1558, of her oldest son, Francis, to Mary, Queen of Scots, and the June 1559 wedding of her oldest daughter, Elizabeth, to Philip II of Spain.

As part of the latter wedding, a grand jousting tournament was held. During the ceremonial joust,

your father, who honored me more than I merited, but I loved him so much that I had always fear, as you know, in many ways, and God has taken him away from me. For this my dear daughter, remember me and let me serve as an example, so that you do not trust so much in the love which you bear your husband and in the honor and the ease which you have at this present moment, as to forget to recommend yourself to Him who can continue your happiness and also when it pleases Him put you into the state in which I am: for I would sooner die than see you there, from the fear that you could not carry so much trouble as I have had and still have, which I am sure without His help I would not know how to carry.

* Paul Van Dyke, *Catherine de Médicis*. New York: Charles Scribner's Sons, 1922, vol. I, p. 107.

to the horror of all the guests, King Henry II was accidentally wounded in the eye. Ten days later, he died. At the age of 40, Catherine de' Medici was a widow, and Queen Mother.

For the next 30 years, Catherine de' Medici served as Queen Mother, as three of her sons succeeded to the throne. First was the oldest, Francis II, who became king at the age of 16. Francis II's reign coincided with a growing religious conflict in Europe between followers of a new religion, known as Protestantism, and Roman Catholics. In France, the conflict would erupt into a religious war.

Francis II was young and often sick, and he entrusted much of the management of France to two of his wife's powerful uncles, the Guises. The Guises were fiercely opposed to the Protestant movement, and began a campaign of persecution against followers. Catherine de' Medici was horrified by the beatings and torture. She advocated a policy of religious tolerance, believing that a war over religion would mean devastation for France, but she had little power over King Francis and his advisors.

Francis II's reign lasted only 17 months. He died on December 5, 1560, and was succeeded by his younger brother Charles, who was only ten. Because of his youth, Catherine de' Medici was named queen regent of France. She quickly acted to bring an end to all religious persecution, ordering that Protestants should be freely allowed to practice their religion in France. She was criticized by Roman Catholics for her tolerant policy. By May 1562, France's first religious war had begun. It lasted nearly a year, ending only as England threatened to invade France and Catherine de' Medici was able to unite the French to drive off the invaders.

By the time he was 14, Charles was ready to assume the duties of king, and he was installed as King Charles IX in the spring of 1564. Catherine de' Medici accompanied him on a tour of France, introducing him to the people in the more remote areas of his kingdom. Later, returning to Paris, she continued to focus on the simmering religious conflict. She became the first member of the French royal family to live in the palace of the Louvre, the construction of which had been started by her father-in-law and completed near the end of her husband's life. She also oversaw the construction of the famous palace of the Tuileries, connecting it with the Louvre by a long gallery. Today they are no longer connected, but instead separated by a beautiful park.

For four years, France remained relatively peaceful, but in September 1567, a second religious war broke out, following an attempt by Protestants to seize young King Charles IX and murder him. For six months, fighting raged between Protestants and Roman Catholics, until a tentative peace treaty was signed. The treaty endured for only five months, before a third religious war was once more dividing the citizens of France.

The war allowed religious anger to rise to an even greater intensity. Rumors reached Paris of Protestants tearing apart holy Catholic cathedrals and destroying precious religious symbols. Catholics responded with fury, angrily denouncing Catherine de' Medici, who had attempted to legalize tolerance for Protestantism. As the violence grew, Catherine de' Medici ordered priests to read from their pulpits the law demanding religious tolerance, but the priests refused.

Finally, by August 1570, Catherine de' Medici had once more established peace between the two sides. She quickly turned her attention to arranging marriages for her children. The unions were meant to demonstrate her desire for peace and tolerance. Her son Charles IX was married to Elizabeth of Austria, the daughter of the Austrian emperor who also advocated a policy of religious tolerance. Her daughter Marguerite was married to Henry of Navarre, the son of one of Navarre's most prominent Protestants. (Navarre was a province of France.) Finally she began arrangements to marry her son Henry to Elizabeth, the queen of England. This last marriage never was finalized, however.

The marriage plans, rather than ensuring tolerance, further angered those who perceived Catherine de' Medici's attempts to marry the king's siblings to Protestants as a sign that France was becoming a Protestant nation. In August 1572, violence once more broke out, this time resulting in a horrific massacre of Protestants in Paris. War quickly followed, and the religious conflict endured for 12 months, ending only with a temporary truce, before a fifth war broke out in February 1574.

As war raged on, Charles IX died. He was succeeded by his brother Henry III, who was then 23. While Henry III reigned, it was his mother, now

One of Catherine de' Medici's sons became France's King Charles IX. King Charles (shown here) married Elizabeth of Austria, the daughter of the Austrian emperor who also advocated a policy of religious tolerance.

in her 60s, who traveled around France attempting to make peace. Catherine de' Medici's efforts were, however, only temporarily successful. War again broke out, and Paris was taken by ardent supporters of the Guises, who erected barricades in the city and forced the king and his wife, and Catherine de' Medici, to take refuge in the Louvre. Finally, as revolution threatened, King Henry and his wife escaped, while Catherine de' Medici set out across Paris, passing through the barricades, to meet with the leaders of the opposition. She was able to arrange a peaceful settlement to the conflict— although the revolutionaries were granted enormous power—and King Henry was able to return to Paris.

Catherine de' Medici's efforts at peacemaking were physically and emotionally exhausting. When she learned that King Henry had authorized the assassination of the leader of the revolutionaries, she knew that war would, once more, be the result. This time, however, she would not live to make peace. She died on January 5, 1589, at the age of 69.

Even after her death, Catherine de' Medici remained a polarizing figure. Many criticized her for her supposed role in the religious wars, arguing that her policies contributed to, rather than alleviated, the conflicts. She was a suspect in many plots, and rumors of her role in the murders of many leading figures continued for centuries after her death. She was denounced by both Protestants and Catholics. Among the few who kindly remembered her, her doctor noted:

> We all remain without light, or counsel, or consolation, and to tell the truth, with her died what kept us alive. From now on we must turn our thoughts elsewhere and find some other support. The kingdom will suffer more than is believed, and the King remains without the most faithful and necessary support that he had.[22]

Test Your Knowledge

1 Which countries were vying for power in Florence during Medici rule?
   a. France and Spain
   b. Germany and England
   c. England and France
   d. Spain and England

2 Which member of the Medici family became known as Pope Clement VII?
   a. Lorenzo de' Medici
   b. Giuliano de' Medici
   c. Alessandro de' Medici
   d. Giuilo de' Medici

3 Which Italian city was captured by Spanish-German forces during Medici rule?
   a. Venice
   b. Florence
   c. Rome
   d. Pisa

4 Catherine de' Medici spent part of her childhood
   a. in an art school.
   b. in a convent.
   c. at the Vatican.
   d. in a hospital.

5 How many children did Catherine de' Medici have?

    a. Ten

    b. Three

    c. Twelve

    d. Six

ANSWERS: 1. a; 2. d; 3. c; 4. b; 5. a

A Dynasty's Decline

The death of Catherine de' Medici effectively brought an end to Medici power in France. The struggles of the Medici family in Italy, specifically in Florence, however, had continued throughout Catherine de' Medici's life.

When Catherine de' Medici left Italy for France to be married, Alessandro de' Medici was ruling in Florence, while her cousin Ippolito had been called by Pope Clement VI to Rome to serve as a cardinal and his aide. He was with the pope in 1534 when he died.

Alessandro de' Medici's rule over Florence marked a period of tragedy in the city. He was a tyrant, who demonstrated complete disregard for the people he governed and took every opportunity to use his position for his own personal gain. He was well aware that the people of Florence hated him, and he feared that some might make an attempt to replace him with the better-loved, more attractive Ippolito de' Medici.

In 1535, Ippolito de' Medici was traveling through Naples to Tunis, to meet with Emperor Charles V. His mission, made at the request of many in Florence, was to plead with the emperor that he might be made Duke of Florence, rather than Alessandro de' Medici. Before he could complete the journey, however, he was dead, the victim of poisoning. Most believed that Alessandro de' Medici was responsible.

Less than two years later, Alessandro himself was assassinated. The 24-year-old duke was murdered while lying in his bed at the palace. His killer had been hired by a distant cousin of Alessandro's,

Alessandro de' Medici's rule over Florence marked a period of tragedy in the city. He was not well liked, demonstrating complete disregard for the people he governed and taking every opportunity to use his position for his own personal gain.

who decided that Alessandro's tyrannical rule of Florence must be brought to an end.

With this act of violence, the reign over Florence by the descendants of Cosimo de' Medici came to an end. Florence was without a ruler. While the family of Cosimo de' Medici had no other male descendants, there was, however, another branch of the Medici family in Florence. If we look back in history to the place where Medici rule truly began, with Giovanni de' Medici, we remember that Giovanni had two sons—Cosimo, whose descendants we have followed up until now, and a younger son, Lorenzo.

Cosimo de' Medici's descendants were the high achievers in the family. They were the skilled bankers and diplomats, the popes and princesses. Lorenzo de' Medici and his descendants had remained in the background—many of them working in the family banks, many of them quite wealthy, but still followers rather than leaders. With the death of Alessandro de' Medici, things began to change.

SON OF A WARRIOR

As supporters of the Medicis looked to the other branch of the family for a possible successor to

Alessandro, the most obvious candidate was 17-year-old Cosimo. Cosimo de' Medici was the only son of Giovanni de' Medici, who had been an extraordinarily successful military commander, serving under Pope Clement VII. Giovanni de' Medici had died as a result of wounds suffered during battle, and was celebrated as a patriotic hero for his service. Young Cosimo was also distantly related to the other side of the family, through his mother.

With a father who was a war hero and family connections to both branches of the Medicis, young Cosimo was a logical choice to become duke, which he did in 1537. He ruled as duke for nearly 40 years, becoming known as Cosimo I—to distinguish him from the Cosimo of several generations earlier, known as Cosimo il Vecchio or "the elder." Under Cosimo I, Florence would grow in territory with the acquisition of Siena. Later, in 1569, Pope Pius V would name Cosimo I as the Grand Duke of Tuscany.

Cosimo I proved a worthy choice as successor to the Medici power. He was hard-working, firm, and shrewd. He married a Spanish princess, Eleanora of Toledo, and became a father to ten children. He also, through his marriage, gained a Spanish army, which aided him in his efforts to secure and expand Florence.

Cosimo I followed in the family tradition of patronizing the arts, and supervised the construction of a series of public buildings, designed to centralize the many government offices that, up until that time, had been scattered throughout the city. They became known as the "Offices," or, in Italian, *Uffizi*, and today the Uffizi galleries house an impressive collection of art. Having seen how quickly previous Medicis had fallen victim to assassinations and political revolts, Cosimo I took steps to cement his own power. He hired and trained expert guards to protect him from attack, and was always moving about the city wearing armor beneath his clothes, and carrying a knife. Fearing attack, he moved his family from the Medici Palace to a huge fortress on the other side of the Arno River, known as Pitti Palace.

He publicized his own accomplishments and those of his family, commissioning grand paintings to celebrate the achievements and courage of the Medicis, particularly his branch of the Medicis. Under Cosimo de' Medici's sponsorship, Florence's

Cosimo de' Medici, the only son of Giovanni de' Medici, continued Medici rule when Alessandro de' Medici was killed. Cosimo de' Medici proved to be hard working and shrewd. He was a worthy successor to the Medici ruling dynasty.

wool and silk trades once more began to flourish, and new roads and harbors were built.

In the fall of 1562, Cosimo de' Medici's wife and two of his sons died of malaria, during a trip to Pisa. He never fully recovered from this tragedy. He placed his remaining children in important positions, either through marriage—his oldest son, Francis, was married to the sister of Emperor Maximilian II of Austria—or through appointments to the Catholic Church. His fourth son, Ferdinand, was named a cardinal at the age of 14. After 37 years of firm reign over Florence, Cosimo I died on April 21, 1574, at the age of 55. He had reshaped Florence into a stronger state, built up its army and navy, developed its industries, and reorganized its government. His rule was often heavy-handed, but he left the city-state much more powerful than it had been when he first assumed control. Cosimo de' Medici represents the final high point of Medici power. The end of his reign marks a sharp decline in the family's fortunes and in the quality of its leaders.

THE DECLINE

Cosimo de' Medici's oldest son, Francis I, had actually

begun to govern Florence during the final four years of his father's life. His 13-year rule was weak and incompetent, and corruption quickly began to mark the government. Crime rose and violence increased.

Cosimo I had focused his attention and energy on developing Tuscany. Francis I, instead, focused much time and money on his passion, science, and often held government meetings in his laboratory, while performing experiments. One of Francis de' Medici's most notable accomplishments was the transformation of the Uffizi from government offices to an artistic gallery, placing much of the Medici family art on display there. Francis de' Medici died in October 1587, and although he had fathered six children, only two, neither of them male, survived. With his death, rule over Florence passed to his younger brother, Ferdinand, who was a cardinal in Rome, and who had disagreed with his brother on practically every point.

FERDINAND I AND COSIMO II

Upon the death of Francis de' Medici, his brother Ferdinand decided to abandon his religious calling to assume the throne of Tuscany. Ferdinand I, as he was now known, determined that Tuscany should abandon its recent policy of siding with Spain in any conflicts, and instead should establish closer ties to France. Ferdinand I had maintained a relatively close relationship with his distant cousin Catherine de' Medici and in 1587 she agreed to his request to marry her favorite granddaughter, Princess Christine of Lorraine, who was then 22. It would be several years, however, before the marriage could take place. France was in the midst of its ongoing series of religious wars, and Princess Christine remained by Catherine de' Medici's side during her final illness and death. Finally, in the spring of 1589, the wedding took place; the celebration lasted for a month.

Princess Christine had been raised by her grandmother following the death of her mother, and she was intelligent, spirited, and loved, both in France and in Tuscany. She proved to be a good wife, and Ferdinand ruled for 22 years. During his time in power, a sense of order and dignity was restored to the throne, following the corrupt years under Francis. He increased the size of the navy, and like many in his family, was a great sponsor of the arts.

He was the father of eight children, and died on February 7, 1609, at the age of 60.

Ferdinand de' Medici was succeeded by his oldest son, another Cosimo, known as Cosimo II. He was 19 when he became Grand Duke of Tuscany, and both his father and mother had trained him to be tolerant, generous, and friendly. He and his young wife were enthusiastically supported in Tuscany, and he was determined to launch a new age in Florence. Much as his earlier ancestors had focused on making Florence a center for art, Cosimo II was determined that Florence should become a leader in scientific research.

Cosimo II became a sponsor of the great scientist Galileo Galilei, who had been his mathematics teacher. Cosimo II appointed Galileo to the position of "Chief Mathematician to the Grand Duke," and gave him a villa in Florence and an annual salary that left him free to continue his research. For 23 years, Galileo developed the discoveries that would earn him a place as one of science's greatest pioneers. He invented the telescope during the first year of Cosimo II's reign, and later developed his theory that earth did not form the center of the universe,

Cosimo II sponsored scientist Galileo Galilei (shown here). Cosimo II appointed Galileo to the position of "Chief Mathematician to the Grand Duke," and gave him a villa in Florence and an annual salary.

but was merely one relatively small planet in the solar system.

Cosimo II was the final banker of the Medici family. He closed the family banks after he became Grand Duke of Tuscany, believing that a conflict of interest was created when the ruler of Tuscany was also its chief financier of trade and commerce.

Cosimo II might have been a great ruler, but he became severely ill at the age of 24 and never fully recovered. He died on February 28, 1620, at the age of 30, leaving behind his wife and eight children. His will specified that his mother and wife would serve as joint regents of Tuscany, until his oldest son, Ferdinand II—only ten at the time of his father's death—was old enough to serve as Grand Duke of Tuscany.

FERDINAND II

The two women who became joint regents of Tuscany, Grand Duchess Christine and Grand Duchess Maria Maddalena, were good women who, sadly, lacked good instincts and sense for governing. They loved splendor and celebrations, and quickly began a period in which the court of Tuscany was notable for its elaborate clothing, extravagant parties, and excessive spending. The eight years in which they oversaw Tuscany, until Ferdinand II came of age, were a time in which much of the Medici fortune was spent, and generous sums were granted to religious orders and monasteries, while the people of Florence sank into poverty.

Even after Ferdinand II became Grand Duke in 1628, his grandmother and mother still maintained considerable influence over the policies of the government. He quickly came into conflict with Pope Urban VIII, who was determined to demonstrate his power by attacking one of Florence's most famous citizens.

From 1609 to 1632, Galileo had been busily developing the scientific theories that would later make him famous. He had made important discoveries about gravity, astronomy, momentum, and time. His theory that the earth revolved around the sun, however, made him a target for papal questioning. In 1616, this theory was condemned by the members of the Inquisition, and he was forced to agree to avoid further discussion of this idea. For the next 17 years, Galileo continued to be the target of religious criticism. By 1633, he was again called before the members of the Inquisition in Rome, charged with having broken his promise. The pope charged that Galileo's theory directly contradicted the Bible, and the 70-year-old scientist was threatened with torture. He was forced to say that his theories were false and was kept as a prisoner.

Galileo, shown here presenting his telescope to the Venetian senate, was persecuted for his theory that the earth revolved around the sun. He was forced to say that his theories were false and was kept as a prisoner.

Ferdinand II had an opportunity to denounce the pope's actions and stand firmly by the man his father had named as "Chief Mathematician to the Grand Duke"—the man who had patiently taught himself and his father, and who shared his extraordinary scientific discoveries with all of Tuscany. Instead Ferdinand II chose the easier path, bowing to the will of the pope and refusing to support Galileo.

Some scholars suggest that Ferdinand II's unwillingness to stand up for Galileo marked the fall of the

Medicis, and the end of the Renaissance in Florence. The family that had once supported new thinking and new discoveries—in art, sculpture, architecture, and science—now bowed to religious pressure and allowed extraordinary talent to be suppressed.

THE END OF A DYNASTY

The grand dukes who followed were weaker men, and their time of rule over Tuscany was a time of decline for the Medici family. In 1670, Ferdinand II died, and his son, 28-year-old Cosimo III, took the throne. While Cosimo III was officially ruling, his mother—Grand Duchess Vittoria—was the power behind the throne. She constantly interfered and offered advice, replacing the officials and advisors. While Cosimo III's reign was marked by religious intolerance and weakened government, it was also noteworthy for its length. He ruled Tuscany for more than 50 years, from 1670 to 1723, and during this period citizens were subjected to strict codes of morality and severe punishment, for even the most minor of offenses. He adopted a short-sighted policy toward defense, refusing to properly fund or train Tuscany's military.

Cosimo III's cruel treatment of his citizens was mirrored in his bullying, intolerant attitude toward his sons. He forced his two sons into marriages with wives who were ill-suited to their husbands' personalities, and refused to allow them to participate in any way in the government. Both marriages produced no children, and, as Cosimo III grew older, the question of how Medici rule would continue became critical. In 1713, Cosimo III's oldest son, Ferdinand, died at the age of 50. After his death, the Grand Duke of Tuscany and the senate passed a law stating that, should Cosimo III's second son, Giovanni Gastone, die without an heir, then Cosimo's daughter, Anna Maria Luisa, would take the throne.

On October 31, 1723, when Cosimo III died, his son Gian Gastone took the throne, and, with his sister, moved into the Pitti Palace. Given he and his widowed sister's lack of children, it was not surprising that the question of succession became of international interest. Spain and Austria were both eager to obtain control of Italy, and their allies—England, Holland, and France—were soon drawn into the conflict. Tuscany was viewed as the prize.

Finally a peace treaty was signed in October 1735 that, when ratified in January 1736, became known as the Peace of Vienna. In the terms of the

Galileo

Galileo Galilei was born on February 15, 1564, in Pisa, Italy. He was the first child of Vincenzio Galilei, a music teacher from Florence, and Giula Ammanati. When Galileo was eight, his family moved to Florence, but Galileo remained in Pisa for two years, in the care of a relative, before rejoining his family.

When he was old enough to be educated, he was sent away to a monastery southeast of Florence. Young Galileo liked the life there enough to consider becoming a monk, but his father had decided that Galileo would become a doctor, and he ordered his son to return to Florence, where he continued his schooling. In 1581, Galileo returned to Pisa to enroll in the university and begin his training to become a doctor, but he quickly found that his true interest was in mathematics.

Galileo became a teacher of mathematics. He was named the chair of mathematics at the University of Pisa in 1589, later taking a better-paying position at the University of Padua.

In the early 1600s, Galileo began experiments that would result in his creation of a telescope—which he called a perspicillum—superior to those that had previously been created. He used it on the sky at

peace agreement, upon the death of Gian Gastone, the Grand Duke of Tuscany would be given to the emperor of Austria's daughter, Maria Theresa. In

night, discovering new bodies and formations, including four small objects orbiting Jupiter, which he named "the Medicean stars." (They were actually moons, but this was discovered later.) The name— and the loan of one of his new telescopes—impressed Grand Duke Cosimo II, who named him the chief mathematician of Tuscany.

Galileo continued to make numerous important discoveries while being supported by the Medicis, but his theories would bring him into conflict with Pope Urban VIII, and ultimately to trial under the Inquisition. Galileo was condemned to life in prison, but the sentence was ultimately lessened to allow him to return to his home, where he spent the rest of his days under house arrest.

Galileo died in early 1642, suffering the public embarrassment of the charges of heresy made against him. It was not until October 31, 1992, some 350 years after his death, that Pope John Paul II made a speech, noting that errors had been made in the case of Galileo. He did not, however, say that the Catholic Church had been wrong to prosecute Galileo for his belief that the earth rotates around the sun.

exchange, France would receive the state of Lorraine on its western border.

Gian Gastone was horrified by the way the European powers were carving up his land before he was even dead, but his protests were ignored. Austrian troops arrived in Tuscany, and upon Gian Gastone's death, on July 9, 1737, Tuscany left Medici hands forever. The Medici family's ruling dynasty came to an end with the death of its last male member.

A RENAISSANCE FAMILY

For more than three centuries, the Medici family helped shape the fate of Florence. From a middle-class family of bankers, they became royalty, transforming their base of power from a few banks in Florence to a banking empire that dominated Italian commerce, and expanding their rule to encompass all of Tuscany.

The Medicis were extraordinary not simply for their rise, but for the number of exceptional, powerful leaders the family produced. There was a clear inheritance among many of the Medici men—and some of the women—that resulted in an ability to become the right ruler at the right place and time. There were, of course, weak and corrupt rulers, as well, but for any family to dominate a single city-state for so long, during such a period of change and turmoil, is exceptional.

Perhaps most important, the Medicis supported, nurtured, and funded others of extraordinary talents—artists, sculptors, architects, and scientists who, for a time, made Florence the center of the Renaissance. The Medicis encouraged new ways of looking at the world, and brought the talents of Michelangelo, Botticelli, Galileo, and countless others to light.

The legacy of the Medicis is still clearly visible throughout Florence. The homes of the Medicis—Medici Palace and Pitti Palace—still stand as evidence of the powerful family that once resided within their walls. The Uffizi galleries offer ample evidence of the importance of Medici support for the arts. Throughout the world, the masterpieces created by artists whom the Medicis sponsored continue to provide for contemporary viewers, a sense of what life was like during the age of the Medicis.

Test Your Knowledge

1 What event effectively brought an end to
Medici power in France?
a. The death of Lorenzo de' Medici
b. The death of Catherine de' Medici
c. The start of the French Revolution
d. The end of the Renaissance

2 Who was the most obvious candidate as a
successor to Alessandro de' Medici?
a. Catherine de' Medici
b. Piero de' Medici
c. Cosimo de' Medici
d. Giovanni de' Medici

3 How many children did Cosimo I have?
a. Ten
b. Six
c. Three
d. Five

4 Who did Cosimo II sponsor?
a. Machiavelli
b. Botticelli
c. Michelangelo
d. Galileo Galilei

5 What are the names of the Medicis' two homes?

a. Pitti Palace and Medici Palace

b. Florence Palace and Medici Palace

c. Uffizi Palace and Medici Palace

d. Pazzi Palace and Medici Palace

ANSWERS: 1. b; 2. c; 3. a; 4. d; 5. a

1360 Giovanni de' Medici is born.

1389 Giovanni's son Cosimo de' Medici is born.

1393 Giovanni de' Medici forms his own bank in Rome.

1421 Giovanni de' Medici becomes gonfaloniere in Florence.

1429 Giovanni de' Medici dies and is succeeded by his son Cosimo.

1433 Cosimo de' Medici and his family are forced to leave Florence; they are welcomed back within a year.

1449 Lorenzo de' Medici is born (Cosimo's first grandson).

1464 Cosimo de' Medici dies and is succeeded by his son Piero.

1434 Though lacking an official title, Cosimo de' Medici becomes a political force in Florence

1523 Giulio de' Medici becomes Pope Clement VII

1488 Michelangelo is sponsored by the Medici family

1430

1478 Pazzi Conspiracy sparks assassination attempt on Lorenzo de' Medici and his brother Giuliano, on April 26; Giuliano is killed

1513 Giovanni de' Medici becomes Pope Leo X

1469 Piero de' Medici dies and is succeeded by his
      son Lorenzo.

1478 Pazzi Conspiracy sparks assassination attempt on
      Lorenzo de' Medici and his brother Giuliano on
      April 26; Giuliano de' Medici is killed.

1479 Pope Sixtus IV excommunicates all of Florence;
      war begins; Lorenzo de' Medici travels to Naples
      in December to negotiate peace.

1480 Peace agreement with Naples concluded in April;
      Lorenzo de' Medici returns to Florence in triumph;
      Lorenzo's son Piero is born.

1569 Cosimo I is named the Grand Duke of Tuscany by Pope Pius V

1737 Gian Gastone de' Medici dies on July 8, bringing an end to reign of Medicis over Florence

1740

1547 Catherine de' Medici becomes queen of France

1633 Galileo is summoned before the Inquisition; Ferdinand II drops his support of his former tutor

1485 Dominican friar Girolamo Savonarola begins to preach against the Medicis.

1488 Michelangelo is sponsored by the Medici family.

1489 Lorenzo de' Medici's 14-year-old son Giovanni is named the youngest cardinal in history.

1492 Lorenzo de' Medici dies on April 9; he is succeeded by his son Piero.

1494 Piero de' Medici surrenders to French army and is forced to flee Florence.

1503 Piero de' Medici dies.

1512 Giovanni and Giuliano de' Medici are aided by Pope Julius II in retaking Florence.

1513 Giovanni de' Medici becomes Pope Leo X.

1516 Pietro de' Medici's son Lorenzo becomes Duke of Urbino.

1519 Catherine de' Medici is born (daughter of Lorenzo, Duke of Urbino) and quickly orphaned; Cosimo de' Medici (who will become Cosimo I) is born.

1523 Giulio de' Medici becomes Pope Clement VII.

1527 Rome is sacked and Pope Clement VII forced into hiding; Florence overthrows the Medici reign and Alessandro and Ippolito are forced into exile.

1529 The army of Pope Clement VII retakes Florence.

1532 Alessandro de' Medici abolishes the Florentine republic and is named Duke of Florence; his cousin Ippolito is named a cardinal.

1533 Catherine de' Medici marries Henry, the second son of the king of France.

1534 Pope Clement VII dies.

1535 Ippolito de' Medici is poisoned by his cousin, Alessandro de' Medici.

1537 Alessandro de' Medici is assassinated; a new branch of the Medicis, under Cosimo I, takes over the rule of Florence.

1547 Francois I, king of France, dies; Catherine de' Medici becomes queen of France.

1549 Ferdinand de' Medici (who will become Ferdinand I) is born.

1569 Cosimo I is named the Grand Duke of Tuscany by Pope Pius V.

1574 Cosimo I dies and is succeeded by his son Francesco I.

1587 Francesco I dies and is succeeded by his brother Ferdinand I.

1589 Catherine de' Medici dies.

1590 Ferdinand I's first son, Cosimo (later named Cosimo II) is born.

1609 Ferdinand I dies and is succeeded by his son Cosimo II, who closes the Medici companies and bank.

1610 A son, who will become Ferdinand II, is born to Cosimo II.

1620 Cosimo II dies; until ten-year-old Ferdinand II is old enough to rule, Cosimo's mother and wife govern as regents.

1633 Galileo is summoned before the Inquisition; Ferdinand II drops his support of his former tutor.

1642 A son, who will become Cosimo III, is born to Ferdinand II.

1670 Ferdinand II dies and is succeeded by his son Cosimo III.

1671 Gian Gastone de' Medici is born to Cosimo III and his wife.

1723 Cosimo III dies; Gian Gastone takes over reign of Florence.

1737 Austrian troops occupy Tuscany; Gian Gastone dies on July 8, bringing an end to the reign of the Medicis over Florence.

CHAPTER 1
Murder in the Cathedral

1. G. F. Young, *The Medici*. New York: The Modern Library, 1988, p. 172.
2. Ralph Roeder, "Lorenzo de' Medici," in J.H. Plumb, *Renaissance Profiles*. New York: Harper & Row, 1961, p. 63.

CHAPTER 2
Bankers to the Republic

3. Young, *The Medici*, p. 31.
4. Roeder, "Lorenzo de' Medici," p. 55.
5. Ibid.
6. Ferdinand Schevill, *Medieval and Renaissance Florence: The Coming of Humanism and the Age of the Medici*. New York: Harper & Row, 1961, vol. II, p. 370.
7. Young, *The Medici*, pp. 98–99.
8. Ibid., p. 94.

CHAPTER 3
Lorenzo the Magnificent

9. Young, *The Medici*, pp. 115–116.
10. Roeder, "Lorenzo de' Medici," p. 59.
11. Ibid., p. 60.
12. Schevill, *Medieval and Renaissance Florence: The Coming of Humanism and the Age of the Medici*, p. 381.

13. E. Armstrong, *Lorenzo de' Medici*. New York: G.P. Putnam's Sons, 1906, p. 299.
14. Herbert M. Vaughan, *Studies in the Italian Renaissance*. Port Washington, N.Y.: Kennikat Press, 1921, p. 8.
15. Roeder, *The Medici*, p. 68.
16. Ibid., p. 69.
17. Schevill, *Medieval and Renaissance Florence: The Coming of Humanism and the Age of the Medici*, p. 436.

CHAPTER 4
A Medici Pope

18. Young, *The Medici*, p. 303.

CHAPTER 5
Catherine de' Medici

19. Vaughan, *Studies in the Italian Renaissance*, p. 13.
20. Paul Van Dyke, *Catherine de' Medici*. New York: Charles Scribner's Sons, 1922, vol. I, p. 38.
21. Ibid.
22. Ralph Roeder, *Catherine de' Medici and the Lost Revolution*. New York: The Viking Press, 1937, p. 609.

Armstrong, E. *Lorenzo de' Medici and Florence in the Fifteenth Century.* New York: G.P. Putnam's Sons, 1906.

Burke, Peter. *The Italian Renaissance: Culture and Society in Italy.* Princeton, N.J.: Princeton University Press, 1986.

Channel 4. "History." Available online at http://www.channel4.com/ history.

"Michelangelo Buonarroti." Available online at http://www.michelangelo .com/buonarroti.

Public Broadcasting Service (PBS). "Medici: Godfathers of the Renaissance." Available online at http://www.pbs.org/empires/medici.

Rice University. "Galileo Project, The." Available online at http://galileo.rice.edu/

Roeder, Ralph. *Catherine de' Medici and the Lost Revolution.* New York: The Viking Press, 1937.

———. "Lorenzo de' Medici" in Plumb, J.H. ed. *Renaissance Profiles.* New York: Harper & Row, 1961.

Schevill, Ferdinand. *Medieval and Renaissance Florence: The Coming of Humanism and the Age of the Medici.* New York: Harper & Row, vol. II, 1961.

Van Dyke, Paul. *Catherine de Médicis.* New York: Charles Scribner's Sons, vol I, 1922.

Vaughan, Herbert M. *Studies in the Italian Renaissance.* Port Washington, N.Y.: Kennikat Press, Inc., 1966.

Young, G.F. *The Medici.* New York: The Modern Library, 1988.

Books

Frieda, Leonie. *Catherine de Medici.* London: George Weidenfeld & Nicholson, 2003.

Kent, Dale. *Cosimo de' Medici and the Florentine Renaissance.* New Haven, CT: Yale University Press, 2000.

Martines, Lauro. *April Blood: Florence and the Plot Against the Medici.* New York: Oxford University Press, 2003.

Plumb, J.H., ed. *Renaissance Profiles.* New York: Harper & Row, 1961.

Young, G.F. *The Medici.* New York: The Modern Library, 1988.

Websites

Discovery Chanel: Medici Project Turns Up Mystery Bodies
http://dsc.discovery.com/news/briefs/20040719/medici.html

End of Europe's Middle Ages: The Medici in Florence
http://www.ucalgary.ca/applied_history/tutor/endmiddle/
bluedot/cosimo.html

Medici: Godfathers of the Renaissance
www.pbs.org/empires/medici/

Heather Lehr Wagner is a writer and editor. She is the author of more than 30 books exploring social and political issues and focusing on the lives of prominent men and women. She earned a B.A. in political science from Duke University, and an M.A. in government from the College of William and Mary. She lives with her husband and family in Pennsylvania.